Black South African Women

In the first anthology to focus exclusively on the lives of black South African women, this volume represents the work of both emerging playwrights and national and international award-winners, including

Gcina Mhlophe
Duma Ndlovu
Maishe Maponya
Ismail Mahomed
Muthal Naidoo
Fatima Dike
Sindiwe Magona
Lueen Conning
Thulani Mtshali
Magi Noninzi Williams

Written before and after apartheid, the plays present varying approaches and theatrical styles from solo performances or one-handers to collective creations. This volume presents an array of women's and men's voices, and includes interviews with the playwrights themselves, who candidly discuss the theatrical and political situation in the new South Africa.

The plays dramatize issues as diverse as women's rights; displacement from home; violence against women; the struggle to keep families together; racial identity; health care; and education in the old and new South Africa.

Black South African Women: An Anthology of Plays is a unique and valuable sourcebook for anyone interested in the drama and politics of South Africa.

Kathy A. Perkins is Associate Professor at the University of Illinois. She is the editor of *Black Female Playwrights: An Anthology of Plays Before 1950*, co-editor with Roberta Uno of *Contemporary Plays by Women of Color* (Routledge, 1996) and co-editor with Judith Stephens of *Strange Fruit: Plays on Lynching by American Women.*

To the memory of
Marion Perkins, Sr. (1922–1998)

Black South African Women

An Anthology of Plays

Edited by Kathy A. Perkins

London and New York

First published 1998 by Routledge
11 New Fetter Lane, London EC4P 4EE

Simultaneously published in the USA and Canada
by Routledge
29 West 35th Street, New York, NY 10001

Typeset in Goudy by Routledge
Printed and bound in Great Britain by TJ International
Ltd., Padstow, Cornwall

British Library Cataloguing in Publication Data
A catalogue record for this book is available from the British Library

Library of Congress Cataloguing in Publication Data
Black South African women: an anthology of plays/edited by Kathy A. Perkins.
p. cm.
Includes bibliographical references.
Contents: Introduction/Kathy A. Perkins — A Coloured place/Lueen Conning — So what's new?/Fatima Dike — House-hunting unlike Soweto/Sindiwe Magona — Cheaper than roses/Ismail Mahomed — Umongikazi/The nurse/Maishe Maponya — Have you seen Zandile?/ Gcina Mhlophe — WEEMEN/Thulani S. Mtshali — Flight from the Mahabarath/Muthal Naidoo — Sheila's day/Duma Ndlovu — Kwa-landlady/Magi Nonzini Williams.
1. Women, Black—South Africa—Drama. 2. South African drama (English)—Women authors. 3. South African drama (English)—Black authors. 4. South African drama (English) 5. Blacks—South Africa—Drama. 6. English Drama—20th century. I. Perkins, Kathy A., 1954–.

PR9366.7.W65B58 1999
822—dc21 98–18547
CIP

ISBN 0–415–18243–3 (hbk)
ISBN 0–415–18244–1 (pbk)

Contents

Acknowledgements

I am extremely grateful for the support and guidance of the numerous people who helped make this collection a reality.

I would like to thank sincerely the following individuals for their assistance in guiding me to the plays, festivals, writers, and various research information: Walter Chakela, Kendall, Lizbeth Goodman, Deva Govindsamy, Khubu Meth, Gita Pather, Kriben Pillay, the United States Information Service (USIS) – Johannesburg and Durban, and Ian Steadman.

For the personal support from the many friends and colleagues who made my visits to South Africa a wonderful experience: Ben Cashden, Michael Kaiser, Nomvula Meth, Shereen Mills, Matthew O'Leary, Mahomed (Babs) Abba-Omar, Margery Moberly, Logan Shunmugam, Zodwa Shongwe, and Juliet Walker.

For those individuals who were instrumental in assisting with the manuscript, providing guidance and inspiration: Nancy Davis, Jane de Gay, Richard Gibbs, Ann Haugo, Kwaku Kurang, Kathryn Marshak, Dawn Plummer, Libya Pugh, Sandra Richardson, and Sandra Seaton.

My four trips to Africa would not have been possible without support from: University of Illinois (UIUC) Research Board, Dean Kathleen Conlin (UIUC College of Fine & Applied Arts), and the UIUC International Programs and Studies.

Finally, for personal support from family, friends, and colleagues here in the United States: Daniel Anteau, Timothy Eatman, Steve Pelphrey, Alphonse Perkins, Linda Perkins, Minerva Perkins, Judith Stephens, Barbara Cohen Stratyner, Kristina Stanley, Vincent Wimbush, and Paul Zeleza.

Many thanks to my editors at Routledge, Talia Rodgers and Sophie Powell, for the opportunity to work together again. Special thanks to Glenda Younge, at University of Cape Town Press.

My greatest gratitude is to the writers who made this collection possible. Thank you for sharing your wonderful stories!

Kathy A. Perkins
Champaign, Illinois

Introduction

> South African women do things, but very little is known about us. Even during the era of protest theatre, most of the plays produced were by men and about men in the struggle. One of my pains that I've had to live with was the fact that a lot of these women were the ones left behind by men who had to go into exile, to prison at Robben Island or were dead. So who do you think was keeping this country going? It was us!
>
> (Fatima Dike interview, July 22, 1997 – Cape Town)

I have always been fascinated by drama's unique power to educate audiences about histories and cultures. My hope is that this anthology, one of the first to focus exclusively on the lives of black South African women through drama, will contribute to the reader's understanding of the position of these black women. This anthology fills a major gap, since the majority of published plays on South Africa focus primarily on men. These plays, written during and after apartheid, represent the work of black South African men and women. (The term "black" in South Africa refers to Africans, and a segment of both Coloureds (people of mixed race), and Indians who identified with the Black Consciousness Movement of the 1970s; my collection reflects the work of all three groups.) The writers range in age from their late twenties to early sixties and come from diverse educational and theatrical backgrounds. This anthology marks the first publication for some, while others have already garnered national and international reputations.

My interest in South Africa dates back to 1979, when my sister introduced me to a group of South African exiles studying here in the States. These students occasionally came by to the apartment my sister and I shared in New Jersey, where they discussed events in South Africa and the impact of apartheid. Having grown up in Alabama during the Civil Rights movement of the 1960s, I had little difficulty relating to their stories of racial oppression and violence. One of the students who visited us, Duma Ndluvo, went on years later to write *Sheila's Day*, a play exploring the parallels between apartheid and segregation in the United States.

In the early 1980s, I took the opportunity to design lighting for several South African artists in the New York area. Through my contact with these artists, I was kept abreast of the cultural and social situation under apartheid. Throughout the 1980s, South African plays such as *Sizwe Bansi is Dead*, *Bopha!*, and *Sarafina*, gained tremendous popularity in the United States, offering insight into the terrible conditions under which black South Africans were forced to live. By the end of the 1980s, rumors abounded regarding the release of Nelson Mandela and the debanning of the African National Congress (ANC). On February 11, 1990, Mandela was released from prison at Robben Island, and a year later apartheid was legally abolished. In April of 1994, black people voted in South Africa's first non-racial election. The following month the world witnessed Mandela's inauguration as the country's first black president. With these various events, my interest in South Africa heightened. I kept hearing talk about the *new* South Africa and the emerging rainbow nation. What was this new South Africa, and where did black women fit into the scheme of things?

I began seeking some answers in the dramas of the old and new South Africa, but discovered there were very few plays that dealt with the role of black women, and even fewer written by black women. While stories by and about the lives of black South African women tend to fare better than their counterparts throughout the continent, there still remains a tremendous absence of literature on their lives. According to South African writer Ellen Kuzwayo, "I always felt there was this great heroic contribution and achievement by women, but nobody knows about it outside of the country, and maybe even within the country. Because of the structure of society, with women right at the bottom, they did not come out to be seen as the real motivating element in the lives of the people, or the country as a whole."[1] In terms of drama, I should not have been surprised by the lack of available material on women. Even in the United States, African American women have been publishing in significant numbers only in the last decade and their numbers are still small when compared to black men and whites.

SO WHAT'S NEW?

Through attending, reading, or working on South African productions in the United States, I became aware of the limited opportunities for black South African women playwrights and performers. Most accessible published South African plays are by males such as white playwright Athol Fugard, and black male writers Mbongeni Ngema and Percy Mtwa. Because there are so few published plays by and about black women of South Africa, dramatized interpretations of the role women play in that society are minimal. The available plays by black women are usually published through small South African presses.

On the international scene, roles for women in South African productions often feature them as exotic characters in musicals such as *Ipi Tombi* (*Where are the Girls?*). During the 1970s and 1980s, lavish musicals like *Ipi Tombi*, primarily produced and marketed by whites, enjoyed successful runs internationally and with mainstream theatres in South Africa. Such productions have been criticized for exploiting indigenous cultures for commercial gain and for their appeal to mainly white audiences. A few plays by black women, such as *Have You Seen Zandile?* and *You Strike the Woman, You Strike the Rock*, received significant recognition at home and abroad during the 1980s.

Women are practically invisible in the internationally acclaimed male-authored protest plays of the 1970s and 1980s; such plays as *Woza Albert* and *Asinamali* focus primarily on the oppression of blacks by whites. Given the nature of apartheid, many black male-authored dramas focused on employment, since most men labored in the cities and had greater exposure to whites than women did. But very few works included other aspects of black life, except for such black male writers of the same period as Matsemela Manaka and Gibson Kente. Both wrote plays focusing on family life and featuring female protagonists. However, these works were rarely seen outside of the townships and did not gain international exposure. In much South African theatre, according to Zakes Mda

> peasants and other rural dwellers were ignored as subjects of artistic attention. Once in a while, on very rare occasions, there would be a bright spark that would illuminate other aspects of the people's life, such as Gcina Mhlophe's (1988) *Have You Seen Zandile?* Other exceptions were *You Strike the Woman, You Strike the Rock*, which examined the role women played in the South African liberation struggle, and *Imfuduso*, which was on the questions of forced removals, in this case at Crossroads in Cape Town. It is significant that these plays were either wholly created (written, directed, and performed) by women, as in the case of Mhlophe's play, or women played a major role in creating them.[2]

In recent years, a number of male playwrights have written plays that focus on black women and the dilemmas of daily life. While numerous male writers have included women in their works, only a few have portrayed women in a sensitive and realistic light. This minority group includes Zakes Mda with his anthology *And the Girls in their Sunday Dresses*, and the works by several men included in this collection. Most

1 James, Adeola, editor, *In Their Own Voices: African Women Writers Talk*, Portsmouth, New Hampshire: Heinemann Educational Books Inc., 1990.

2 Mda, Zakes, compiled and introduced, *Four Plays*, Florida Hills, South Africa: Vivla Publishers, 1996.

recently Athol Fugard has featured black women as his subject in his post-apartheid plays *My Life* and *Valley Song*.

ZANENDABA (TELL US A STORY)

In June of 1995, I made the first of four trips to South Africa to seek out women playwrights willing to tell *their* stories. I was somehow not convinced that women in South Africa were as silent as I had been led to believe. Within eight hours of my arrival in Johannesburg, I visited Kippie's, a popular club in the heart of the city, which at the time hosted a women-only night once a month. At Kippie's I was introduced to South African women from all walks of life – class, education levels, and racial classifications. The night featured poetry, music, and dramatic readings for an enthusiastic crowd. A large table prominently displayed international and national literature by and about women, including material on health issues. Since I was a recent arrival to the country, the women were as anxious to share their stories as I was anxious to hear them. One theme that reverberated throughout the night was the feeling that the centrality of black women's accomplishments had not been recognized in the struggle against apartheid, but were overlooked in South Africa's colonialist and patriarchal society.

What struck me most about that first night were the many similarities between black women in South Africa and those in the United States. The issue of affirmative action is being debated in South Africa as in the States. Several black women were finding themselves in the workplace on an equal level and in authority often over black men and in a few instances in authority over whites for the first time. They were curious to know how African American women were able to cope with being thrust into these situations, how to socialize with whites, and how to gain general respect from whites and black men. Some spoke of their frustration at the problems finding adequate housing even when they were financially able to do so, because of discrimination – even in the new South Africa. The conversations flowed into the early hours of the next day, and thus began my first of many sleepless nights in South Africa.

During my visits, I was pleased to find a host of women who were having their works produced, albeit on a smaller scale than those of men. I met such pioneering artists as Fatima Dike, Saira Essa, Nise Malange, Thobeka Maqhutyana, Fatima Meer, Gcina Mhlophe, and Muthal Naidoo. Emerging writers Lueen Conning, Khubu Meth, and Magi Williams offered an insight into the views of a younger generation of black South African women. These women expressed concerns regarding the production and publication of plays in South Africa. I learned that in traditional South African cultures, women were primarily story-tellers, and, as is typical throughout Africa, the oral tradition dominates in theatre. Traditional theatre in black South Africa is designed for performing and not primarily to be written and published. This explains why the works by many cultural workers, including Nisa Malange in Durban, have never reached a wide audience. Also, a great deal of Malange's work with women is performed in the various languages of South Africa. South Africa recognizes eleven official languages, including English, Zulu, Afrikaans, Venda, Xhosa, and Sesotho.

Censorship under the former apartheid system contributed in part to the lack of plays by blacks in general. Writers such as Saira Essa spoke of their plays being censored and sometimes banned. Fatima Meer explained that segments of a script would be distributed among different individuals to prevent the authorities from gaining access to a complete work. When these government officials attended plays considered questionable, there would be no complete text to examine, and cast members would often improvise a new plot. Meer also emphasized that the few plays that were written at the time became lost or destroyed because of the transience caused by forced removals, or the fear of authorities discovering the work.

While censorship affected both men and women, domestic responsibilities play an important role for black women as theatre practitioners. It is easier if one is a poet, because a poet needs only pencil and paper. A playwright needs not only pencil and paper, but additional resources like a cast and a place to perform. In Africa women are still the primary nurturers and caregivers. Women spoke of the problems of finding time for rehearsals and dealing with the logistics of staging their works, usually with little to no funding.

The issue of publication drew many comments during my interviews with women as well as men. South Africa had a tradition of theatre long before the arrival of Europeans. Traditional theatre in South Africa includes dramatic enactments such as solo narratives known as "praise poetry" by the Zulus, and the Xhosa *intsomi*. These forms of theatre were prevalent in the various townships. Publishers who sought works structured along the lines of Western drama ignored these theatre forms. To be published, playwrights had to write in English and adhere to Western standards for the most part. Because black men had greater access to whites and the English language, they were more likely to create publishable written material. Most women playwrights in South Africa are self-taught, as is true of most of the women in this collection. Many of them spoke of the need to find mentors or workshops to develop their skill. In contrast, many of the male writers have already had the opportunity to study outside the country, to be mentored, or to engage in various workshops to develop their craft. For all the women interviewed, writing was a vital necessity; they had stories that needed to be shared. They also spoke of the need for exposure on an international level.

The 1990s have provided greater opportunities for women to have their works produced. Increased visibility has been due in part to the gradual dismantling of apartheid and recently implemented affirmative action policies. Venues such as the Windybrow Center for the Arts in Johannesburg provide a showcase platform through its annual playwrights' festival. Since 1995, the venue known as the Playhouse in Durban, KwaZulu-Natal, has presented the Women's Arts Festival, under the leadership of Gita Pather. The festival commissions new works to foster and promote women in all areas of the arts – dance, music, visual arts, and theatre. Black women are gradually having plays produced at the Standard Bank National Arts Festival, popularly referred to as the Grahamstown Festival, although their works are performed primarily on the fringe stages and not in the main venues. (The Grahamstown Festival, which runs for about ten days during the month of July, is one of the world's largest arts festivals.)

THE PLAYS

The six full-length plays and four one-act plays presented in this anthology represent a range of black South African women's experiences. These plays are *stories* that reflect the lives of women, a subject often absent from written work, and in most instances from the stage. They are stories that speak not only of abuse, disappointment, identity, racism, and sexism, but also of resilience, resistance, survival, liberation, and the hope of a better life for themselves and their families. Some of the plays are taken from actual events in the writers' lives.

Internationally acclaimed storytellers Sindiwe Magona and Gcina Mhlophe bring autobiographical pieces to the collection with *House-Hunting Unlike Soweto* and *Have You Seen Zandile?* Compelling and steeped in the language of the oral storytelling tradition, these two stories lend themselves beautifully both to the stage and as written text. Magona's short story *House-Hunting Unlike Soweto*, taken from her collection *Push-Push and Other Stories*, comically dramatizes the difficulty involved in finding an apartment in New York City. Although it was not originally written for the stage, I could not help but visualize *House-Hunting* as a performance piece. Gcina Mhlophe takes us on a journey from her childhood to her early teens in *Have You Seen Zandile?* In both *House-Hunting* and *Zandile?* we find African women uprooted from their original homes attempting to adapt to their new environments. Both plays also focus on the importance of education and the family.

Duma Ndlovu's *Sheila's Day* and Maishe Maponya's *Umongikazi/The Nurse* are two plays centering on resistance to a racist system, both in the United States and South Africa. Written during the apartheid era, the plays shed light on black women's participation in these struggles. Unlike most protest plays of the 1980s, *Umongikazi/The Nurse* and *Sheila's Day* examine oppression from a personal level. *Umongikazi/The Nurse* delves into health issues of blacks, and the inadequate labor conditions of black nurses during the apartheid era. *Sheila's Day* parallels the history of racial oppression among domestic workers in the American South with that of South Africa. Both plays are based on actual events.

Magi Williams' *Kwa-Landlady* and Thulani Mtshali's *WEEMEN* both focus on the abuse of women – mentally and physically – in the home environment. The plays not only bring to light a topic not often addressed in South Africa, but they present women who take a stand against their abusers. *Kwa-Landlady* examines the abuse of a landlord toward his female tenants and, at the same time, the play makes a statement about the abuse of black people toward each other. *WEEMEN* explores physical and mental spousal abuse, and is one of the few plays that take us into the home of a township couple to address this issue. Instead of remaining passive about their abuse, the women in both plays seek a solution.

A group that has virtually been invisible in terms of dramatic works is the Coloured community. Lueen Conning's *A Coloured Place* and Ismail Mohamed's *Cheaper Than Roses* provide an intimate view of the lives of Coloured women. Both plays are "one-hander" or one-woman pieces. *A Coloured Place*, based on actual interviews with Coloured people in the Durban community, takes a look at the lives of a diverse group of women and their search for identity. *Cheaper Than Roses* presents a young Coloured woman who had passed for white during the era of apartheid but must come to grips with how she will classify herself in the new South Africa. The plays are about identity both in the old and new South Africa.

Muthal Naidoo's *Flight from the Mahabarath* and Fatima Dike's *So What's New?* are plays about women's liberation. The plays address independent women who are seeking their own identities in a male-dominated society. *Flight from the Mahabarath* allows women to free themselves from the stereotypes they've been forced to portray in the great Indian epic *The Mahabharata*. The characters literally step out of the epic to share with the audience their desires for a more fulfilling life. *So What's New?* is a domestic comedy about three township women who work in and outside of the legal system in the new South Africa. The play is also an exploration of sisterhood and survival in the new South Africa.

I have found the plays in this collection, along with the many I was unable to include, to be a compelling education in understanding and appreciating the lives of black South African women. This body of work is only a sampling of theatre being produced and written by and about black women in South Africa. This collection focuses on writers who write mainly in English. It is my hope that this anthology will create a greater interest in black South African women – a group that has been invisible far too long – and will encourage the publication of related works in Zulu, Xhosa, Sesotho, and other indigenous languages. This anthology, like my previous anthologies focusing on African American women, provides a forum in which women from Africa and throughout the African Diaspora can share their stories.

THE INTERVIEWS

Eight writers were interviewed in person during my visits to South Africa. Duma Ndlovu and I communicated for the most part via phone/fax. Sindiwe Magona was interviewed in New York City, where she currently resides. In addition to providing biographical information, the writers responded directly to specific questions. I felt it important for the writers to answer questions in their own voices, rather than in less eloquent paraphrase. I posed three questions to each writer, with an additional question to the women. They were:

- Artistic statement, or what inspired you to write the play?
- What is the role of theatre in South Africa?
- Have things improved in general in the new South Africa?

In addition I asked the women:

- Have situations improved for black women in theatre in the new South Africa?

In some cases, I met with the writers on more than one occasion. I was intrigued by many of the responses, and the writers spoke candidly about their feelings on what was happening in the new South Africa. Many of the writers responded at length, so it was difficult trying to condense responses for this collection.

I am indeed honored to have the opportunity to present the works by these wonderful South African storytellers. They have been instrumental in my gaining a greater knowledge of the lives of black South African women.

Lueen Conning

> I consider myself African. But this is not a general Coloured perception. In fact a lot of Coloured people deny their African heritage. There is an aspiration toward white beauty although it's not overtly stated, but they furiously straighten their hair so you can't see the African kink, they still consider a straighter nose, thinner lips, lighter skin as beauty. And that's the aspiration. Apartheid still lives in our minds.

Actor, poet, and writer Lueen Conning was commissioned to write her first professional play, *A Coloured Place*, for the 1996 Women's Arts Festival at the Playhouse in Durban Kwa-Zulu-Natal. *A Coloured Place*, a multimedia one-woman show, has a unique woman's perspective about growing up Coloured in South Africa.

Lueen was born and raised in the Durban area, and until the age of 15 she attended state Coloured schools. She later gained admittance to a private school, a Catholic convent that accepted a few black pupils during the later apartheid era. In our interview Lueen shared her frustrations surrounding the Coloured schools during the 1980s:

> As an individual I was not acknowledged as an artist. My creativity was seen as a hobby that you couldn't make a career out of. There was no subject that related to art. English was my only source of expression. I was highly frustrated because I realized that there were so-called white schools or private schools that offered drama as a subject. And I wanted to study that badly. I knew from an early age that I wanted to perform and that I was an artist.

Lueen isn't exactly sure how she became interested in professional theatre, but she realized that storytelling was an inspiration. Her family environment included her father, a plumber, and her mother, a nurse and social worker. As a child Lueen's mother took her to political rallies that were mostly conducted in Zulu. Lueen believes that she gained a lot of her activism and dramatic flare from her mother.

When Lueen began attending the multiracial convent, some of her Coloured peers felt that she had sold out.

> There was a sense of animosity from friends because I wanted to achieve things they didn't believe people like us could achieve, and started to go places that many Coloured people didn't go – like the theatre.

Her writing career began with poetry at the age of 8. After high school she freelanced as an actor for a short period, touring South Africa with the highly acclaimed Theatre for Africa Company. She later obtained her Performing Arts diploma from Natal Technikon, and one year later she completed her training as an arts administrator at the Playhouse, where Gita Pather served as her mentor.

For the inaugural Playhouse Women's Arts Festival in 1995, Lueen wrote *U-Voice*, a series of poems/monologues which she directed, performed, and stage-managed. Her work has been performed mainly in small venues, and her writings center primarily on women's issues, such as women's contribution to society and abuse against women. Lueen has utilized festivals, which are growing throughout the country, as a means to gain exposure.

Following the success of *A Coloured Place* at the Women's Arts Festival, the production returned to the Playhouse several months later, where the show played to capacity audiences. Lueen resides in Cape Town, where she is pursuing her writing career, and works as an Arts Project Manager for the Robben Island Museum.

ARTISTIC STATEMENT

It's something I've avoided – the issue of Coloured people, and even relating myself to the term Coloured has always been a problem for me. Doing this play is a lot like a personal journey. The idea came from having so many strange questions in the new South Africa and South African people asking me what are you, and I would assume they would know the apartheid boxes we come from. But also there's not one particular face, or type of hair, or skin that you can say is Coloured, or can really define us. Also, if you don't have a typically Coloured accent, it's hard to tell.

I decided to interview Coloured people from all walks of life in terms of age, class, levels of education, gender, etc., in the Durban area. I started with friends and moved on to strangers. Unfortunately, there are very few highly visible Coloured role models, particularly in Durban. The ones who have accomplished things have left the country or the community area itself. They are the non-stereotypes. I also spoke to people of other racial groups to get their perception of Coloured people.

The aim of the play is to feed and stimulate the questioning about identity and the significance of where we come from, and why, as Coloured people, we've never acknowledged our roots. The play says out of this acknowledgement we can define our true identity, and be at peace with that. A Coloured place means that there is a rightful place for Coloured people in South Africa – we do belong somewhere, but many lack this sense of belonging. Coloured people were marginalized during apartheid and many believe that they are marginalized in the new South Africa because of policies like affirmative action. The most disadvantaged people and the majority, who are pure Africans, are being dealt with first in terms of reconstruction, development and support, which is as it should be. Coloured people feel low on the waiting list, so there is a kind of bitterness that exists.

Because of not having an overt cultural or collective identity or something they could call their own, Coloured people have experienced, in a sense, a major identity crisis. In the old South Africa they didn't fit into any of the prescribed boxes. African, Indian, and white communities had very distinct cultures and parameters. Coloured people were dumped into a separate box, lived in their own areas and, in a sense, purely out of the circumstances, there was a sense of community.

Unfortunately, the urban Coloured community is on a trip that is all about escapism. Everything I see is about people escaping who and where they are. Whether through alcohol and drug abuse, gangsterism, or denial of their African heritage. Not a love for whites, but almost an aspiration towards that because white is still seen as beautiful and privileged. Coloured kids are aspiring toward the African American gangster-hero image or glossy inner-city images they see on TV. Also, the trend of seeing African Americans via the media being free, accomplished, having wealth, and exposure – all of that has inspired a sort of interest and a bit of pride in being black, but it's still not recognition of our *Africanness*. There is no pride that you have an African grandmother. I've seen that as part of my coming to terms with my identity – a path of self-discovery and empowerment. I have to know where I came from. To acknowledge your Africanness is also part of the liberation process, especially in terms of where we come from with apartheid. The whole perception that African is inferior, that there is nothing to aspire to, no beauty, no pride, nothing to revere, is an apartheid ideology, an apartheid illusion. These ideas are still prevalent. Passed down.

Gangsterism is common in the Coloured community. Kids aren't getting a stimulating education and have nothing to do after school. There are not enough recreation facilities, most families are poor, and there are usually problems at home. Alcoholism, domestic violence, and teen pregnancy statistics are high in the Coloured community. Coloured people are seldom seen outside their community boundaries in great numbers. I want to shake the apathy within the Coloured community through this play and celebrate the potential and rich heritage we possess. Very few plays have been written about the Coloured experience. *A Coloured Place* reflects a reality, it's a voice for Coloured people and a chance to look at ourselves in the mirror.

THE ROLE OF THEATRE IN SOUTH AFRICA

Healing.

HAVE SITUATIONS IMPROVED FOR BLACK WOMEN IN THEATRE IN THE NEW SOUTH AFRICA?

Although black female writers in South Africa have been active for a long time, they have been fairly invisible to the public eye, and those who have gained recognition through their work have been primarily exposed to international audiences. Most of them have yet to be acknowledged and supported at home by the major players in the field of local theatre and the publishing industry. Basically these platforms have been dominated for too long by usually white male writers, particularly in theatre, and quite honestly it's our turn!

Black women are faced with the enormous challenge of stepping into new territory in terms of what *we* have to say, what *we* believe needs to be addressed, and in defining and expanding our role in South African theatre. At the very foundation of the local theatre industry, we have old South African traditions to break, but we also have a wealth of talent, powerful voices that will not stop until they are heard. We are often natural storytellers and, now more than ever, we have tons of indigenous stories to tell!

HAVE THINGS IMPROVED IN GENERAL IN THE NEW SOUTH AFRICA?

This is a trick question! I'd love to support the media-enforced perception that we are "one happy rainbow nation", if that were the truth. At the end of the most exhausting but important discussion around this issue, I usually say, but at least we are moving in the right direction. A great deal has changed – politically, socially, economically, etc. Not all of it has been for the better. Because of the turbulent and complicated transitional process toward a new South Africa, I would say that the one thing that has been purely a step forward has been the end of legal apartheid. As citizens of this country we cannot expect the government to be solely responsible for the improvement of our lives and our collective healing. We have to participate with confidence in this reconstruction process. We have a lot at stake and can't take the risk of leaving our future in the hands of the powers that be.

PRODUCTION HISTORY

A *Coloured Place* premiered at the 1996 Southern Life Playhouse Company Women's Arts Festival in Durban, with Chantal Snyman, and directed by Lueen Conning.

Interviews conducted June 1995, July 1996, and July 1997.

Photo by Kathy A. Perkins.

1 A Coloured Place

Lueen Conning

INTRODUCTION

The performance begins with a slide presentation depicting various locations, faces and aspects of Coloured life in Durban, easily identifiable to the community for and about whom this play is written. Similar projections are interspersed throughout the play and are accompanied by a voice over which incorporates extracts from interviews, quotes from source material and improvised dialogue.

Scenes

1 Born in-between
2 Rehabilitation
3 Tips on types
4 Celia in me
5 When the cycle hurts
6 What's new?
7 A Coloured place

Cast

A young Coloured woman

Setting

Time

Contemporary life in a Durban Coloured area

Space

A symbolic set which can be used to represent various domestic interiors and exterior locations.

Introduction: A collage of voice-overs accompanied by slides

Sfx:[1] *A cappella Rap song – The Real Ones*

CHORUS Bruin ous, hey x 2
The real ones
VERSE We're kicking up the flow
Here we go x 2
It's time to realise
That you're not a Negro

Listen up x 2
Cos you're in for a blast
We're looking to the future
Free your mind from the past

Sfx: Quotes A–R and matching slides

A

(Brothers squabbling)

BROTHER 1 Hey, what kind with you? Lemme alone, I'm not stealing it, how!

BROTHER 2 Ma lookit Mario, he's wearing my jacket. *(To* BROTHER 1*)* Take it off ha, it's mine!

MOTHER Your'll better shuddup before your father wakes up and fists the both of you. The man's working night shift and your'll got no consideration!

1 Sfx = sound effect

Sfx: Radio tuning into station

B

NEWS REPORTER In 1972, a young Durban Coloured mother of five, Mrs Patricia Justien, turned herself into a human torch and burnt herself to death over the Coloured housing shortage in Wentworth. On her deathbed Mrs Justien said she did it "to persuade the authorities to allocate a house for herself and her family in Wentworth".

C

CHURCH CONGREGATION SINGING
Someone's crying Lord, Khumbaya
Someone's dying Lord, Khumbaya
Someone's praying Lord, Khumbaya
Oh Lord, Khumbaya

D

H.F. VERWOERD One must distinguish between citizenship of a country and...what the components of a homogenous nation are. There is no doubt that the Coloureds are citizens of this country. There is just as little doubt that they are not part of this homogenous entity that can be described as the nation.

Sfx: Repeat

E

Young gangsters talking

GANGSTER 1 Who, ou Gees? Whaa, dat ou got maaiberd 'cos he schemes he knows a span!

GANGSTER2 Hey, you shoulda checked de ou kakking himself. Dey baamered him de by ou Solly's shop and the Y.T.F's were skopping and klapping him. But he kicked down. Dey jaared him into the bushes and ou Vince chooned him: You come back to dis district and we'll fucken steek you, your maader!

(All laugh)

Sfx: Typewriter sounds

F

SOCIAL WORKER People in the ghetto follow the logic of survival, of doing from moment to moment, in apparently random fashion, whatever gives them the most intense sensation of being alive. This insight might help to explain the senseless gang warfare and vandalism that is so prevalent in the Coloured areas of Durban.

Sfx: Repeat

G

Young women talking

VOICE 1 Who...Ha? He's been after em since school days, phoning my house, following me to the club, sending messages with my brother...

VOICE 2 Aah shame man, Babs. The poor man's got feelings for you.

VOICE 1 Hey, please. Just cos he's got that babyface, doesn't mean he's different. The only feelings men have, are when they're feeling with their fingers! *(Raucous laughter)*

H

Men in bar

MAN 1 Hey, my bra chooned me dat his divorce vied through in no time.

MAN 2 Ja, but how much did he have to pay and did he get his fair share, or did she vat everything?

MAN 3 With a vrou ladat bra, it's better to take what you get and chuck. Did I choon your'll about the time ou Nobs vrou caught him in bed with her friend? *(General response – disbelief)*

MAN 1 Whaa...you vatting me!

MAN 3 She fucken threw them with boiling water, Ekse. Njannies! He was still tryna get his pants on when she got stuck into the other stekkie.

(All roar with laughter)

I

POLITICAL SPEAKER As a group the Coloureds have lacked the sentiments of unity, a territorial base and the numbers necessary for a politically effective movement of nationalism.

J

OLD WOMAN It's like the wind that blew all these particles in different directions. A lot of things that originally united Coloured people have changed.

Sfx: School bell rings

K

TEACHER Now class, who can tell me how cross-pollination takes place?
BOY Me Miss, me!
GIRL Ah but Miss, I had my hand up first.

Sfx: Extract of rap song – The Bruin Funk

L

WHITE SOCIAL WORKER Those Coloureds who had European fathers formed a curious intermediate class between the Europeans and the mass of Coloured people. Very conscious of their kinship with whites they clung pathetically to such European standards as they knew, without having any hope of being admitted to that European society.

M

YOUNG WOMAN My white aunty isn't proud of me, so why should I be proud of her?

N

AFRICAN MAN Most of them are proud to be associated with white people, they live very white lives and they have inherited the white man's fears.

Sfx: Computer keyboard typing

O

WHITE SOCIAL WORKER With ambivalent and conflicting aspirations, the neglect by government of the provision of amenities and the constant reference to the uncertain origins, it is likely that Coloureds can be described as culturally deprived.

P

AGGRESSIVE YOUTH What you mean? Of cos we got culture. Bruin ous have their own style and there's a lot of talent in our communities, especially singing and dancing. Have you been to any of our variety shows ha, ha?!

Sfx: Computer beep

Q

PSYCHOLOGIST The imposed conviction of inferiority breeds apathy, low morale and a lack of self-confidence.

Sfx: Repeat

R

Sfx: Reverb on

ACTOR'S VOICE To the majority, Coloured people are just an invisible part of the masses.

Scene 1: Born in-between

Fixed slide image
Sfx: A door shuts
Lx:[2] *Bedroom lighting fades in*

(TRACEY, *high school student, is seated, engrossed in her preparation of an assignment. She is interrupted by a shout from someone off stage.*)

TRACEY Huh? (*Pause*) What?...Who is it?

2 Lx = lighting effect

(*pause*) just take a message. But if it's Shaun tell him...tell him I never came home last night. (*Clicks her tongue in irritation*) Shit!I'm never gonna finish this. (*She reads.*) Misege – what? (*Refers to dictionary, then reads aloud*) Miscegenation...They make it sound like contamination, a flippin' disease!

(*Thinking aloud*) What if God never made Coloured people? I mean, were there "cocktails", mixed people like us in the beginning? Let's say there were these pure nations and they lived in separate corners of the globe and only after years of exploration, they discovered each other. (*Writing enthusiastically*)

Only He (*Referring to God*) knew that when these nations met they would start wars over territory, Earth's gold and even the colour of their skin.

(*Talking to herself*) Now that's where we would have come in, God's answer, People who would form the bridge and prove that unity is possible. (*Writing*) We are the overlappers, the people's people, yes, Man's creation! We are different but we are one. All over the world, but especially here and now, Coloured people represent a union... a blood-bond. (*Thinking aloud*) Instead we are rejected for not belonging to either clan and then what do we do? Reject ourselves. And our next move?

We start copying someone else's image. Some of us follow the wit ous, clutching any piece of evidence that we've got a great-great-grandfather on that side. What about the rest our roots? (*Writing*) We must uncover them and take pride in the richness of our blood.

Lx: Blackout
Sfx: Drum roll and cymbal clash
Quotes 1–3 and matching slides

1

AFRIKAANS CLERK The Population Registration Act (no. 30) of 1950 states: "a White person is defined as meaning a person who in appearance obviously is or who is generally accepted as a White person, but does not include a person who, although in appearance obviously a White person, is generally accepted as a Coloured person."

Sfx: Mini-bus taxi hoots

2

GIRL IN TAXI It's the whiteness in us that black people can't accept and it's the blackness in us that whites can't accept. In the past we weren't white enough and now we can't get jobs cos we not black enough!

Sfx: Typewriter sounds

3

KUGEL I think that Coloureds are as much a part of the continent as the Zulus, the Kenyans or, for that matter, the white tribes who call themselves South Africans or Rhodesians.

Scene 2: Rehabilitation

Slide image – A mother and daughter
Lx: Slow fade in
Sfx: Brahms Lullaby in blackout – Slow fades as actor begins to speak

(CLAUDIA *shifts through a wooden kist full of family relics. Various items evoke memories and she brings their significance to life for the audience.*)

CLAUDIA (*Stroking the dark, polished wood*) Recognize this? A kist, somewhere in your granny's house, usually at the foot of the bed with a special doily on top of it. When I was small, it was a box of untouchables. For some it was a young lady's "bottom drawer", where you kept your trousseau and any family treasures that were due to be passed down when you grew to a certain age or when your gran died and it was time for the relatives to argue over what was rightfully theirs. It looks like a coffin doesn't it? It even opens like one. (*Lifts lid hesitantly*) At six years old my imagination told me that this was where granny kept grandpa's ashes. (*Mock shivers*) Whoo!

(*Imitating mother*) "It's made of solid Embuya wood. It'll be worth quite a fortune one day, but you wouldn't think of selling it Claudie, would you?" (*Reassuring*) No Ma, of course not.

(To audience) So here it is, just not at the foot of my bed with a doily on top of it!

(She opens the chest and picks up a gaudy bib-tie.)

Slide change: Father image

(Laughing) Go dad! So he wasn't always such a stiff bastard. It's hard to imagine him stepping out dressed to the nines. He probably wore a polka dot shirt and purple bellbottoms to go with this.

(Discards tie) Thank God he met my mother. At least she's got some taste. She'd never have allowed him out of the house dressed like that. People used to call her a domineering wife, but she was always trying to put some life into him. His horizon stretched no further than work and home. Oh and soccer on the weekends. So she stopped including him in her plans. Often she went to the dances, meetings or movies with friends and sometimes on her own.

(Imitating grandmother) "That's no way for a married woman to behave!"

(Pause) And my father?

(Imitating father) "You wanna make a spectacle of yourself, you carry on. Me, I know my place. Your bitch of a mother obviously never taught you that."

Slide change: Little girl combing doll's blond hair

(She rummages in the kist and picks out a pair of thick-heeled shoes and parades across stage.)

Ooh, these must have been Aunty Selma's, some real kick-me-deads. They're back in fashion though.

(Imitating Aunty Selma) "These are the 'real macoy'." Aunty Selma would have said, "No-one will have a pair like these."

(Her eye falls on a small cloth bundle in the kist. She slowly unwraps it, smelling the cloth tentatively.) I thought you'd almost still be able to smell it. That familiar whiff of burnt hair.

(Lifting an iron comb from the cloth.) An instrument of torture, if you ask me. One strategic blow and that's it, your brains are on the floor.

(Pause) Actually it's an heirloom, carefully preserved and passed down from my great-granny...to me I suppose. The thing is I didn't need it.

(Mock Indian accent) The Indian genes on my father's side blessed me with gladdes, almost stick straight hair. Combined with my dark skin it earned me nicknames like curryguts and chillipip. It also meant that my mother was asked:

(Imitating inquisitive neighbour) "How come the coolie blood was so strong with her and not with her sister Charlene?" Charlene inherited what most people refer to as croes hair, otherwise known as the bushie hair, frizzy hair, peppercorns, a korrelkop, a kroeskop. She had the fair skin and somehow missed out on the hair to match. That's where the iron comb comes in. The saving grace for Coloured girls before they introduced: *(Sings jingle)* Wella...perfectly you x 2.

A pioneer in the world of hair straighteners!

Lx: Snap to red wash (1)
Sfx: Brahms Lullaby in background

CLAUDIA *(Imitating mother, she dramatizes brusque combing and plaiting of a child's hair.)* "Shame my child. Did God have to give you this unmanageable bush? Dammit! I just wish that you'd inherited your father's hair instead of mine. It would make your life and mine so much easier. At least if you were a boy, you could keep it short and still look decent. Ay, but never mind. We'll try and see what we can do about these phutu-plaits; maybe even try a new style or something. You're still too young for us to start straightening it. Besides, your scalp is so sensitive. But don't worry, when you're a bit older we'll try some of that children's relaxer. OK?"

Lx: Snap back
Sfx: Fade Brahms

That's about when the inferiority complex sets in. Charlene was six or seven when hers started to surface. Then there were the jokes about girls with hair that refused to respond to chemical taming.

Lx: Snap to red wash (2)
Sfx: Crashing window pane

(Imitating jeering boys)"Jarr ekse, even a gale-force wouldn't move that helmet. Real muntu's hair!"

Lx: Snap back

By the end of class two she'd had enough.

Lx: Snap to red wash (3)

(Imitating little Charlene)"Ah please, Ma. I want my hair to be like Claudie's. It won't cost us anything if do it at home, Ma. I'm not scared."

Lx: Snap back

*(Demonstrating)*You'd heat the comb by placing it over the hot coals in the fireplace or on a hot plate or primer stove. When it was ready, you'd wipe off any ash or dust, before getting as close to the scalp as bearable for the victim. With each stroke the numerous unwanted kinks per inch were literally ironed out. I can still see her clutching her ears for dear life as my mother approached with the hot comb. Still, she was sick of her middle path and two thick plaits, weighted down at the ends by a pair of blue or white baubles to match her uniform. Her little set of anchors to prevent those plaits from sticking up in the air. More of a ball 'n chain than ball and elastic!

Without those anchors, Charlene's hair had a mind of its own. Plaits would come undone, or resisting wind and rain, would point to the sky like aerials, mini-antennae from her head. As her hair grew more accustomed to curl-evicting heat and chemicals, it's will-to-frizz was conquered. The result? Charlene with a head of hair she could be proud of. With the aid of rollers, blow drying and swirling she was transformed. She conformed. Of course there were endless compliments to reinforce her new self image.

(Imitating Aunty Selma)"Oh, your hair came out so nice, you can't even see that it's been done. Who did it for you, Lovie?"

(Imitating mother)"Now you look a bit more like your sister. Just watch, even the boys will start taking more notice of you, you'll see sweetheart."

Now for the rest of her life she'll have to maintain that picture, I thought. No matter how much it costs. As long as she avoids wet and windy weather, she'll never have to fear that her hair's gonna "go home". What a joke! Going home means going back to your roots, your natural state.

The hair can dry out, fall out, break, split, thin out and die. You may even have to don a wig to hide the damage, but as long as it's not croes and you're not completely bald, you'll survive.

*(Packing items into kist)*Almost twenty years later, Charlene is beginning the process of rehabilitation. Not only of her hair, but of her being. No more efforts to please family, boyfriends, neighbours who may reject you for not being absorbed into the Coloured crowd. We often speak about it. It's that fear of rejection that cripples you. You get swallowed by what everyone thinks and soon *they* determine what you do, what you wear, where you go and hell, even who you go out with!

I love Charlene's attitude cos it's not the typical.

(Defensive)"So what?" But rather: "Shame. I understand, you're so afraid of who you are." And if she's in a good mood she might smile and say: "You should try it sometime. There's nothing wrong with being yourself. It's what makes you unique!"

Lx: Blackout
Sfx: Quotes 4, 5 and matching slides
Typewriter sounds

4

ENGLISH HISTORIAN Cape Coloureds originated from Khoi San, white and Oriental. Natal Coloureds are different in many respects from the bulk of Coloureds in the rest of the country. Their origins can be traced to three groups, Mauritians, St. Helenans and Euro-Africans.

5

CAPE COLOURED PERSON The term Coloured is not of our own thinking, and if we look at the circumstances of the South African situation then you must ask why. We have no peculiar colour, we have no peculiar language and if other people see these peculiarities, they see them not because they see them...but because they want other people to see them...I don't want to be labelled Coloured...all I want to be known as is South African.

Scene 3: Tips on types

Lx: Ice blue wash
Sfx: Distant highway traffic

(JENNIFER *enters. She is a drunk Cape Coloured "bergie", a middle-aged woman clutching her shabby jersey to keep out the cold. She is looking for Fransie. Her eyes eventually settle on an audience member; she pounces.)*

JENNIFER Ag Fransie, what am I gonna do with you. Sitting kaalgat opie witman se stoep. Wag jy vir iets? Daa's niemand binne daai huis, so you might as well forget it. Margie's looking out for my things there by the bridge and you know I don't trust her. *(Pause)* I saved 'n eintjie for you. Hoor jy, Fransie? Daa's nog iets in my borrel, 'n laaste mondvol plesier. Kom jy saam? Kom moegoe, dis laat!

Sfx: Car crash
Lx: Snap to orange wash
Slide change: A close-up of a teenage girl's face

(JENNIFER *abruptly changes character, speaking directly to the audience as* SAMANTHA, *a vibey, smooth-talking teenager.)*

SAMANTHA *(Stripping off "bergie" clothes)* No, I do not stem from a long line of toothless fishermen and grinning flower sellers. I'm no tourist attraction spicing up the beach front. Neither have I or any of my immediate family been to Cape Town for anything other than a holiday and to see the mountain, like everyone else. Afrikaans is not my mother tongue, yet you will be amused as I'm to note that many of us were registered at birth as Cape Coloured, Cape Malay, or swept under the distinguished umbrella...Other Coloured. *(Provocative dramatisation of each type)* I am also not the knife-wielding-slang-chooning-dagga-rooking-club-crazy-adolescent-alcoholic-type. I am not the taxi-addict-hanging-out-of-windows-in-peak-traffic-to-let-everyone-being-deafened-by-my-amps-know-and-see-that-I-am-here-and-I-am-loud-and there's-F-all-you-can-do-about-it-type.

Play-white? I couldn't even if I tried. Besides it's far more fashionable these days to be pro-black. And please, I don't mean African as it is, but psuedo-homey-nigger-lingo-baggy-jeans-and-jiving-hands-gangsta-black-into-rap-hardcore-rap-at-that-type.

The female equivalent being the tough-and-sexy-beer-and-cigarettes-who-says-girls-can't-rap-so-dress-me-skimpy-cos-a-woman's-not-a-woman-without-a man-type.

It's obvious that I'm not the nice-and-decent-get-me-to-church-so-I-can-strut-my-fashion-down-the-aisle-to-get communion-oh-so-innocent-marry-the-boy-next-door-with-a-veil-over-my-face-cos-believe-me-daddy-I'm-still-a-virgin-at-twenty-five-type. My mother is not the babalaas-rollers-in-the-street-swear-my-father-for-her-Friday-nite-blue-eye-and-fat-lip-type. My brothers and sisters and I have never been the sit-on-your-ass-blame-and-complain-it's-our-parents-it's-apartheid-this-new-government-affirmative-action-welfare-mentality-type.

I fought not to be the abandoned-and-pregnant-at-sixteen-give-up-my-dreams-cos-your-life's-over-and-education-doesn't-pay-so-I-better-just-get-a-saleslady-job-like-my-aunty-so-me-and-my-child-can-wear-nice-clothes-type.

All types! A frame created specially for you, by someone else. An outsider whose opinion matters more than yours or mine. But it's not what they see that robs us our identity. We betray ourselves. We play the part. We stick to what we know, malicious when one of us chooses a life beyond those confines. It takes courage to change your point of view and unashamedly do what your gut tells you to do.

Lx: Blackout
Quotes 6, 7 and matching slides

6

WOMAN IN STREET Coloured people are only a community in that they generally cling to the same ideas.

7

INDIAN MAN We must each follow the path we want to, but bruin ous just seem to follow everyone else.

Scene 4: Celia in me

Lx: Purple wash fades in
Sfx: Gentle falling rain
Fixed slide: Proud young parents posing with their newborn daughter

(ZOE pages through her photo album, reminiscing)

ZOE I was born where most of Durban's Coloured population was born, Addington hospital. My family shifted about fourteen times before I was ten, but somehow we inevitably settled in a historically Coloured area, even after it was legal to live somewhere else. There were never any public signs saying Coloureds only, but like an unspoken law, you went to a Coloured school, a Coloured church, had mostly Coloured friends, listened to popular Coloured music and followed Coloured fashion...or else!

Lx: Snap to bright white wash (1)
Sfx: Rain snap out

(Imitating teenage peers)

GIRL 1 Whehe, that one thinks she shits ice-cream. One-two klaps and she'll come right.
GIRL 2 Ja, she better watch it, cos me I got nancy time for people who think they too clever.

Lx: Snap to purple wash

ZOE I grew more determined to make my own choices, be myself and eventually I got used to not fitting in. My dad built a kind of pedestal for me and through me, my mother saw a dream for herself realised. Being, as my gran would say, "a Coloured girl with her head screwed on right", was a safe place to be. So I thought. But I was now at that age when losing that "precious gift for your husband one day" was the warning on my mother's lips and the gossip on the tongues of the neighbours.

Slide change: Woman hanging washing in backyard
Lx: Snap to bright white wash

ZOE *(Imitating neighbours)*
WOMAN 1 I mean, are our schools not good enough for them that they must send their daughter to a white school. Just watch. Just know she'll start "twanging" like a witou and listening to opera music, as if she's got a clue of what's going on! They need to come out down a peg or two, the lot of them.
WOMAN 2 You know what it is ? It's that mother of hers a real jitterbug, always flitting around. I see her from my kitchen window every Tuesday, dashing off to play tennis in that mini-skirt of hers. Please, at *her* age!

Lx: Snap to purple wash

And then it happened. Yet another Coloured teenager pregnant, straight out of school. The neighbours were delighted.

Lx: Snap to bright white wash

WOMAN 1 What I did tell you? Private school and all. At least my daughter's looked after herself. She will be going to Varsity next year. *(Pause)* Oh. I don't know, but she'll have a degree behind her name when she's finished.

Lx: Snap to purple wash
Sfx: Rain fades in
Slide change: Dejected old woman sitting on porch

ZOE Everything changed. My gran's praises fizzled. *(Imitating grandmother)* "Oh well, my son. She isn't the first and she won't be the last."

While the other granny, on hearing the dreaded news, left my mother speechless as she burst into sobs.

(Imitating grandmother) "Hai no, child. Not her too. Such an intelligent girl wasted like that. Ag no, man. What are these children getting up to these days. What did her poor father have to say?"

Slide change: Father image

ZOE Not much actually. I thought he'd be the one to blow a fuse, but he didn't. Even before I said it, I sensed that he knew. He curled up on my bed with his head at my feet and said: "What is it, my baby?" The speech I had spent almost two weeks agonizing over, fell out of my mouth in monotone.

"Dad, the worst thing that could ever have happened, has happened. I don't know how else to say it…I'm going to have a baby."

I had repeated my mother's pattern to the T, pregnant at the same age from a man I never intended to marry. She was furious that all her attempts to keep me from making her mistakes, had failed. I wanted to scream at her too. *(Shouting)* I'm going away, so you won't face the sniggering neighbours and sorrowful relatives!

Slide change: Close-up of little boy's face

I intentionally had my baby in another city, a distant hospital and as far from a Coloured environment as possible. *I* saw the arrival of my son as a sign for me to change direction. Together we made a new beginning. I went ahead with my career plans, baby at my side.

Lx: Snap to bright white wash
Sfx: Rain fade out

(Imitating peer)

GIRL 2 You going back to study? For what? Whe-ma-me, you've got time.

(Imitating neighbour)

WOMAN 1 Ooh, she's definitely missed the boat. Can't wear white at her twenty-first, that's for sure. *(Laughs)*

Lx: Snap to purple wash

They began to ridicule again and I could feel my old self coming back. I graduated with distinction and my dad resurrected his pedestal. My parents broke tradition too, by not forcing me to marry the boy. Besides I wouldn't let them. Oh and about that prize package "for our husbands one day", I just remind myself that they're talking about a part of *my* body as if it doesn't belong to me.

I guess to let go of an old way of life you have to dare to step outside, choose your own angle. Why the hell not? Nowadays almost everything I do is the breaking of the mould and each time I realise a new part of myself.

Coloured is not always what it seems and I'm not what *you* think I am, but what *I* think I am.

Lx: Snap to orange wash
(ZOE *speaks as* SAMANTHA.)

You could call me the never-surrender-cos-it's-not-over-till-the-coloured-girl-spreads-her-wings-type!

Lx: Blackout

Quotes 8, 9 and matching slides

8

PSYCHOLOGIST There is a tradition of retraction and at the same time violence has become a symbol of manhood.

9

COLOURED SOCIAL WORKER Coloured women are survivors. If they can withstand all the verbal, physical and psychological abuse that they do and still wake up in the morning and find something to laugh about, just imagine how much more powerful they would be in the absence of that abuse.

Scene 5: When the cycle hurts

Lx: Gobo creating shadows and patches of light
Slide: Old wedding photo, bridal couple at church door

(BRENDA *enters in semi-darkness, humming a popular tune. She stumbles and curses, then realises that there is someone in the room. Her mother is not physically present on stage, but* BRENDA *speaks to her as though she is. Her "mother" is seated in a large armchair.)*

BRENDA Mummy? Is that you? What you doing sitting in the dark, Ma why don't you switch the light on? *(She does so and steps back in shock.)*

Oh fuck, Ma! *(Long pause. She stares at the couch on which her mother is seated.)*

Where is he? *(Pause)* Gone where? Flippin' coward. Are you OK, Ma? Can I get you something? *(Pause)*

(Angry) I stay out one night and he has to make the most of it! I'm not that stupid child who can't fight back anymore and he knows it. Why didn't you phone me, Ma. You knew where I was. Or even call the bladdy cops for once in your life. Jesus, I'm sick of this.

(Pause. She sits.) You know Ma, I could have got that flat with Clarissa and Ashley, but I thought of you alone in this house with him and I said never mind, I can wait a bit longer till you pull yourself together. I wouldn't have been able to go to bed in peace anyway, wondering what he's doing to you at night. But Ma you can't go on like this forever. I can't. I'm spending my life being your bodyguard and he hasn't stopped hitting you in all these years. What makes you think he'll ever change? He doesn't even need an excuse these days. You just have to look at him sideways and he says you're asking for it.

I mean, tell me Ma. What was it this time, the food? Did he go off cos of something you said? *(Pause)* Me? Cos you let me go out last night? No, it can't be me. I'm in his good books. I'm not "living in sin" with Ashley and he wanted a teacher or a doctor or a lawyer, so now I'm doing the fuckin' LLB, so he can "broam" about it. I mean, even Bradley's out of his way. Always throwing it in his face that he wasn't his real son, so now he doesn't have one. The dog should be smiling.

(Breaking) Look at you man, Ma, what are you holding on for? So one day he can hit you so bad that the stitches and ice-blocks won't even help. Is that what you want, Ma? And for what? So he can live? *(Long pause)*

You remember that blue floral dress you had, Ma? You made it, hey. The one with the two pockets in front that you used to dig in for your hanky or some tissues. *(Silence)* Well, I remember it, it used to be your favourite. But you stopped wearing it that day after Aunty Sandra's wedding, remember Ma? The day your blue dress turned red. You know, that's one thing about my father. He never leaves a job till it's finished. Standing there breathing like an ox, with his shoe in your face. He knew we were watching. It was like he was trying to show us a point, but he just made us hate him more. *(Pause)*

Ma, listen to me. We could find a flat together, you and me. I could work some nights in the week instead of only on the weekends and you could start working from home like you're always joking about. You've already got the sewing machine and all those stylish patterns in your head. I mean, look at the outfit you made for my matric ball. No-one could believe that you copied it from a magazine and in no time. Ma, are you listening? Imagine Ma, "Gloria's Garments" or better "G. Designs." You could take orders. Half the neighbourhood already knows how good you are. *(Pleading)* Ma!

(Frustrated) Ma, don't sit there like a bladdy statue. You could do it Ma, start looking after yourself, instead of slaving in this fucked up house, just waiting for your next hiding. Ma…?

(Her eyes follow her "mother" crossing the room and exiting the stage.)

(Raging) Ma. Ma! For fuck sakes, at least tell me what's wrong with what I'm saying. Please Ma, don't just walk away, I'm serious. I'm prepared to take the chance if you are, he can't touch you!

Sfx: Dishes being cleared and washed up off stage

*(Defeated)*What do you think you teaching me, Ma? How to stay faithful to a man, even if it kills me? How to make a dead marriage work, so I won't be a "divorcee" or cause a scandal. "The wife packed up and left her husband, just like that!" At least you stuck it out till the children were old enough and when is "old enough" Ma? You're not going anywhere and Bradley's already following his stepfather's example. Am I supposed to follow yours?!

(To herself) Well you are one outstanding example, Ma. A fuckin' classic. Just like your mother.

Lx: Slow fade to blackout
Quotes 10, 11 and matching slides

10

Middle-aged Coloured women talking

VOICE 1 It's always some old white lady or a bladdy Indian winning the jackpot and what about us?

VOICE 2 Ja, hey, people like us don't win lotteries.

11

COLOURED HOUSEWIFE In the twenty years that I lived in that block of flats, I watched the mother, the children then the grandchildren sitting and drinking on that same staircase.

Scene 6: What's new?

Sfx: "Opskiet" music heard in the blackout
Lx: Slow fade in
Slide: Large family with raised glasses, at New Year's Eve bash

(EVETTE *is doing a "langarm" dance by herself. As the song ends, she relaxes, pours herself another drink and collapses into a couch. She is a witty and outspoken woman in her mid-forties, who becomes progressively drunk and abrasive through the scene. At times she speaks directly to the audience and then sometimes she seems to be talking to herself.)*

EVETTE You must be wondering what I'm doing here all by myself, like some old cow in a nursing home on New Year's Eve, mind you. He's gone to that stupid party alone this time, cos me, I'm not a false person and I'm sick of pulling a mask for those in-laws. His family never took to me in the first place, so it's no skin off my face. Besides, I'm in no mood for the same boring conversations about how big the children have grown and comparing husbands who can cook to husbands who won't. They're a bunch of liars anyway.

Everyone knows that Shirley's man is forever getting some young fool pregnant and Pasty acts so shocked, like Andre's any better. As for poor Merna, she'll get a allergy one of these days, with all that cheap make-up she plasters on to hide her bruises. Oh and let's not forget madam Cookie herself. The party's at her house this year, and I'm dik of hearing her stories about how Jerry bought her this gold ring last year and that gold chain for her birthday and for the tenth time how he sent her this huge bouquet of flowers when she went into hospital to have her *(Gesturing)* "wardrobe" taken out. Dripping in jewellery like a bladdy coolie! Looks like a damn Christmas tree, if you ask me.

I doubt she ever asks where that money comes from or thinks how it would feel if it was *her* son buying those drugs from Jerry. Poor Tyrone, that's their son. Imagine what it's like for him, knowing what his father does on the side. Watching his father buy anyone and anything he wants. No bladdy principles, like money's the answer to all your problems. Me? I may be poor, black and ugly but at least when I sit in church, my conscience is clear. *(Makes the sign of the cross)* My child knows the difference between right and wrong. He knows that if I catch him hanging around with those button-head cornerboys, I'll klap him, pull his ears in front of them, no matter how big he thinks he is.

(Suddenly overcome with pride) My boy...He just started this nice job my friend's husband organized for him. Every Friday he comes straight home with his pay packet, not even opened yet. After he's paid his board and given me some money towards a carton of cigarettes, a box of wine or something nice for myself, only *then* does he think of himself. I just hope he doesn't let me down now that he's out of school. You know how they get. Full of big ideas, like buying a car and shacking up with that girlfriend of his. Ay, but what can a parent do to stop them? He keeps saying that they're in no hurry to get married, so why must they live together is what I can't understand. *(Panicking)* Maybe she's pregnant and he's too skrik to tell me. Ooh and she's from one of those snotty uppercut families too. They're not exactly rich, but they live in a white area and it'll be a big disgrace, you know what I mean. They'll say it's all his fault and then what'll he do?

(Calming herself) Anyway I told him not to bring shame to this house, just because his father's not here to put him in his place. You see Barney's not his real father and they never really hit it off, so it's only me he

listens to. *(She sighs and takes a long sip of her drink.)*

Ooh, it's almost half-past eleven, they must be really making a noise by now. With those people, once they've had a few shots, all that stiffness is out the window. The woman are screeching with laughter, the kids are running amok and the men are babbling about engines and what have you or else they're showing off with their guns. Hmph! No thank you. I'm quite happy having my own private celebration for a change. Anyway Cookie probably wasn't expecting me to show my face at her house after the fight we had.

We haven't spoken to each other for...must be five months now. I told her off about minding other people's business and you know what she had the nerve to tell me? That I'm forever living in other people's houses and that I don't know when to go home. That's the problem with her type of person. You can't put a mirror in front of them, 'cos they won't like what they see.

I hope Barney remembers to bring my share of the food home, especially my favourite potato salad and Granny Williams must have made her usual delicious trifle. Mmm. The old lady can bake, man! Sponge cake, chocolate cake, koeksisters, biscuits, Christmas pudding, you name it. She makes everything the old way, using the recipes her mother gave her. She refuses to give away her baking secrets. Ja, I suppose she just loves being told that her cakes come out the best and she's bang that one of us will outshine her.

Bladdy old cow! *(She pours herself another drink)*

Now Cookie, on the other hand, loves to tell everyone how to cook and it got to the stage where I used to hear her starting to preach and I'd just get up and walk out. I'm not gonna sit there acting polite, while madam tells me how to do better in the kitchen, as if that's the way to improve my marriage!

(Whispering) Of course *she* knows men inside out and she's not shy to tell you. *(Aside)* That's because she slept with so many of them before she became the faithful housewife, that she can't even remember their names! *(Chuckles to herself)*

Oh, I better phone Barney to remind him about the food before they start the countdown, cos that's all he's gonna have for lunch tomorrow. I refuse to stand and sweat over those pots, when there's only two of us eat it. I don't know what's so special about New Year's anyway.

Slide change: Large family posing with raised glasses, at New Year's Eve bash

(She lights a cigarette, dials and waits for someone to answer.)

Hullo...who's that ? Oh Tyrone sweetheart, you sound so big over the phone. It's Aunty Evette here. Please can you call Uncle Barney for me, lovie. He's wearing a green-and-white stripe T-shirt and denim bermudas. Thank you, boy. I'll hold on.

(To audience) Just like I said, a bladdy madhouse. Oh and Merna's smoking too much, sounds like a dog barking. They probably had a good scandal about me already. No-one will stand up for me too, except Pasty maybe. She's the only one I can tolerate from that whole Williams clan.

(She is interrupted) Barney, is that you? Here! You sound like you drank a whole case by yourself. But listen, I'm phoning about the breyani, don't forget to bring me some. *(Pause)* You can put it in my Tupperware that I sent the beans salad in and bring some meat and potato salad too...What you mean you can't hear me? Since when do your ears get blocked just 'cos your tongue is thick? *(Raising her voice)* I said don't for...Oh, so now you heard me. Just bring back my bladdy bowls; I know how those sisters of yours are forever snatching other people's Tupperware by mistake. OK? *(Pause)* I'm watching TV, so if I fall asleep in the lounge don't disturb me when you come in. Ja, and let someone sober drive you home, alright? OK. Bye.*(Abruptly replaces receiver and pours herself another drink.)*

*(To audience)*As I was saying, this thing about New Year. What exactly are we celebrating ? I'm not getting any younger and this place hasn't gotten any better. The bladdy kids are growing up too fast. It's all that American trash they listen to, blasting a person's eardrums in the taxis. If the girls are not pregnant, then it's the boys stabbing each other or trying to drink themselves to death. It was exactly the

same when I was young. Only that time you were forced to marry the boy who spoiled you and the gangsters were much more sophisticated and organized. Not like these goofballs we have today. Lucky for me, my parents were a bit strict. If it wasn't for my mother forcing me to go to church and my father checking up on my friends, I might have ended up a whoring alcoholic like Tessa down the road. Tessa the "town mattress", "There's a screw just waiting for you."

(She notices the countdown on TV, quickly turns the volume up and tops up her drink.)

Oh, just listen to me selling my mouth for-a-win-and-a-place. I nearly missed it. *(She raises her glass motioning for the audience to join in.)* Five...four...three...two...One? What the hell, Happy New Year!

Sfx: "Opskiet" music rises
Slide change: Fireworks
Lx: Fade to blackout as she dances alone

Scene 7: A Coloured place

Lx: Fade in. A warm interior
Sfx: Scorpio Song at low volume
Slides of Coloured children (groups and individuals) in various settings

(An older TRACEY *during this scene randomly covers parts of the set with white sheets, as if to put each story and its characters to rest.)*

TRACEY There is a gap, an emptiness in the local history museum. That space waits for us. It is opening.

We must know where we come from, to understand how we've come to be where we are. Our stories remain untold, our triumphs unheard of, our voices...unrecognized. We have to show ourselves or there will always be a hollow place where our pride should be.

I want my children and their children's children to know of a Coloured place not rotting with division and inertia, but a Coloured place of power and diversity, that they will not be ashamed to call...home.

Lx: Fade into green tree-shaped Gobo
Sfx: Scorpio Song rises

Concluding voice over: Quotes A–K accompanied by matching slides

Voice over: Conclusion

A
I think of Coloureds as outspoken people, down-to-earth.

B
A Coloured person does not believe that he can invent anything. He can only watch, take, copy and buy, because he cannot see himself as a creator. With me, with everything I touch I ask myself: hey, why can't I do that?

C
Our Coloured youth are far too Americanized, but what we see on TV is not reality. Americans are selling us their garbage and we're buying it!

D
The future of Coloured people lies in the hands of each Coloured individual. It's the universal question of choice.

E
The term "Coloured" is something other people identify me by.

F
I think Coloured people are beautiful and as soon as they can realize it, the sooner they can make the world around them beautiful. You know, spread that beauty.

G
I've always thought that having mixed blood in my veins makes me an interesting person.

H
To me, Coloured women are the most beautiful women in South Africa.

I

May the new year bring into our minds and souls an awareness that we are our own bondsmen and by our endeavours free ourselves. And in this awareness we will find the beginning of the thread of oppression and subjugation which permeates the entire fabric of our being. And finding it is not enough. We must eradicate and destroy it, first in our souls and, then, wherever else it may manifest itself.

End

> What I managed to do after the protest period was over and we've gotten freedom in this country, was to start writing specifically for women. And that's what I'm doing. I'm not writing plays about men anymore.

In 1977, Fatima Dike became the first African woman to publish a play in South Africa, *The Sacrifice of Kreli*. Born Royline Fatima Dike in the township of Langa, in Cape Town, her family was part of the forced removal in the 1930s. Dike was educated at church schools in Langa until they were taken over by the government in the 1950s. She later went to a boarding school run by Irish nuns in Rustenburg in the old Transvaal until graduation. Because she loved English and reading, Fatima knew she wanted to do something in these areas, but opportunities were very limited for black women.

> I was in school during the late 1950s, 1960s and the early 1970s, and at that time there were three outlets for black girls. You became a teacher, a nurse and, if your parents had money or were educated people, you became a social worker. So in my day, there was really no variety.

She decided to choose a teaching career and consulted a teacher friend about the possibilities of going to college in order to return to Langa to teach in one of the high schools. The friend explained to Fatima that under the Bantu educational system you were placed wherever there was a vacancy regardless of whether or not you knew the subject matter.

> After that comment, I realized why the quality of education was so bad. It was a take it or leave it matter in which you've gone to college and at the end you are given those options.

After high school, Fatima went to work in her brother-in-law's bookshop, where she became engrossed in reading. During this period of the early 1970s, Black Consciousness groups were emerging, many presenting poetry readings and other so-called radical materials. With the support from a local record shop, Fatima was able to smuggle banned records into the country. She obtained books such as Eldridge Cleaver's *Soul on Ice*, material on the Black Panthers from the American Information Services, Dr. Martin Luther King's "I Have a Dream" speech, and even a record of Angela Davis's speech from her prison cell.

> These things were so motivating to us, along with the poetry we were writing. But this was a beautiful period that ended quite suddenly and we lost friends because of the banning of groups. People started disappearing and there was silence. Then things were revived in 1975 when Sue Clark, who was a poet, started having readings at her house.

In 1972, Fatima began to volunteer her services at the Space Theatre, a nonracial theatre in Cape Town known primarily for producing Athol Fugard's early plays. She participated in a fundraiser where she presented a poem. She met Robert Amato, a white writer/director who had gathered information about a king of the Gcalekas. He was interested in writing a play, but as a white person he felt he was not the best one to pursue this project. He suggested that Fatima take on the task, because she knew the customs and language of the people.

The Sacrifice of Kreli is a play based on black history, including ceremonial pageantry that looks at black resistance to colonialism. Ironically, the play was produced during the 1976 Soweto uprisings. The play examines the life of a king who goes into self-exile instead of being enslaved by the British. Written in both Xhosa and English, the play was performed in Cape Town, toured the Eastern Cape, and later appeared at the Market Theatre in Johannesburg.

Fatima's second play was *The First South African* (1977), based on a true story, which explores the issue of racial identity. In 1978, she wrote a children's play, *The Crafty Tortoise*, based on an African folk story. Her next play, *Glass House*(1979), was inspired by the 1976 uprising of students in Langa and the black child, Hector Petersen, murdered by the South African Police.

> It hit me when I realized that these people [whites] would rather kill us all off, or they will all die before they give us our land. I was very angry. But in a country like South Africa, during that period, you became very careful. You learned to suppress your anger, but never let it die because you wanted to survive the next day and the next. That's how I survived. I just squashed my anger, so that I could write about these things.

Glass House is a two-woman piece about the relationship between a black and a white woman, and was the final production at the Space Theatre in 1979.

From 1979 to 1983, Fatima went into self-exile in the United States. While there, she participated in an international writers' conference at the University of Iowa. The remainder of her time was spent in New York City working with various theatre groups. In 1980, *Glass House* was produced at Ellen Stewart's La Mama Theatre and also toured the East Coast with actress Mary Alice performing in one of the productions. Fatima took courses at New York University, where she enrolled in a playwriting class with Ed Bullins, who told her she was too experienced to be in his class. Dike considers herself to be primarily a self-taught playwright, but she credits those from the Black Consciousness Movement for nurturing her work.

Fatima's latest piece, *Street Walking and Company Valet Service*, is aimed at young people. The play focuses on the escalating drug scene in South Africa.

> What's happening in the new South Africa is that drugs have been glamorized. To us it's a shock because it's new and is happening so fast. The play is based on the lives of four women from different backgrounds.

She also intends to work on a play based on the Truth and Reconciliation Commission. Fatima resides in Langa.

ARTISTIC STATEMENT

In 1990, we knew when Mandela was released from Robben Island things were going to change, and that our theatre also had to change. Protest theatre couldn't live forever. I was living in Johannesburg with Nomhle Nkonyeni and she had brought a woman from Port Elizabeth to look after her grandchild. And the other lady who lived in the building, Gertrude, ran a shebeen on the top floor of the building. And every day, religiously at 4:00 P.M. Gertrude used to go out with four cases of beer bottles and would return with the bottles filled and leave them in Nomhle's kitchen. By 5:30 she had finished buying all the booze she needed for the evening. She would then sit in front of the television with Nomhle's caretaker watching *The Bold and the Beautiful*. One afternoon I happen to come and these two women were sitting together watching *The Bold*. Now Gertrude hated sex, but she enjoyed watching it on the soap. And the caretaker loved sex. So the two of them were sitting there arguing over the soap. For two weeks I'd stop whatever I was doing at 5:30 and be at Nomhle's house to watch these two women argue over *The Bold and the Beautiful*! And that's how the story began. But I couldn't just write about two women watching a soap; I had to do something else. I went to stay with another woman in Albertina, at the height of the violence, when they were killing people in what was the Eastern Transvaal. So the violence that we hear outside of the window in the play is that reality.

What I want the audience to get from this play is that black women are funky! We can be very brave. When we get together and get down we can be fun. The difference between African American women and South African women is that African American women are out there and doing things and you can see them everywhere. South African women do things but very little is known about us. We can be very inventive.

THE ROLE OF THEATRE IN SOUTH AFRICA

Theatre always has to be an educator. It reflects the society in which we live. Sometimes we try to write plays to change the society's view of things.

HAVE SITUATIONS IMPROVED FOR BLACK WOMEN IN THEATRE IN THE NEW SOUTH AFRICA?

Yes. There is a lot more freedom. If one wants to do something, you don't have that fear of what are the brothers going to say. You just go in and do what you want to do. You see, what governed us before was the struggle. I couldn't have written *So, What's New?* in the 1970s, as much as I would have loved to. The whole idea was that we had to harness our power together to fight the struggle through theatre.

HAVE THINGS IMPROVED IN GENERAL IN THE NEW SOUTH AFRICA?

Yes. The feeling for me is that I have the freedom to do what I want because I have the vote in the land of my ancestors. And if I don't like what's happening, I don't have to vote for that person or party. On the other hand, people think government makes things happen overnight and there'll be abundance. It's never going to happen like that. We are the citizens of this country. When we were fighting for freedom, we knew that in the end this freedom would bring responsibility. We should not just wait for the government but do things on our own. No country has ever been prosperous in three years. It takes a long time. If we're expecting fruit now, it will be unripe and then we'll have stomach cramps.

PRODUCTION HISTORY

So What's New? premiered at the Market Theatre in Johannesburg in September, 1991. Directed by Barney Simon, the cast included Doris Sehula, Pat Mabuya, Motshabi Tyelele, and Nomsa Xaba.

Interview conducted July 22, 1997, in Cape Town

Photo by Kathy A. Perkins

2 So What's New?

Fatima Dike

Preset

The lounge/kitchen of BIG DEE*'s house. The lounge is decorated in bold, nouveau riche style, a large couch with a matching two-seater and armchair. A coffee table, a long counter which separates the kitchen area. Beyond the kitchen, through a beaded curtain, the storage area for* BIG DEE*'s shebeen is visible, the shebeen is beyond that, outside. Another doorway, also curtained by beads, leads to the rest of the house – the bedrooms, the bathroom. Downstage centre is the focal point of the room, a large TV set.*

Blackout. The signature tune of The Bold and the Beautiful *comes up. Lights up.* BIG DEE *rushes in, grabs a plate of raisins and settles in her favourite seat on the big couch. Voices of soap opera characters.* BIG DEE *settles ecstatically, immediately absorbed. After a few beats,* PAT *enters carrying a battered briefcase.*

Act I

Scene 1

PAT Hello Dee. I am fine thanks. What about you? (DEE *ignores her.*) Hello Dee. I'm fine, thanks – what about you?

(PAT *goes straight to the fridge to get a beer.*)

PAT Tyhini ntomibi? – ndiyakubulisa. [What's the matter, girl? – I'm greeting you.][1]

DEE I'm fine Pat. (PAT *takes a big gulp of beer.*) Uya bona ke sisi [you see now sister], now you owe me R178.

PAT Ou Dee kawuyeke man [come on, Dee, be sweet], you are the richest shebeen queen in Soweto an I'm starving. Yazi, selling houses in Soweto can be hell. Hayi, I must find myself another job.

(DEE *laughs, still absorbed in the soap opera.*)

DEE I told you to go back to showbiz.

PAT And starve!

DEE You are starving anyway.

PAT *(Settling into armchair)* Hey, what's this? Is it Capitol or…

DEE No, it's *The Bold and the Beautiful.*

PAT Have I missed much?

DEE You've missed everything.

PAT Damn! Indlela endibaleke ngayo and the damn taxi got caught in the rush hour traffic.

DEE Shhhhhh!

PAT I felt like killing the taxi driver.

DEE Shhhh! Hayi if Sally falls for Clark's lies again I'll throw up s'trues God [honest to God] ngiza ku me nyanya.

PAT Yho! When SPECTRA was going bankrupt who saved Sally? It was Clark my dear she owes him.

DEE Clark needed Sally too my dear. His wife Chris Forrester had dumped him and his career with Eric Forrester's was finished. What he has done to Sally is the straw that broke the camel's back.

PAT But Dee, this is not your usual marriage. This is a case of beauty and the beast. Clark is young, handsome, virile…

DEE Uya bona wena [do you see now?], this is why I don't like you here. You always spoil *The Bold and the Beautiful* for me. Sally is experienced. Besides she owns SPECTRA, what has Clark got?

PAT What has Clark got?

1 Translations into English included in this text have been provided by the author.

DEE Shut up!

PAT Dee, do you really think Sally won't give up all her money to be with Clark? I mean, beside her money what has she got?

DEE Sally has a brain in her head like me, *not* between her legs like some people I know. Clark will not get away with his bullshit!

PAT I hope so for your sake.

DEE Oh khawuthule [shut up]! *(Pause)* What do you mean?

PAT I'm thinking about you and Willie.

DEE Clark is a slut, he'll sleep with anything on two legs if it wears a skirt. If Willie tries anything like that, I will cut his b...e...e...s off.

PAT Now that's my kind of man. I want a man to sweep me off my feet, and when I wake up in his bed the following morning, I'll say. "My God what happened, where am I?"...I don't want a guy who will say, "Please asseblief [please] tog Pattie."

DEE You want a sex maniac?

PAT Don't you?

DEE Hey nkazana [woman] we are talking about you not me?

PAT Hey, I told what I want from a man, what do you like?

DEE I like them to be sexy and gentle and passionate.

PAT Then we agree Clark is sexy.

DEE He's not my type.

PAT What's your type?

DEE Shut up and watch.

(They watch TV for a moment.)

PAT Margo's marriage to Bill is falling apart.

DEE Owu Pat u va nxa kusithiwani? [Oh Pat, why can't you behave?]

PAT It's true, ever since Margo discovered that Bill had lied to her about his trip to Hawaii and about the diamond bracelet, they are moving further apart.

DEE Shhhhhhhh!

PAT Ridge and Brooke are still in love. I'm a woman, I know.

DEE She has slept with all the men in that family but she's still hungry for more. Women!

PAT I don't blame the poor girl, which woman can resist Ridge?

DEE You can't resist any man, that's for sure.

PAT Ridge and Brooke shared something so strong, it will always come between her and Eric.

DEE Oh please, Pat, don't talk nonsense. Brooke does not know the meaning of love, she confuses it with lust. She is going to spend the rest of her life running between Eric and Ridge if Stephanie does not do something about her soon.

PAT Do you think Eric will go back to Stephanie?

DEE Eric is just too dumb.

PAT Dee, you know men, you know them.

DEE I know they can't resist a fuck. *(Pause)*

(PAT *laughs.*)

DEE Hey wena [you], Pat, if men could have babies would they sleep around as much as they do?

PAT *(Laughing)* That is an interesting thought.

DEE They are too scared to watch their wives giving birth. *(Laughs)* Can you imagine what would happen if they gave birth just once?

PAT Yho! They'd use contraceptives just like us.

DEE Not when they are too lazy to use condoms.

PAT This reminds me of something I read in a magazine recently. Picture this: Bra Willie is polishing the floor on his knees, with a baby on his back. You come home from work, throw your briefcase on the sofa in the lounge, throw yourself over to grab the remote control and watch the news on TV while you kick your shoes off one by one. Bra Willie comes, and ever so gently peels your socks off while he makes sure that he is not standing in front of the screen. A hot cup of tea makes its way into your eager hands, you sip and swallow, no sugar. You tell Bra Willie rudely that the tea has no sugar; he apologizes profusely as he makes his way into the kitchen to get the sugar, saying "Mama, I am so sorry, but I went to the clinic today and the doctor told me that I was pregnant again."

DEE Oooo, I'd love to finish this off. "Willie", I'd say, "besides being a bad housekeeper you're a bad cook and now you want to be a breeding machine. Unfortunately, I can't let you do that here. Pack your bags and go home, tell your father I'll be coming to demand my lobola [dowry] back, I'm sure there are many men out there who could do what you have failed to do, better."

PAT Right on!

DEE Hey, that's reverse sexism! *(They fall about laughing.)*

(A commercial interrupts the programme.)

PAT Hey, I love ads. They give me chance to grab another beer.

(PAT *goes to the fridge to get another beer.*)

DEE Sisi yi fridge yam leyo ayiyo yethu. [Sister, that fridge is mine, not yours.]
PAT Ag, I know it's your fridge but my favourite beer is inside.
DEE Now you owe me R180.
PAT Uligqolo [you're a miser]. What is your money beside my friendship? Where's the baby?
DEE U Mercedes? She hasn't come back from school.
PAT She is late today.

(DEE *stands up from the couch and goes to switch the television off.*)

DEE Eyona nto ke [the problem is] Pat. I want to go somewhere, Willie took my car. I don't know where he is. I am supposed to go to the supermarket! to the bottle store! to the butchery and I am sitting here wasting my time.
PAT Does he know you were going to need it?
DEE Hey nkazana, we have a standing rule, if he takes the car he has to check with me. Uyandi caphukisa ubona nje [he makes me angry] when he acts so irresponsibly, if you care to know.
PAT Ag Dee! it's the rush hour.
DEE Hayi suka [go away], he knows about the rush hour. He knows he should be here.
PAT But the car could be giving him problems?
DEE What problems Pat? Huh? That car gets serviced every three months. I'm the woman who pays, I know. I wonder where Thandi is? I could borrow her car and go about my business.
PAT Hey, did you say Thandi? Is Thandi back in town? Uyazi Dee, I could kill that little sister of mine. My mother is forever asking after her, "Where's Thandi, where's Thandi?", as if I don't exist.
DEE *(Laughs)* Are you blaming her?
PAT Hayi suka, just grab a beer and sweeten your tongue, it's on me!
DEE Njongapha sumanu undifuxuza ngotywala [look here, stop filling me with booze]. You know that I don't touch booze during the week, and besides if Willie came home and found me drinking, you know what would happen.
PAT *(Raising her bottle)* Since I don't have a Willie, here's to life!
DEE I've got someone to keep me warm, what about you?
PAT Up yours, lovie!

(Both laugh.)

Pat Yazi [you know] Dee, I must still go home and cook, or else my son will divorce me. Suku hleka.
Dee *(Laughs)* I don't worry about that! Willie and Mercedes take turns to cook for me.
Pat Yoo, if my son had a woman who made him cook, I'd throw the bloody bitch out personally.
Dee Hayi Pat man, wena you are just jealous. If your son really loved the woman, he'd pamper her.
Pat Hayi Dee that's my child uyazi [you know], my one and only son. I am going to choose his wife.
Dee *(Laughing)* Come on Pat maan, Sandile is only twelve!
Pat Yhu, I can wait, I'll choose.
Dee *(Laughs)* Inene, I feel sorry for her, whoever she is, akalibonanga.

(Both laugh.)

DEE Hey, it's seven o'clock. Where's that child of mine? anga linge nje ande nze l' izimanga ngoba ndakumbonisa impundu zenyoko. [She mustn't do things that will shock me otherwise I will show her the burns of a snake.]
PAT *(Laughs)* Why do I get the feeling that you are going to cook your own supper tonight?

(MERCEDES, *sixteen years old, dressed in a tracksuit, enters through the kitchen door. She throws her school bags down on the kitchen floor.*)

MERCEDES Hello Ma. Hello Sis' Pat!
PAT Hello my baby. Your mother and I were just talking about you. How's school?
MERCEDES School is fine Sis' Pat.
PAT Aha!
MERCEDES Ma, what's cooking I'm starving?
DEE Mercedes, what time is it?
MERCEDES Has your watch stopped, Ma?

DEE I asked you a question? Lixesha lokungena endlini eli? [This is no time for a girl to be out on the street.]

MERCEDES Hayi.

DEE Uyabonake mtwanam [listen here my child]. In this house we have rules. If you feel you can't obey them, move out.

MERCEDES But Ma, today is Wednesday. We have netball practice.

DEE Netball practice my foot, Mercedes! If netball is going to keep you out this late, you'll have to give it up.

MERCEDES Give it up?

DEE Yes.

MERCEDES But Ma, I've been picked to play in the first team.

DEE Today your excuse is netball practice, tomorrow it will still be netball practice. You are still a baby. I don't want you dropping another baby on my lap. Your father died mtwanami without leaving us a cent. I want you to learn and make your own future. I want you to bring me a degree, not a birth certificate, siyavana?

(*Pause.* MERCEDES *gets her bags off the kitchen floor and exits to the bedroom.*)

PAT Mmm, mmm, yhu choman, Kodwa, I think you are a bit hard on her.

DEE Pat, what do you expect me to do? Hee? Ubona nje amaxesha ajikile [times have changed]. If I don't tell her now what's right and what's wrong, tomorrow will be too late.

PAT Amaxesha a jikile [times have changed].

DEE And so what?

PAT Ha, today children know a lot more at an early age. If you are that worried about Mercedes, why don't you just take her to the doctor. Heh. You know what I mean.

DEE And give her the green light to sleep around.

PAT It's going to happen sooner or later.

DEE Pat, just leave me alone wena [you] man.

PAT Sorry for butting in. Thanks for the beer, I must go.

(PAT *stands and puts the two empty beer bottles in a cardboard tray next to the bin.*)

DEE Don't thank me.

PAT Ag, just call it good manners.

DEE Pay me.

PAT Uyazi wena Dee, one of these days when I'm gone you'll remember me my friend s'trues God. Bye bye Mercedes.

MERCEDES *(From the bedroom)* Bye bye Sis' Pat.

(PAT *goes out.* MERCEDES *comes into the living room and stands just outside the bedroom door.*)

MERCEDES Ma, why are you so angry with me? I've done nothing wrong; it's the truth. I've worked so hard to get into the first team, please don t stop me from playing.

DEE Mercedes come here, yiza pha mntanam, yiza ku mama.

(MERCEDES *goes and sits next to her mother on the sofa.*)

DEE Mercedes, when your father died I was young, you were a baby. Your grandmother was too poor herself to help me. All I knew to do was sing. One day there was a talent contest in the township, I went there with my friends, you were on my lap. My friends said, "Come on Big Dee go up and sing you are better than these people." I was shy. I went up. I just closed my eyes and I sang, "Ndililolo ndodwa ndenziwa zizenzo Zam, ndenzwa ziinyembezi zomzali o waye hlel'e lindile." The people clapped, even you. Ben Moloise was there, he said, "Baby you've got the job." I was so happy I was a Music Maker, that is where I met Sis' Pat and Sis' Thandi.

MERCEDES The Chattanooga Sisters?

DEE Yes, the Chattanooga Sisters. What a job! For five years, sleeping in cars, sleeping on cement, two months no pay. But I said mm mm no more. I went to work in a factory so I could have you with me again. Ja my baby and the men it wasn't hard to find a man. But how many do you remember? It's not the thing I'm proud of. Do you think I'm happy to run a shebeen with drunks banging on my door? I want something very very different for you. I want you to be strong, to be clever, I want you to go out into the world and say I want this I want that I am a woman. If I fight with you it's because I love you. You are the best thing that has happened to me. You have given me something to live for.

(PAT *and* THANDI *enter through the front door singing "Chattanooga Choo Choo".*)

DEE Thandi where did you get that dress?

THANDI You like it?
DEE Do I like it? I love it!
THANDI Well in that case I'm not telling.
DEE Aha! You got it from Milady's back door[2] exclusive!
THANDI Wrong! But I'll get you one within the week. Bye for now.
PAT By the way where's Willie?
DEE If you want me to throw up ask me about Willie.

(THANDI *and* PAT *exit singing the "Chattanooga Choo Choo".*)

Fade

Scene 2

(SIS' DEE *is sitting at the kitchen counter reading a newspaper.*)

THANDI Andise naar nje, itraffic iya dika phandl'a pha. [I am nauseous because there is a traffic jam on the roads.] Hello Dee no TV?
DEE I didn't want to watch anymore. Brooke is breaking my heart. She is still carrying on with Ridge, and Ridge is still carrying on with Brooke. If I watch anymore I'll break this TV.
THANDI Willie's not here?
DEE Don't talk to me about him, if my car is not back by tomorrow I'm going to the police.
THANDI Awuke uza ku si bambisa? [Are you going to have us arrested?] If you arrest Willie you'll get us all into trouble.
DEE That's your problem not mine. Tomorrow I'm throwing all his clothes out on the street, whoever wants them can have them, they can have a jumble sale.
THANDI Polo, Pierre Cardin, Yves Saint Laurent...yhoo Big Dee! I can imagine him running around in his underpants...I can also see war on this street...people fighting over Willie's clothes...in fact that's a sight I wouldn't miss seeing.
DEE In fact if you want them you can have them. You can start a flea market at the gate, you'll make a fortune, I know how much I paid for those clothes.
THANDI I've just come from Armstrong's house he's not there either.
DEE I know. I went there this afternoon, Armstrong was sitting outside looking like Mickey Mouse, "I haven't seen him Sis' Dee, I thought he was at your place, in fact I was about to phone him there." The way they were all looking at me, I could tell there was shit! I felt like giving Armstrong a kaffir klap. I know he is with that bloody Thoko again. That woman...I swear I'll kill them both if I catch them together, u Thixo uyazi hii strue.
THANDI They told me he went to Paarl.
DEE Paarl se moer [ass]! He's with Thoko wherever he is.
THANDI E yona nto ke ulibazisa umnxilo [the problem is that he is delaying us]. There's work coming in and it needs him personally. There might be a delivery from tonight if everything goes well. I don't have space. In fact I have to get rid of everything I've got.
DEE Hey, I've told you I don't want to know anything about your business. I don't want to know about anything. When the police come here looking for you, they must find me blank and they must go away blank. Have you seen the papers today? Fighting, killing everybody's blaming everybody else. I don't care whose fault it is, I want it to stop. I want the whole world to stop.
THANDI Amen!
DEE It's no joke, I mean it. I don't want to know what's coming from Botswana or what's going to Durban or what's here for that matter.
THANDI Dee, you're my friend, I trust you.
DEE I know, but in this game trust is not enough. Pain is the question. The pain of being questioned by the police, the pain of being physically abused if they feel I'm hiding the truth from them. Will I be able to endure that pain without selling you out?
MERCEDES *(Entering)* Hallo Ma, hallo Sis' Thandi.
THANDI Hallo baby.
MERCEDES Are you driving that Mercedes Benz station wagon parked outside?
DEE Before you start talking cars it's half past six. What was it today, netball practice? Where's your tracksuit?
MERCEDES Ma, I told you about the youth club meeting today.
DEE And your skirt?
MERCEDES What about my skirt?
DEE Is that the latest length in school skirts?

2 Stolen goods.

Next you'll be telling me that your school uniform is hot pants.

MERCEDES Ma you said I could wear it like this.

DEE Two feet above the knee?

MERCEDES Hayi ma! Do you want me to walk around dressed like a nun?

DEE I want your skirt to touch your knees!

MERCEDES Yhoo ma they'll laugh at me at school.

DEE I pay, so you'll do as I say. *(To* THANDI*)* Yesterday she brought me the list for her summer uniform, R400! You can thank God your mother isn't a poor domestic servant.

THANDI In our day, we wore one uniform right through the year, a black gym and a white shirt.

MERCEDES Even in summer Sis' Thandi?

THANDI Even in summer.

MERCEDES Yhoo, it must have been hell for you guys.

THANDI It was, but we never thought about it. You know what? I used to sleep on my gym dress.

MERCEDES Sleep on it?

THANDI *(Demonstrating)* I used to put a newspaper inside, and spread it out on my mattress, I'd put another newspaper on top, an old blanket, then my bottom sheet, I used to iron in my sleep.

DEE All the lazy bums used to do that, and, if you were careless in your sleep, your gym could come out wrinkled like a prune.

THANDI Ag, unomona wena Dee. Baby, go take a look in the boot of my car there's something grand in there far you. *(To* DEE*)* I'm not going to let you spoil my day.

DEE I don't want her looking in your boot.

THANDI It's clean. Look for a white plastic bag.

MERCEDES Okay Sis' Thandi. (MERCEDES *exits through the front door.)*

DEE You spoil her.

THANDI I love her. *(Pause)* She's growing up.

DEE Don't tell me.

THANDI I wonder what her father would say if he were alive?

DEE He would be worried like me.

THANDI I remember when she was born, he said to me,"Thandi, this is my Mercedes Benz. The man who marries her will have to pay me enough lobola to buy a car like that."

DEE Was he sober when he said that?

THANDI Sober, why?

DEE Then he was serious. We discussed lobola once, long ago, and we came to the conclusion that if we accepted it from any man who wanted to marry Mercedes, we'd give it back to them after they were married as a wedding present from us.

THANDI Promises are broken when pockets run dry.

(MERCEDES *enters singing and holding a red dress.*)

(MERCEDES Sis' Thandi, it's beautiful.)

(She embraces THANDI.)

THANDI Go try it on.

MERCEDES *exits singing into the bedroom and changes into her new dress.*

THANDI Come on Dee, smile, God loves you. I've got troubles too you know?

DEE What troubles?

THANDI Dee, do you know that on top of everything, my brother has moved back into the house? As if that is not enough, his friends have moved back in with him.

DEE Did his girlfriend kick him out?

THANDI Yes!

DEE So? Do the same, say good riddance to rubbish!

THANDI You know the house is in his name.

DEE You pay the rent.

THANDI The City Council doesn't care.

DEE Move out, then. He'll understand.

THANDI And leave my Jet Master fireplace, sliding doors, Italian tiles and burglar bars for him? You'd better think again.

DEE It's your life baby.

THANDI You know how much I've spent renovating that house.

DEE Get some of your own boys together bagqibe ngaye qha! [and let them work him over!]

THANDI I've just had a big fight with him. I told him, "That food you're eating, that bed you're sleeping on, the blankets you sleep under and that couch your friends spill booze on are mine, I paid for them."

DEE And what did he say?

THANDI Fock off.

(MERCEDES *enters, wearing a red dress! Her hair done punk style, singing.*)

MERCEDES How do I look Sis' Dee?

DEE Like a prostitute punk.
THANDI *(Laughs)* Baby, you look sensational! I knew it was just right. Phone Victor now, tell him to come and see you. Quick!
DEE *(To* THANDI*)* Hey, hey, hey, not in my house.
THANDI What's wrong with Victor now?
MERCEDES He's out of favour right now.
THANDI Why, he's such a nice boy?
MERCEDES Ag Sis' Thandi, leave it alone. Ma, what do you want for supper tonight?
DEE I'm not hungry; do your homework first.

(MERCEDES *winks at* THANDI *and exits to her room.*)

THANDI Maybe *she's* hungry.
DEE It's my house, it's my food.
THANDI Sorry.
DEE It is.
THANDI I ve got stuff in my car.
DEE I thought you said the boot of your car is clean?
THANDI It's not in the boot.
DEE Don't tell me.
THANDI It's Willie's.
DEE I'm not interested.
THANDI Can I leave it with you till he comes back?
DEE NO! You don't give up do you?
THANDI That's what makes me a good sales lady. Dee, you know I wouldn't want you to get mixed in all this, but I've got a problem.
DEE You've got a problem and I want it to stay that way, yours.

(PAT *enters through the front door, throws her bag on the couch and goes to the fridge for a beer.)*

PAT Hey Dee, what a day, andi sa nxanwe [I'm so thirsty]. This job is not working out I swear!
DEE Now you owe me two hundred rand and I don't want any stories at the end of the month.
PAT Okay Dee, I'll give you your two hundred rand month end.
DEE *(To* THANDI*)* Why don't you ask *her*; she's your sister...
PAT Ask me what?
DEE Your sister wants a favour from you.
PAT What favour? *(To* DEE*)* Where's Willie?
DEE Where's Willie, where's Willie...You're asking me?
PAT But Dee, your car's parked outside.
DEE My car!? And him?
PAT I thought he was here with you.
DEE The bloody bastard! Uqhel'u ukuty'i mali ya bafazi, aka soz'a ndinyushe mna. [He's used to living off women. He won't get a penny out of me.]

(DEE *exits through the front door talking angrily under her breath to check her car.*)

PAT Where is he?
THANDI With Thoko.
PAT What?
THANDI 'Strue, Armstrong told me.
PAT Does she know?
THANDI She knows.

(PAT *looks at her suspiciously.*)

THANDI Nobody told her, Armstrong said he would bring the car back. So I thought I'd find him here. Now, I don't know what to do.
PAT Why don't you go back to Armstrong? He'll know where Willie is.
THANDI I can't. She'll get suspicious. Besides, I've got stuff in the car, I must unload it, can I leave it with you?
PAT Hey, wait a minute, I don't know anything about these things.
THANDI I know. Look, you don't have to do anything, we'll leave the stuff with you, I'll go and look for Willie, as soon as I get hold of him we'll come and pick it up and when we've sold the stuff there'll be something for you. Deal?
PAT Okay, but remember, I don't want that stuff in my house for too long.

(DEE *enters wielding red bikinis, she is furious.*)

DEE Look at this, look at this! Do I wear bikinis? Have you ever seen me in a red bikini for that matter? To make matters worse the keys were hanging there for anyone to take. Thandi, give me that stuff I'll keep it till he gets back!
THANDI Sorry Big Dee, the job's taken.
DEE Fine. I'm going to put the police on you.

(PAT *and* THANDI *start laughing.* DEE *exits to bedroom area,* MERCEDES *enters through the bedroom.*)

MERCEDES What's happening?
PAT We're banishing all men under the age of sixty.

THANDI Only the very old and the very rich may remain.

(*They begin to perform the song, "U Sugar Daddy".* DEE *enters with a pile of men's clothing which she dumps outside the kitchen door.*)

DEE Mercedes, where did you learn that, from your netball practice? Hee, uya fetsha ngoku?

(*Lights fade to blackout.*)

Scene 3

(*Lights come up.* DEE, PAT *and* THANDI *are sitting with drinks.* MERCEDES *is sitting at the kitchen counter doing her homework.*)

PAT What happened to Caroline?
DEE She and Ridge kissed and confessed their love for one another.
PAT I was right, Ridge had her.
DEE YES! Yes!
THANDI I don't know how you can worry about those Barbie dolls.
PAT Hey girls, let's phone SABC and tell them to do a soap opera about us.
THANDI We're not rich enough.
DEE We're not beautiful enough.
PAT Between you and Big Dee we're rich enough, and I'm beautiful enough for all of us.
DEE Raaaaa!
THANDI Speak for yourself.
PAT Alright then, it can happen in the future, in the New South Africa. I'll be Patricia Mahambebuza of the Mahambehlala Estate Agency and I'll sell houses only to the rich and the famous. I'll run advertisements in all the Sunday papers in the country.
DEE Dream on. I love this. And me – what will I be in the soap?
THANDI You'll be a shebeen queen[3] of course.
DEE What?
PAT Oh ja, you'll run a high class shebeen. Remember that Italian's house in Saxonwold? I'll sell it to you. Everyone will want it. Ridge will want it, even Ridge. He'll offer me money, big bucks, but I'll tell him, "Nothing doing, this house belongs to Big Dee my friend." Then he'll offer me the world, still, "Nothing doing". Finally, he'll ask me what he should do to get the house. I'll tell him, then, he'll make love to me in Sun City, on the beach at the Wild Coast. Then, just when he thinks he's got it, I'll sell that house to you Big Dee. Mercedes will have her own private apartment upstairs with a separate entrance, and when Ridge realizes that I don't want him anymore he'll go after her.
DEE I'll shoot Ridge through the heart.
MERCEDES Ma!
DEE Do your homework!
THANDI Ag, she won't want Ridge, she's got Victor.
DEE She won't have time for anybody because she's got homework, school and university to look forward to.
MERCEDES She's talking about the future Ma!
DEE You won't have a future if you don't do your homework.
THANDI Oh come on Dee, don't be a spoil-sport.
PAT Yes, come on tell us about your shebeen.
DEE Yes, of course. It has a beer garden with a swimming pool the size of Green Point Stadium next to it. We have life guards of both sexes, hunks and hunkettes. The hunks will save all the girls and the girls will save the boys from drowning. Mercedes that part of the house will be out of bounds to you.
THANDI Tell us about the inside, Big Dee.
DEE The living room is built like a swimming pool, with a marble floor and cushions scattered all over for comfort.
MERCEDES People who drink in that section won't be able to get up.
DEE (*Gives her a look*) We have the morning after section. This is for all our customers who have passed out and slept over. For a small fee they can use the jacuzzi or the sauna to clear their babalas if they don't want to drink it away.
THANDI That room ought to be good for Monday mornings if you can't get a doctor's certificate.
PAT Hey Dee, you've hit the nail on the head my friend; that is genius!
DEE I had you in mind Pat when I planned all of this. I know how hard Mondays are on you.
MERCEDES (*Sings*) Hee babalas khawu ndiyekele ngo Mvulo. [Hangover, leave me alone, it's Monday, I have to work].
PAT Yazi u sile? Usile wena. [You are silly.]

3 A woman who runs a pub from her house.

DEE I'll ground you till you're twenty-one if you don't watch your mouth, u Pat akay'o ntanga'kho [Pat is not your mate.] Nobody can come in with takkies and jeans.

PAT And no bare feet.

THANDI Only tuxedos and evening dress.

MERCEDES Evening dress at a shebeen? That's a bit much!

DEE I thought *I* was the shebeen queen, not you. She's right Thandi, I don't want uptight assholes in my joint. I'll settle for oo mashwabana [linen pants].

MERCEDES That's my mum!

THANDI No cars below BMW.

DEE Ja. No VW Golfs and definitely no Toyotas.

PAT No Mazdas.

DEE No Willies.

PAT That's for you to decide.

DEE We'll get Eddie Murphy to come and do stand up comedy.

PAT And when he hears you laugh he'll fall in love. They say he goes for big mamas.

DEE Who says?

(MERCEDES *laughs.*)

DEE Who told you?

PAT About what?

DEE That he likes big mamas?

PAT That's for me to know and for you to find out.

DEE Pat, I like that man, he makes me laugh, and he's sexy too on top of that. So, if you value your life you'll tell me all there is to know about him.

THANDI Come on girls,we said no more toy boys remember?

DEE Eddie Murphy is no ordinary toy boy, he is a hunk, I love the way he laughs, the way he walks, his bendy legs, his...

MERCEDES Mum, if you don't put your mind on your business I'll ground you till you're eighty.

DEE Are you listening to us or are you doing your homework? Go to bed this minute.

(*Three gunshots are heard. Blackout.*)

Act II

Scene 1

(*It is late Sunday morning. A figure is sleeping on the sofa, wrapped in a blanket.* DEE *enters from the bedroom area. She is groggy. The phone is ringing.* DEE *complains loudly and answers it.*)

DEE Ja? Hee? Uthini kanyekanye? [What are you saying exactly?]...You've got the wrong number...Who?...Why are you phoning so early?...She's not here! (*Slams the phone down*) Bloody Victor!

(MERCEDES *enters from the back door with a bucket and rags. She starts cleaning the basin, then she sweeps the carpet and dusts the TV.*)

MERCEDES Morning Ma.

DEE What's the time?

MERCEDES Quarter to twelve.

DEE Why didn't you wake me?

MERCEDES I did but you were fast asleep.

DEE Don't be cheeky! Why aren't you at school?

MERCEDES You asked me the same question yesterday, remember? Don't tell me you're growing senile.

DEE I'll send you to that convent in Umtata if you don't watch your mouth.

MERCEDES It's Sunday, Ma.

DEE Don't be smart. Sister Magaritha is still waiting to straighten you out with her fists.

MERCEDES She must be related to ET.

DEE Her fists are the same size as Terreblanche's.

MERCEDES (*Laughs*) Do you want some coffee, Ma?

DEE No, I want Panados, they are not in the cupboard.

MERCEDES There's a box next to the sink.

DEE That bloody Dixon! I told him I don't want to drink. But no, he had to persuade me. "Let me mix you my famous Manhattan." So I say yes because I thought he was talking about Manhattan the white wine. It's so mild a five-year-old can drink it and not get drunk. The next thing I know I'm drinking brandy Manhattans and I'm knocking them back as if they are going out of fashion.

MERCEDES So why do you blame Dixon? He didn't force you.

DEE He tempted me. (*She looks out the kitchen door.*) Hayi this yard looks worse after a Saturday night than after last week's shooting. What a night that was. I had a terrible dream.

MERCEDES I know, Ma, you told me.

DEE My house was surrounded by men with

axes, guns, and knives. They were shouting and singing, banging the doors and burglar bars trying to get in. I ran all over the house closing the windows, but they were pulling them open from outside. I kept closing all the windows. I ran to my room, two women were sitting on the floor praying and crying, they were terrified like I was. How did they get in? What if the men outside wanted to kill them, to kill me for harbouring them? They could easily smash my windows through the burglar bars or break my doors down. You came out of your bedroom screaming that there were men and women hiding in your room. We had nowhere to go. Suddenly it was quiet again. There was a knock on the window, a soft knock, a friendly knock. It was a man with wild hair and red eyes. He pointed a gun at my head and said, "We are coming to get you all, wait and you will see."

MERCEDES Ma, it was just a bad dream. I remember, when we got to bed the noise was terrible, we could hear people fighting in the yard. I suggested to you that we get under the bed and you said, "No, if I'm going to die, I want to die in my bed not under it." You told me I could do what I liked. So, I stayed with you, I never slept. We were all too scared to look and see who was fighting outside. Was it the township residents fighting the hostel dwellers, or was it the youth fighting the taxi drivers? Maybe the police were doing a house to house search for dangerous weapons or the hostel dwellers were helping the defence force search the township for members of APLA.[4] Maybe the white people balaclavas were there too helping the police and the army. Even when it was quiet again I could not sleep. I heard the dogs barking and the roosters at dawn. I saw lights coming up through the curtains; I couldn't move. You slept through everything. How you did it I don't know. Just once you frightened me more than the shooting when you screamed, "Get out of my house...Phumani [get out]!" in your sleep, I shook you just to wake you up. You stared at me and said, "What?" You fell asleep again. Sometimes I feel like your mother, s'trues God.

(*There's a call from the front garden.*)

PAT Good morning ladies. Am I in time for the morning service? Are the choirboys sexy or just plain good looking?

DEE *(Mumbling)* Oh please God don't let it be her.

DEE *sits at the table resting her head in her hands.* PAT *enters.*

PAT *(Sees the body on the sofa.)* What's that?

DEE I'm holding a bomb in my hands.

PAT Not you – that.

DEE Hey, I'm warning you: you have entered a minefield.

MERCEDES Sssssssssssshhhhhhhh! *(Starts pulling the blanket from the head of the body)*

DEE *(Sees the body for the first time)* Nkosi yam Mercedes don't touch it: fingerprints.

(MERCEDES *pulls the blanket away and reveals the sleeping* THANDI.)

PAT How did she get there?

MERCEDES I put her there.

PAT When?

THANDI *(Still sleeping)* Six o'clock this morning.

PAT You bitch! Where have you been? (PAT *pulls the blanket off* THANDI. THANDI *holds on to it.)*

THANDI Hayi maan Pat, come on. I haven't slept in two days.

PAT Is that all? I haven't slept in a week. But you, you drive off before the shooting starts and disappear for a week. You don't bother to call and let us know that you are safe.

THANDI Hey sis, I didn't know you cared...

PAT Not me, your mother. She nearly went crazy, she almost drove me crazy too. I had to take her to every bloody police station, mortuary, your dagga friends and your mandrax dealers.

THANDI I've been to Durban and back.

PAT Why didn't you phone me, why didn't you send a message?

THANDI Because there were no phones where I was.

PAT You're a missing person now. Do you know how hard it was for me to report you to the police knowing what you carry in the boot of your car?

THANDI Danger follows me wherever I go dear sister.

4 African People's Liberation Army.

PAT Voetsak! I know whose car that was.

THANDI What car? I haven't got a car anymore. I lost it when the shooting started at Crossroads.

PAT What were you doing there in the first place? Don't answer that.

MERCEDES She was going to make a drop or pick up we all know that.

THANDI Undiqhel'i nonsense.

PAT I wasn't talking to you in the first place.

MERCEDES Would you like a cup of coffee Sis' Thandi, Sis' Pat?

PAT Secondly, I don't know what you're doing in the company of adults.

THANDI Make that coffee black and strong. *(To* PAT*)* I went to Crossroads to collect money from my dealer. We had just finished counting the money when there was a loud explosion. Everybody runs for the door. At the door there was a big ball of fire, so, we all jumped through the window, but then a spray of gun fire meets us halfway. The next thing I know is my car blowing up in all directions. One of the people in the mob happened to be a friend. Were it not for him I would be dead now.

PAT Okay Rambo, put your shoes on we are going to tell your mother all this. She thinks I'm the gangster and you're the hairdresser and my tsotsi [gangster] friends have kidnapped you.

Scene 2

(That evening, MERCEDES *is on the telephone. She has the ironing board out and is ironing a shirt,* THANDI *is sitting on the sofa reading* Tribute *magazine.)*

MERCEDES Hey, I never got a message. Did you leave one? With who?...No, it's too much now...We're going to have a big fight one day soon...very soon. No, but she must give me my messages. Ag, no maan Victor she mustn't...Why don't you come here?...She's out – she drove Sis' Pat to Vereeniging to pick up her mother from a church gathering there. *(Sudden announcement)* Guess who's here?...Sis' Thandi...ja she appeared from nowhere...she's reading...*Tribute*...she's just blown me a kiss...

THANDI It's for him.

MERCEDES It's for you. She's had lots and lots of adventures which we can't talk about over the phone. How long will you be?... Oh...then it's no good they'll be back by then. Okay...sweet...ja...bye. Sis' Thandi, he sends his love and I'm getting jealous. *(*MERCEDES *goes back to her ironing.)*

THANDI Don't worry, the feeling's mutual. Remember our oath, no toy boys? It's still standing. Victor reminds me of Sipho, a toy boy in my not so distant past. He had a bright little face and loved to dress in blue jeans and white Adidas. He had a cute little butt.

MERCEDES Sis' Thandi!

THANDI Did he phone this morning?

MERCEDES Ja, he says so.

THANDI I think I heard your mother on the phone this morning. *(Mimicking)* Why do you phone so early? She's not here. Bloody Victor!

(They both laugh.)

MERCEDES Hey Sis' Thandi, mama's unfair. He's always telling me to understand her better.

THANDI What has she got against him?

MERCEDES It's not him, it's the times.

THANDI The times?

MERCEDES When you stand up for what you believe in, and you play a leading role in the community the way Victor does, you're always open to criticism. He runs the street committee. Sometimes he has to make decisions that are not popular with the rest of the street. When he opened the cultural centre everyone was proud of him, even Mum. He's been detained, exiled, and tortured by the regime, but he doesn't back down because he knows we are going to win in the end. Sis' Thandi, this is Africa, our land, the land our forefathers gave to us. It is our legacy.

*(*THANDI *lifts her hand, palm up.)*

MERCEDES The fingers are not standing together, we're at each other's throats. And as long as this violence continues the solution is going to take a long time to come. The comrades have come up with a way of sorting things out.

THANDI What do you mean "comrades"?

MERCEDES I know what I want. So does Victor. I don't run in front, I don't wave, I go to school. I'll go to university and I'll work with my people.

THANDI I don't want you to get into trouble.

MERCEDES We have no choice. We are born into trouble.

THANDI I don't like the way you talk.

MERCEDES You're not the only one.

THANDI I don't want to hear anymore.

MERCEDES Now you know and it must end here between us in this room.

THANDI Be careful, I don't want you getting into trouble.

MERCEDES Now you sound just like Ma.

THANDI She loves you.

MERCEDES I know she loves me. But when is she going to understand me the way I understand her? Do you know how many men propose to me every night in this shebeen? Yet she worries about who walks me home from school.

THANDI A lot can happen between school and home. Nothing can happen here. The guys who propose to you here know they'll [stop] before their lips can touch yours. They just do it to feed their egos.

MERCEDES You see, you talk just like her.

THANDI Come here.

(MERCEDES *joins* THANDI *on the sofa*.)

THANDI Ag, you're so nice to hold, you're still my baby.

MERCEDES You see, you're as bad as she is.

THANDI I just don't want you to get hurt that's all.

MERCEDES You can't protect me all my life. You guys must learn to trust me.

THANDI That's true. It's terrible being a parent.

MERCEDES It's worse being a child.

(*They look at each other and laugh*.)

MERCEDES I worry about you. I wish you were a hairdresser, seriously.

THANDI Hey, no sermons.

MERCEDES I mean it, Sis' Thandi. Do you think about the stuff you sell?

THANDI Every minute.

MERCEDES It's in our schools now.

THANDI Maybe I should have gone to this prayer meeting.

MERCEDES Do you want us to get hooked?

THANDI God help us.

MERCEDES I hope He does, but that is not the solution.

THANDI You see, your mother and I had a problem finding work that paid well. So, she chose the high road and I chose the low road.

MERCEDES My mother doesn't sell liquor to children. You sell drugs. Do you know where yours end up?

THANDI An adult can walk in here now, buy liquor and give it to a kid outside; it's the same thing.

MERCEDES Oh no it's not! My mother does not sell take-aways, period.

THANDI If I don't sell them somebody else will.

MERCEDES That is no answer, Sis' Thandi.

THANDI I really don't know what to say. I can say to you I'll stop, but I can't because I have a spare wheel full of tablets which is going to help me pay my bills and buy a house maybe.

MERCEDES My friend Billy was very clever in school. The other night I saw him sitting outside his house. I waved and called out to him. He was so bombed he couldn't lift his arm to wave. All he talks about nowadays is mandrax!

THANDI Oh, that is disgusting! Mercedes, I can't be held responsible for all the fools in the world. Besides, if your mother felt she was cheating some woman out of food or money for her children every time she sold a nip, she wouldn't be where she is today. Do you think cigarette companies feel guilty every time a younger person lights up? No. They know that they have a potential customer for life. They are worse hypocrites than me, they put signs on their packs about the surgeon general warning people about the dangers of smoking. So, you see, it's everybody for himself and God for us all.

MERCEDES Our war is against racial injustice now. Next it could be against drugs. I hope we won't be on different sides when that time comes.

THANDI (*Takes* MERCEDES' *face between her hands and kisses her*) Mercedes Benz!

MERCEDES What?

THANDI I love you.

MERCEDES I love you too Sis' Thandi.

Fade

Scene 3

(*Some days later. Shebeen noises from outside.* PAT, *in dark glasses, is watching TV.* DEE *bustles in through the back door and straightens her hair in the mirror on the fridge.)*

DEE Mercedes...Mercedes...*(She notices* PAT.*)* Hey, when did you come in here?
PAT Ten minutes ago.
DEE Where's Mercedes?
PAT She left two minutes ago. She said there was an emergency meeting.
DEE I'm taking a court order against Victor, I swear!
PAT Come on Dee.
DEE Why aren't you out there? Have you joined the AA or are you increasing your bill from my fridge?
PAT I'm drinking water today, last night nearly killed me.
DEE There's a good looking guy out there, he's looking for you. He says he's Cokes.
PAT He's most of what nearly killed me last night.
DEE He's looking for you and I told him he'd find you home.
PAT Are you crazy? I have a son, a small child, I can't bring a man home in front of Sandile.
DEE I sent him to your mother's house.
PAT Nice. Very nice. Dee my mother can smell a married man a mile away.
DEE So he's married?
PAT I can't go home now, I'll have to spend the night with you.
DEE Over my dead body! He's not bad looking; why are you running from him?
PAT Do you fancy him?
DEE Who wouldn't?
PAT Love on the rebound is bad.
DEE Where did you meet him?
PAT At the taxi rank.
DEE Oh, a true romance of taxis.
PAT Something like that.
DEE What does he do?
PAT He drinks like a fish and keeps going all night!
DEE No, I can see that. What does he do by day?
PAT He says he works in the stock exchange.
DEE Not bad! At least he's not after your money.
PAT What money? And he didn't say what he did on the stock exchange? Maybe he's a messenger.
DEE Could be worse! You dirty slut, you lucky bitch!
PAT *(Mimicking* DEE*)* Ja, I've got someone to keep me warm, what about you?
DEE Up yours!
PAT *(Raising her glass)* Cheers!
DEE Anyway taxi romances are tickey-line [cheap]!
PAT So, you met Willie in a shebeen, what's that?
DEE *(Coyly)* Who's Willie?
PAT And if you want to know. He's been asking after you...
DEE I don't want to know.
PAT I thought you might.

(There is a loud noise from the shebeen outside. A fight. DEE *goes to the door and yells at the customers to quieten down.)*

DEE Hey, if you don't know how to behave, you know where to go. *(She turns to* PAT.*)* What? Did Thoko kick him out?
PAT Who?
DEE Willie!
PAT *(Laughing)* Who's Willie?
DEE No! Come on man, did she kick him out or did he kick her out?
PAT He didn't say.
DEE Didn't you ask? I thought you were my friend.
PAT Hey! Two seconds ago it was "Who's Willie?"
DEE No, come on man.
PAT I'll tell you if you'll let me off my bill.
DEE You're asking to die!
PAT Okay. Keep your money. I don't want to die. Not tonight. He says he's missing you.
DEE How much?
PAT Like hell.
DEE Good!
PAT I think you should see him.
DEE *(Coy again)* Why?
PAT I think he's in trouble.
DEE Good riddance!
PAT Are you sure of that?
DEE *(Despite herself)* What kind of trouble?
PAT He'll have to tell you himself.
DEE Let him tell Miss Red Bikini!
PAT Ag, come on Dee, you know what Thoko means to him: goodnight – goodbye!
DEE He chose her bed, let him burn in it!
PAT Come on Dee, where's your heart? Boys like Willie burn quick.
DEE *(Pretending reluctance)* Alright, tell him to come and see me.
PAT He already has.
DEE What do you mean?
PAT He's waiting outside in a white BMW.

DEE You bitch, why didn't you tell me in the first place? *(Runs off)*

Scene 4

(THANDI *is sleeping on the sofa in the lounge;* MERCEDES *comes in. She goes to her mother's bedroom but the door is locked. She wanders about the room, pours herself milk from the fridge and eats lemon creams from the cupboard.*)

MERCEDES Hey, I go out and leave one Chattanooga Sister behind and I come back and find another one. Look at you. Look how you sleep. And you call me baby. What happened to you tonight? Sometimes I just sit and think about the world, especially since I met Victor, I think about all the people there are. How many people there are in the world. Yhoo! And I think ja, something is happening to all of them every second that passes on this earth. If they are sleeping that's something. If they are dreaming that's something more. Right now, how many babies are getting born and breathing for the first time? And how many old people are dying, and young people? I've been to the funerals of lots of my friends. Funerals always make me cry, but those are the worst. You stand with your friends and cry for your friends. I've stood by the graves of kids killed by the police, and by our own people too and I've thought, "Hee, will I ever leave this place?" and "Will I be next?" Sometimes I've just wanted to lie down with them, because it seems impossible that I will sleep in my own bed and wake up and go to school the next morning. But that happens and other things happen too. No second is ever the same. Does everybody think about these things? Do white children? They don't know what we know. What do they know? I'm not sure. Do I want to know? I'm not sure. Sometimes I understand about the world, sometimes I can't think beyond my nose. *(Laughs)* You see, this is how I am when I've been with Victor. When I'm with him he talks and I listen. And I meant to tell mama all these things when I got home. When I went to her room the door was locked. I hope she and Bra Willie make up.

Scene 5

(MERCEDES *is sitting in the kitchen, folding political leaflets.* PAT *enters through the front door carrying a bag of gifts.*)

PAT Hallo my darling.

MERCEDES Sis' Pat, where have you been?

PAT A weekend in Durban my dear. The Maharani Hotel, all expenses paid.

MERCEDES Who paid?

PAT My loving sister.

MERCEDES You don't say.

PAT She even went one step further: she bought me a plane ticket there and back.

MERCEDES You don't say, and what did you bring back?

(PAT *puts a two-litre Coke bottle of seawater in the fridge and gives* MERCEDES *a gold chain.*)

MERCEDES Alright Sis' Pat, I'm going to wear this at the students' conference next week.

PAT And watch your friends turn green.

MERCEDES Sis' Pat, this chain must have cost you a bit. Who paid?

PAT None of your business.

MERCEDES Did you bring back something green and leafy for Sis' Thandi?

PAT Your feet are getting too big for your shoes, my girl.

MERCEDES Was it white and round and costs twenty rand each?

PAT Sukusa!

MERCEDES Sorry Sis' Pat, it's my mouth. I don't know what to do with it.

PAT Where's your ma?

MERCEDES Out shopping.

PAT And how's the happy bride?

MERCEDES Not so happy. Willie took the weekend off. Don't tell her I told you.

PAT The bastard! He asked me to take this trip for him, so that he could be with her.

MERCEDES They were supposed to go to Sun City.[5]

PAT I know, I suggested it.

MERCEDES She waited for him all of Friday night, watching TV till *Good Morning South Africa!*[6]

PAT The bastard!

MERCEDES I tried to get her to bed three times, we ended up having a terrible row.

5 A holiday resort similar to Las Vegas.
6 i.e. until the TV comes on air in the morning.

DEE *(Off stage)* Mercedes!...Mercedes!

MERCEDES *(Grabs her pamphlets)* Sis' Pat, tell her I've got a headache and I'm sleeping, please. *(Exits)*

DEE *(Entering)* Where's Mercedes?

PAT She's sleeping, she's got a headache.

DEE Ag, no maan, she's still got that headache from yesterday?

PAT I don't know from when. I found her in bed when I got here.

DEE Ag, come and help me unload the booze in my boot.

(They go out and come back carrying crates of beer.)

PAT You look tired: happy tired.

DEE Hey you know Sun City: it never sleeps. How was your weekend? Don't tell me your dirty business, tell me the weekend part.

PAT The mission was accomplished safely and swiftly. There's a bottle of seawater in the fridge compliments of the Indian Ocean.

DEE And you can have a beer on me after we've finished.

PAT So, otherwise, how are you apart from no sleep?

DEE That's for me to know and for you to find out. How's Thandi?

PAT She's having more problems with her brother.

DEE He's your brother too.

PAT An accident of birth.

DEE You made a wise decision when you moved out of your mother's house.

PAT I had no choice. I went out of my way to look for the perfect house for Thandi and I showed it to her today.

DEE Pat, that's very nice. Who's going to look after your mother when Thandi moves out?

PAT Her son will.

DEE On what, he hasn't got a job?

PAT They'll live on mother's pension.

DEE R370? Maybe that will open your mother's eyes.

MERCEDES *(Enters from the bedroom)* Ma when did you get back?

DEE How's your head?

MERCEDES It's better. I had a good sleep.

DEE Come inside, I want to talk to you.

MERCEDES *(Sits next to her mother on the sofa)* Ma?

DEE What's this I hear about you being involved with the comrades?

MERCEDES What?

DEE I know all about you and your plans.

MERCEDES What plans, Ma?

DEE I know about your sit-ins. I know about the pamphlets in this house. I can see more trouble ahead, but most of all I don't want you to see Victor anymore because he is the cause of all this.

MERCEDES Sis' Pat...

PAT Mercedes I swear...

DEE You knew and you never told me?

PAT Dee, I swear...

DEE Stay out of this, I'm talking to her.

MERCEDES Ma, what are you talking about?

DEE Do you know who I met at the bottle store? Mr Sithole. He spoke to me about your plans as if I was in on the whole thing. I felt stupid. If you want to march, march out of my house and don't come back. If you want to sit in, you have a choice, you can do so in the comfort of your bedroom or in a police cell – take your choice.

MERCEDES Can I talk now?

DEE NO! *(To PAT)* This is the best part. Victor wants to clean up our streets, he is taking the Ntsaras on.

PAT Intoni, intsara, the ntsara gangsters? Yhoo.

DEE Do you know who told me? Willie. The whole location is laughing at him.

MERCEDES Let them laugh. But they won't be laughing when we've cleaned our streets out. They will invite us to dinners. They will hold benefits, they will lay the red carpet wherever we go.

DEE If you think you are going to be part of Victor's roadshow you'd better think again. This time I'm not joking about the convent in Mthatha.

MERCEDES Ma, I don't care what you think you know, you don't know how to listen, so how can you understand?

DEE Okay, carry on, but I swear, nobody will come to this house and tell me you are dead. Nobody will bring your dead body to this house. No prayers will be said for your departed soul in this house, finish! Now, if you want something to do take a broom and sweep the yard – it needs it.

MERCEDES We do not want a nation of illiterates. South Africa has no place for illiterates. We want to learn and build the black nation, make it strong.

DEE Let the politicians do their thing not you. Now go and sweep that yard, come on!

(MERCEDES runs out sobbing in frustration.)

PAT Whether we like it or not, we have to acknowledge what the children have done and are still doing. They saved this country!
DEE From what? All we got out of the uprising of '76 is a generation of lost youth.
PAT What can I say? Beauty is in the eye of the beholder.

Fade

Scene 6

(*The three ladies are sitting in the lounge, drinking.*)

PAT If you are mad at Willie why take it out on Mercedes?
DEE I'm not mad at Willie.
PAT Shame the devil and tell the truth.
DEE I want to kill Willie. But I don't want my child to end up sitting here like me, waiting for *Good Morning South Africa*.
THANDI Mercedes is too smart for that.
DEE I told you I don't want to hear about her.
PAT Whether you like it or not, we are not going to bed till this whole matter has been cleared out.
DEE In that case, this well is declared to be dry as of now. (*She makes to clear the table.*)
PAT Touch that booze at your own risk.
THANDI You know what our problem is? We don't think.
PAT That's true! In fact that was my New Year's resolution this year, to spend at least ten minutes every day thinking, but I keep forgetting.
THANDI No, I'm serious. What I do is dirty, what you do is dirty.
DEE But it puts bread on the table.
PAT What I do is mad.
THANDI Speak for yourself.
DEE Have you been talking to Mercedes?
THANDI I'm telling you, that child is wise.
DEE And naive.
THANDI But what she says is true. I'll be a drug dealer for the rest of my life. I may wash my money and open a hair salon, but that money is like small change to me. This money is in my blood.
PAT Do you know what really kills me? Are nice couples like the couple this morning, buying their first home, all the dreams, the future is written on their faces, in a couple of years that house is re-sold because they couldn't afford it any longer. Or going back to those clients a couple of years later to find the house still without furniture because they are having a tough time meeting the mortgage.
THANDI Maybe we should all have our heads examined.
DEE Speak for yourself.
THANDI Don't you feel a twinge of guilt?
DEE Ask me in a few years' time after Mercedes has graduated from university.
PAT I thought you'd disowned her.
DEE Shut up wena.
THANDI We're too old to start all over again. Our only hope is to make sure that our children get a good education so that they won't have to make money our way.
PAT You have no choice. You've just chased your child into the streets.
THANDI Shut up Pat!
PAT Luck is mine, touch white.
THANDI Mercedes is fine. She's with her grandmother.
PAT Bad is yours.
DEE Is that so? And when did you hear all this?
THANDI She phoned me just before I came here.
DEE What else did she say?
PAT She doesn't want to talk to you.
THANDI YET!
PAT I love that child; I wish I had one like her.
DEE You've got one. But I wonder if he knows his mother?
PAT Would you like to swop?
DEE She's going to need a change of clothes.
THANDI She said she'll wear her grandmother's clothes.
DEE That's my Mercedes, alright.
THANDI You know what she said to me? "Sis' Thandi, why don't you start the Chattanooga Sisters again?"
PAT That's a good idea, why don't we?
DEE You two do what you like, I'm too old to work for no pay.
PAT Dee, the music business is different today. Look at The Mahotella Queens; they have made a come-back, they are making money. If we find a good producer what is there to stop us? We can make a name for ourselves and a cosy nest to line our pockets at the same time.
THANDI You know Pat, some of the young musicians today can't sing to save their lives. They are either monotonous or they try to be American. If we got back together we could show these kids the real music of this

country. Mbaqanga will take the world by storm.

PAT We could go to the SABC archives and dig out songs from the fifties. Manhattan Brothers.

THANDI That Nathan Mdledle was a hunk.[7]

PAT Remember the days of Alf Herbets African Jazz?[8]

DEE Yes, when we were kids.

THANDI Or the excitement of the opening night of *King Kong*? *(Starts singing)* "The earth turns over, the clocks are ticking and I sit waiting for something new."

(They join THANDI *in the song.)*

PAT *(To* DEE*)* How about that?

DEE Ag, talk is cheap, money buys the whiskey. If you want something to do, phone Cokes.

THANDI Who's Cokes?

DEE Pat's boyfriend.

THANDI Pat's got a boyfriend? Congratulations!

PAT Congratulations se moer. His wife is a nursing sister.

THANDI And he's got you too. Lucky guy.

PAT U theth'i kaka [you are talking shit].

DEE Come on phone him, maybe he's got nice friends for us.

PAT You phone, and when the nursing sister answers the phone tell her to send Cokes and two of his hunkiest friends over for dinner.

THANDI Hey girls, here we are, black. Single. Successful. Our love lives are up to shit. The only men in our lives are either married, hangers-on or just pure scum. What is wrong with us?

PAT Men don't like women who own houses, drive their own cars, have their own bank books, open doors for themselves. They scare the shit off their pants.

DEE I'll drink to that!

PAT Hey, just think, a week ago you wouldn't be drinking with us in case Willie came home and found you drunk. Let's drink to your liberation, Big Dee.

THANDI I'll drink to that.

PAT Hey, I must go home, Sandile will have to do with Kentucky Fried Chicken for supper tonight.

THANDI He'll be fast asleep by the time you get home.

PAT Then I'll wake him. He loves it. Come on Thandi, drive me to the shops.

THANDI I'm a danger to myself and the road. Try next door.

PAT *(To* DEE*)* Knock knock, next door. Will you please drive me to Kentucky Fried Chicken, I want to win the love of my son back.

DEE Let me see. *(She gets up unsteadily.)* I can stand. *(Walks around the table)* I can walk.

THANDI Can you drive?

DEE Am I walking straight?

THANDI I thought you were driving?

DEE I am. I have to walk straight if I'm to drive straight. *(She bends over* THANDI*.)* How are my eyes? *(She puts on dark glasses.)*

THANDI Mmmmhhh, that's better.

DEE Okay, now, where are my keys?

PAT How should I know? I walked here.

DEE If you don't know, just say you don't know.

PAT I don't know.

DEE Thandi, have you seen my keys?

(MERCEDES *appears at the kitchen door.)*

THANDI I don't see your keys but I see your daughter.

(The other two turn to MERCEDES*.* DEE *takes off her dark glasses.)*

DEE Nkosa yam, uvelaphi? [Good Lord. Where did you come from?]

MERCEDES Mother, and your ladies at large, I love you all with all my heart. I don't know how my life began, I don't know how it will end, but I do know that with you three funky mamas it will not be boring. That is why I feel strong, here. *(Patting her heart)* It is because of you, I am going to live with you and wear you down with my love.

DEE Come here, my child.

MERCEDES Sorry, but I've got to finish my homework.

(MERCEDES *exits to the bedroom.* PAT *and* THANDI *clap.)*

7 Nathan Mdledle was lead singer of the Manhattan Brothers. He played the lead in *King Kong: The Musical*.

8 Alfred Herbet was a Jewish man who promoted stage shows with blacks.

Scene 7

MERCEDES Ma, do you think Stephanie will show Brooke those tapes?
DEE She will be a fool if she doesn't.
MERCEDES But Ma, what if Brooke tells Eric that Stephanie is blackmailing her, that could drive Eric and Stephanie even more apart.
DEE What if the man who is making love to Brooke on those tapes is Ridge, then what?
MERCEDES Oh Ma, this is so confusing, why can't Ridge walk out of that screen into my life and I'll love him to death?
DEE I wouldn't mind as long as he loved you only.

(*There's a knock on the door.*)

DEE (*Shouts*) Come in!
PAT (*From outside*) The door is locked.
DEE Go home.
MERCEDES Ngu Sis' Pat ma.
PAT (*Still outside*) Dee why is the door locked? It's early.
DEE These are dangerous times my dear.
PAT Come on Dee.
DEE And wena, you are the biggest danger.
MERCEDES Ma, let Sis' Pat in please.
DEE I wonder uyaphi? She is just coming to make noise and stuff herself with my beer on credit. (*To* PAT) One minute! (*She carries on watching the TV. There is another knock on the door, this time louder.*) Hey voetsek maan! (DEE *goes to open the door.*) Hey voetsek maan this is my house!
PAT (*Goes to sit on the sofa in* DEE*'s place*) Why don't you kill yourself? I'm not going to stop coming here.
DEE That's my place. Sit on the armchair.
PAT Hey this is a bloody shebeen I can sit anywhere I like. (*To* MERCEDES) Have I missed much?
MERCEDES No.
PAT What has happened so far?
DEE I am not talking till *The Bold and the Beautiful* is over.
MERCEDES Clark went to ask Eric for a job, Eric ordered the security to escort him out of the premises, then he told him in no uncertain terms what he thought of him. He told Clark never to set foot on his doorstep again.
PAT Poor Clark.
DEE Poor Clark, kaak!
PAT Dee, you've got a heart of stone.
DEE Good. I like it that way.
THANDI Sanuku ngxola [shut up], we are watching.
PAT Don't shout, we are listening too.

(*A single shot goes off in the distance.*)

DEE Did you hear that?
THANDI What?
DEE It's a gunshot.
PAT A gunshot, now? Ag, it's too early.
THANDI Ja, maybe it's a car backfiring.

(*More gunshots go off, as if they are coming from a machine gun.*)

THANDI Are all the doors locked?
MERCEDES I'll check, Sis' Thandi.
DEE (*To* PAT) What would you do if you were in Sally's shoes?
PAT What has Sally got to do with this?
DEE She's married to Clark and on top of that she is expecting his child.

(*Another rapid round of gunshots goes off, this time closer.*)

MERCEDES Ma, it's starting again.
THANDI Okay, let's check the bedrooms.
DEE If I were Clark I'd go back to Sally.
PAT Why does Clark always mess his relationships up?
DEE Because he is arrogant and he thinks he is God's gift to women. He is not afraid to stand in a church and promise to love and cherish any woman till death parts them in front of a minister before God.
PAT "Till death do us part". I think that line is stupid. Nobody knows what the future holds.
DEE That's life, Pat. Clark should have learnt his lesson by now.
PAT Amen. Dee, you've got a heart of stone.

(*Another loud explosion. The TV goes off.*)

DEE Not again.
PAT Oh shit, it's off!
DEE Uya bona ke [you see] Pat you mustn't come and watch soaps here anymore – watch soaps in your house. Ulibadi.
PAT Uya ndi gezala ke ngoku nyani [you are pushing crap down my throat].
DEE I mean it.

PAT Hayi uya ndisukela [you are intimidating me].
DEE Starting tomorrow.
PAT Are you serious?
DEE Ucing'u kuba ndi ya dlala [do you think I'm playing]?
PAT One day I'll walk out of the front door and I won't come back, you'll be sorry.
DEE No, Pat I won't be sorry. I'll be fat with happiness because you won't control me in my house anymore.
PAT You're the one that's bullying me in your house.
THANDI You shut your fucking mouth, we are listening.
DEE The TV is off, wena maan.
PAT Hee wethu ntombi what happened to...
DEE Oh no, please Pat.
THANDI Pat u va nxana ku sithiwani?
PAT Ma ka ndibalisele kaloku. She promised to tell me after *The Bold and the Beautiful.*
DEE Look here Pat, my life does not revolve around soaps alone. I've got other things to do.

(A loud explosion followed by a long battle of fire power.)

PAT Hey this is serious. If I'm going to die I want to die next to my son.
THANDI You stay where you are or you'll get to your son in a coffin. *(*THANDI *crawls across the floor to the window.)*
DEE *(Whispering)* Can you see anything?
THANDI Something's burning.
PAT *(Crawling to the window)* Where?
THANDI There.
PAT *(Takes a peak)* Kuse matyotyombeni e Crossroads.
DEE What could it be?
PAT They could be burning the shacks.
DEE Mm, mm, that smoke is white.
PAT Yi tear gas Thixo [God] wam.
THANDI Tear gas! Ivasoline e bathroom. *(Runs to the bathroom)*
MERCEDES I only hope Victor is not there.
DEE You stay where you are wena.

*(*THANDI *lets out a blood-curdling scream from the bathroom. Runs into the living room laughing.)*

PAT Thandi, what is it, yintoni?
THANDI I saw myself in the bathroom mirror and thought it was an intruder.

(The phone rings.)

DEE Halloo?...Who?...Sellinah?...Sellinah is that you?...What? *(*DEE *replaces the receiver and rushes to the window.)*
THANDI Who was that?
DEE Ngu [it was] Sellinah.
PAT Sellinah from next door?
DEE Ewe [yes]. She says there are men outside the house.
THANDI What the hell are you doing?
DEE *(Peeking behind the curtain)* They are stealing our cars.
THANDI *(Running to the window)* My car?
PAT *(Laughing)* Her car.
THANDI Hey voetsek wena. *(She goes to the phone and dials.)*
Hello?...Armstrong?...Armstrong?...*(Loud explosion.* THANDI *drops the receiver and throws herself on the floor. The gunfight continues.* THANDI *crawls to the window and peeps.)*
They're gone.
DEE Our cars?
THANDI No, the men.
PAT Thank God.
DEE I need a man in the house.
THANDI No, you need a gun, it's more reliable.

Scene 8

(Morning. PAT *and* THANDI *are sleeping on the sofas. The phone rings. The women stir.)*

PAT Answer the damn thing maan!
THANDI You've got two legs too.
PAT Yours are younger.
DEE *(Enters muttering)* Are you crippled? *(She picks up the phone and listens, curses.)* We don't want AIDS in this house. *(She slams the receiver down.)*
PAT Shu!
THANDI Who was it?
DEE Willie.

(She sits smugly next to the phone. It rings again.)

PAT Dee, pick it up.
DEE Let him suffer.
MERCEDES *(Enters)* Ma, what's going on here?

*(*THANDI *exits to the bathroom.)*

DEE It's a private matter.
MERCEDES Then let me answer the phone for the sake of peace.

DEE Touch that phone and you'll die.
MERCEDES Maybe it's Victor.
DEE It's not Victor.
MERCEDES How do you know?
PAT Dee, be kind to animals.
DEE That rat?
MERCEDES Ma, something may have happened to Victor.
DEE Good. One less rat to deal with.
MERCEDES Ma, if Victor is dead or hurt or...
DEE Okay, I'll answer the damn phone. *(Picks up the phone)* Ja...didn't you hear what I said last time?...Who the hell do you...I must shut up and listen to you? Uya geza [you are silly] Willie, use, ukrazukile [you are crazy]...I wouldn't marry you if you were the last man on...what did you say?...Hello, hello, Willie? He's put the phone down on me.
THANDI What does he want?
DEE None of your business.
PAT He wants to marry her.

(The phone rings. MERCEDES *picks up the receiver.)*

MERCEDES Hello Victor...
DEE Put that phone down.
THANDI Come on, Big Dee, give the kid a break.
DEE I'll give her a broken head if she doesn't put that phone down.
MERCEDES Listen, I'll call you back. *(She puts the receiver down.)* It's all yours.

(The phone rings. DEE *picks up the receiver.)*

DEE Yes?...It's my phone and it can be engaged any time I want it to...I think I've had enough of that now...ja. Ja...*(She starts smiling.)* and then?...ja...*(Her smile broadens)*...Okay, I'll think about it.
THANDI What did he say?
DEE That's for me to know and for you to find out.
PAT Your business is our concern.
DEE Stick to your own dirty business and I'll stick to mine.
PAT That man is poison.
DEE One girl's poison is another girl's plum.
THANDI Amen.

(The phone rings. MERCEDES *picks it up.)*

MERCEDES Hello...hold on...*(To her mother)* It's for me. Okay shoot...no...yho...come here and we'll go together...okay then, I'll come to you.
DEE What did he say?
MERCEDES It was a private matter.
DEE Kwe yakho i phone, that phone is mine.
THANDI More troubles at Crossroads?
MERCEDES No.
THANDI What was that "yho" really for?
PAT You'll never get the truth from her – she's a comrade.
DEE Not in my house. Phandle [outside]. Over my dead body. And if she thinks Victor is going to convince me, he'll have Willie to deal with.
MERCEDES He's not coming to live here, Ma!
DEE This is my house.
THANDI I love to hear you say that. You say it with such...conviction...such confidence...I wish I could say it too...
PAT What's stopping you?
THANDI Pat, I'm buying that house, definitely. And you know what? Fana can keep those Italian tiles, the Jet Master fireplace and the sliding doors.
MERCEDES Sis' Thandi, I love you when you talk like that. You talk with such...conviction...such confidence...
THANDI Of course, why shouldn't I?
MERCEDES Maybe there'll even be a hairdresser in the back.
PAT Commission at last.
DEE Thandi my friend, thank you very much. Now I can get Pat to pay me.
THANDI How about some coffee?
MERCEDES Coffee coming up Sis' Thandi.
PAT We should do a soap based on us, and we should call it *Funky Mamas.*
THANDI Funky Mamas?
DEE Jonga pha, I'm not a mama. I'll never be a mama. I am Sis' Dee the adorable lady.
THANDI Pat, I'm not funky, I can never be funky. Funk went out with Sly Stone. I am black, single and attractive and I dare any man to walk in here now and see if he'll come out alive.
MERCEDES Seriously, why don't you guys get back together and revive the Chattanooga Sisters? You'd be great, I can see you mum charming those guys off their pants, Sis' Thandi will have them eating out of her hands with chocolate tenor, and Sis' Pat will be such a slut they won't be able to keep their hands off her.

*(*PAT *jumps up and runs to* MERCEDES *with hands*

outstretched. She chases MERCEDES *around the room while* THANDI *and* DEE *shout at* PAT *to stop.* MERCEDES *starts an old Chattanooga standard and all three women join her. At the end of the song they collapse laughing. They start arguing in vernacular with great intensity.*

Lights begin to fade. The soundtrack from The Bold and the Beautiful *drowns out their argument. There is the sound of gunfire over the music. Only* MERCEDES *is visible. She is no longer laughing. More gunfire. Music and lights fade.)*

Sindiwe Magona

> When I left in 1984, there was no effective education for African children in South Africa. I had three kids and I believed in education! I had not finished high school when I left school, but in 1976, during the Soweto uprisings, I was doing my last year towards a degree. I had done a General Certificate of Education (G.C.E.) by correspondence. I did my B.A. degree through the University of South Africa, which was the only truly open university in South Africa at that time, because it's a correspondence university. Since it wasn't a residence, anyone could be a student, so there were no problems about toilets.

Sindiwe Magona is one of the most exciting South African writers to emerge during the 1990s. She is the author of four books – *To My Children's Children* (Honorable Mention in the 1991 Noma Award for Publishing in Africa), *Forced to Grow*, *Living, Loving and Lying Awake at Night*, and *PUSH-PUSH and Other Stories*, from which *House-Hunting* is taken. First published in 1990, *To My Children's Children* is a fascinating and powerful autobiographical account of Sindiwe's first twenty-three years. Written as "a letter from a Xhosa grandmother to record her life in South Africa for her grandchildren so they do not lose their history," this first volume of her autobiography provides an intimate insight into the hardships of township life under apartheid. At the same time, *To My Children's Children* is a celebration of Sindiwe's endurance and triumph to survive. The second volume of her autobiography, *Forced to Grow* covers her child-rearing years (mid-twenties to mid-thirties), when as a young teacher and activist she suffered the agonies of single parenting during the turbulent 1970s student revolt. Her two collections of short stories are fiction, although a few stories are based on her life.

Sindiwe was born in the village of Gungululu in the then Cape Province of the Union of South Africa. At the age of 5, her family moved to Blaauvlei location in the urban area of Cape Town. Forced removal uprooted the family once again in 1961 to Guguletu township.

> Although Blaauvlei was also a slum, we had a better quality of life than in Guguletu. Blaauvlei was a smaller community, people knew each other, and children felt safe and were safe. The community was well knit. When you go to places like Guguletu, which is huge, you're thrown next to people you don't know and those bonds are broken.

Although Sindiwe's parents were not educated, they wanted their children to be educated and never hesitated to make sacrifices. Sindiwe attended school in the township, but was later sent to a Christian boarding school. At an early age, Sindiwe wanted to be a writer.

> I was always good with words, and if there was going to be one essay read at school, it would be mine. I used to win prizes a lot. At 17, my ambition was to one day write a book. I didn't know anyone who wrote books. And the only books that we ever encountered were the ones at school. So we didn't live with books, although I did more reading than the average child my age. We never bought books except school books. Reading is not really part of our culture – storytelling is. Unfortunately, storytelling is dying out because of the break-up of the family.

After receiving her teaching certificate in the early 1960s, she embarked on a teaching career. "When I finished my tenth grade education and my two-year teacher's certificate, I was considered highly educated." During her second year of teaching, Sindiwe became pregnant and was forced to resign since it was against departmental regulations for unmarried mothers to teach. "While I was being punished for having a baby, during the two years on forced leave, I became pregnant again. I got married with the second baby and at the age of twenty-three was pregnant with the third baby." During her four-year teaching hiatus, Sindiwe became a domestic worker, where she laments that "it did more to me than it did for me. It introduced me to the fundamentals of racism." The final year of domestic service, her husband illegally moved to Johannesburg, leaving her to care for the three small children. A year after his departure, Sindiwe resumed her teaching career.

Sindiwe's writing career began seriously when she migrated to the United States. She studied at Columbia University from 1981 to 1983 for Master's degrees in social work and business administration. Shortly after she returned to South Africa, a job became available at the United Nations. In April of 1984, Sindiwe once again headed for New York City – this time with her three children.

In New York, she spoke to groups about life in the townships and decided to put these stories on paper. Although she was interested in writing while in South Africa, time was her enemy. Since one job never paid adequately, she always had two or three part-time jobs to supplement whatever full-time job she had. And then there were the political activities.

> Here, in the U.S. I had one job and no real social responsibilities except for going to church. So I had lots of time – something I'd never had in my life. I didn't take any classes, I just started writing. I thought maybe if I write about myself, I will empty my system of myself and then something else will rush in there. And that's how I ended up with the biography. I didn't set out to write about myself. But the more I wrote, the more things came and the more I remembered.

Through a friend of her brother's, she was able to find a publisher while on a trip home to Cape Town. She knew nothing about the publishing business.

> This is true of most African women. There are so many stories floating around the country or rotting in people's suitcases and drawers. Remember for a long time to do anything you had to have a sponsor, someone who knew the other world. That's what happened to me.

Sindiwe is studying playwriting and recently wrote her first play, *Echoes of the Diaspora*, a collaboration with other writers of African descent. She wants to write plays about the South African experience. Her immediate concern is the plight of children in South Africa, particularly of girls, and she is working on a proposal to promote African women at home.

> I see myself returning to South Africa to write. I love writing. I think it's important for us to write. When I write about the new South Africa it will be what I want to write. Work is hard to publish now because people only want to hear about the new South Africa, which is supposed to mean only good things.

Sindiwe resides in New York City, where she works for the United Nations.

ARTISTIC STATEMENT

House-Hunting Unlike Soweto is autobiographical. I was fed up with what was happening in South Africa. It wasn't hard to leave South Africa at the time. The educational system for Africans was bad. Kids were out of school for years.

When my husband left, I decided to make some changes. As a single mother, I knew I needed to do more. From 1976 through the early 1980s I saw my kids' education going down the drain and just wasting away. *Now* you find politicians, both black and white, talking about the "lost generation." I knew at that time that this was going to be a lost generation. I just saw young people who would never be able to recover. I had done a lot of work for various organizations working for change but now I'd got fed up. At that time, I was at a white school teaching Xhosa, and it was difficult for me to educate these kids while my three were rotting at home. The situation was too much to deal with.

THE ROLE OF THEATRE IN SOUTH AFRICA

The little that I know about theatre was that most of it was protest, addressing as it should the issues of the day. Yes, we need to discuss the issue of the day, but like all literature, it would be helpful to expand a little bit and include more universal themes. To also have theatre that is pure fun, especially for young people.

HAVE THINGS IMPROVED IN GENERAL IN THE NEW SOUTH AFRICA?

I'm a little bit cautious in my joy about the new South Africa. My fear about the changes taking place in the new South Africa is that now that apartheid is gone, people are going to forget so fast that it was ever there. In another decade or two – if we're that lucky, and definitely in three decades' time – the world will be very upset with us, very impatient and fed up, if we do not begin to make great strides.

There's this great forgiveness thing with the Truth and Reconciliation Commission (TRC), about which I have mixed feelings. I doubt we are hearing the whole truth. Also, I think to myself, why are we so anxious to forgive people who haven't even said they're sorry? I haven't had anyone telling me they're sorry for all the money I didn't earn when I was busy, as an African woman teacher, earning a sub-teacher's salary, where there was a six-layer system – white male, white female, Indian/Coloured male, Indian/Coloured woman, African male, and African woman. Where is my back pay? It's OK now that anybody can live anywhere, but with all that I'm owed, how am I going to go over there and buy that house? What will I leave my kids when I die? And now I'm supposed to think that since this is the new South Africa, let's forgive and forget. It is really very hard.

And don't come here with your dirty memories. No one wants to hear stories before 1994. As soon as you mention that in mixed company, white people will tell you, you've been out of the country too long – we are in the "new" South Africa, and what you're bringing up belongs in the past. But it's our past! I can see that just as black lives were cheap and still are cheap, our past is cheap. They made the laws, they ruled the country, and now they decide that some things have changed, so forget about the past. It's easy for white people in South Africa to forget. What did they suffer? Those who suffered were the few who were sympathetic and in the struggle with us. I admit there were some like that.

People are forgetting and it hasn't been five years. Things promised haven't happened. Black people really need to start thinking about what we were denied in the old South Africa and how can that be ours. If our children were going hungry in the old South Africa and are still hungry, if our children had a poor education in the old South Africa and are still receiving a poor education, if people lived in shacks and are still living in shacks, something is not right. In terms of number, there are more of us now, but what do these numbers mean? Yes, there are more of us in a position to move things forward but I don't see this happening. There is so much unemployment. And who is unemployed? People who look like you and me!

We have to remember what we're dealing with. We are dealing with a very wily customer. The handing over – if you can call it that – of South Africa didn't happen overnight. It was a well-orchestrated business. Those people have been preparing for this day forever. We just woke up in 1990 when Mandela left jail. When they said apartheid was over, all the things that apartheid stood for were still in place. They still are. Apartheid is everywhere in the world where there are black people and white people.

Interview conducted July 1997, in New York City.

Photo by John Isaac.

3 House-Hunting Unlike Soweto

Sindiwe Magona

I find the whole thing bewildering, I must confess. Not just coming to the United States, after all, this was my third trip to the country. But this time I was not just bringing myself, I was not coming at the invitation of the States Department, furnished with an escort. Neither was I coming as a student to be sheltered in students' dorms, enlightened by student advisors, and have my stay monitored by the time-tested mechanisms of a sound, world-renowned institution. This time, I was at the head of a five-member delegation, my family – my four children and I. The hurricane of the schools boycott had driven me to these shores, so now, what did I expect? What was I in search of? What dreams were pinned inside the hems of my petticoats?

While our children were busy boycotting classes, the time God set was willfully going on its own sweet accord. My children, each one of them five years behind in her or his education, were five years ahead in age – any class you'd put them into. *MISFITS*. There was no kinder way of putting it. The kindest, most sympathetic principal in the City of New York could not just take them and put them into a class. Everything about them was just so wrong: *especially the age*. They were all too old for the classes they were supposed to be in.

On top of that, we had no records of their immunization. Records? Records are kept when there are recognized people to whom those records pertain. In a country where the citizenship of the African was not recognized, why would the government have taken the trouble to keep records that showed that a child of mine had been given this or that immunization? In fact, why would that child be immunized at all? Wouldn't that be counter-productive to the grand plan of culling our numbers – by hook or by crook?

If the education of my children was a key factor in our leaving South Africa, finding accommodation was a priority after our arrival in New York. Where does a poor soul with no experience – first, second, or any other hand – of looking for accommodation begin doing that in, of all places, the Big Apple? Forty years old, new in the country, I wondered.

No, I was not a member of a newly discovered tribe of mountain-dwellers. Neither had I spent my entire life in a mental asylum. I was fresh from a country where, despite my protestation, at times even vigorous, the government insisted on "protecting" me from the vagaries of modern living, including real estate.

In South Africa, urban Africans lived in townships. However, not every African had the right to rent a house (buying was out of the question, illegal). And until recently, only a man could get permission to rent. On condition he "qualified" for residence in the particular urban area; he was married; his wife also "qualified" for residential purposes in the same urban area. It helped the couple's cause greatly if they already had children.

But I, being a woman, never had the shadow of a chance of renting a house although I "qualified" for residential and work purposes in the Prescribed Area of the Western Cape. Moreover, when I married, I had committed the folly of choosing a man allowed only to work in Cape Town – a migrant labourer.

But that was long ago, in another life.

Now, I had left South Africa. New York had no Bantu Administration Boards to regulate every aspect of my life. How do normal people get to live in normal houses, I asked, first myself and then others?

"You have to go through the real estate pages of the newspaper or go to a real estate agent," advised friends, little realizing they might as well tell me to read hieroglyphics.

The real estate section of the paper, in South Africa, is about that...real estate; it has nothing at all to do with the squalid matchboxes we are forced to live in in the African townships. Therefore, this is a section of the paper that we, Africans, did not look at. Why would we have bothered looking into that section since we were not allowed to live in those areas with houses that got themselves listed there?

I had never set eye on the financial section, the vacations section, or the leisure section – for the same or a similar reason: exclusion, whether legal or economic. Thus did I discover the extent of my deprivation. Here I was, one of the lucky few among my people, part of the one percent or so who have somehow escaped government design, our planned dwarfing, and I could make neither head nor tail of a section of the newspaper; so successfully had I been bonsaied.

After wading through numerous real estate sections and with hefty help from several kindly colleagues from the office, I was afire: If I save, I told myself, in two years I will have $20,000 and buy a house on Fifth Avenue!

Greatly encouraged, I began building my American castle. However, as this was clearly a long-term objective, I kept on perusing the paper, looking for somewhere to stay. My heart quickened at this description: Three bedrooms, including master bedroom, two full baths, separate dining room, eat-in kitchen; twenty-four-hour doorman service. Perfect! The jacuzzi was but the crowning glory.

My heart racing, I reached for the phone.

"I'm interested in the three bedroom you advertise in today's *New York Times*," I cooed with what I hoped was my most unfathomable but intriguing accent, evocative of diplomatic links and unlimited wealth.

"Are you calling from the city, Ma'm?" And when I replied that I was, this highly polished voice, warm and reassuring, demanded – "When would you like to see it?"

"Oh, this afternoon...say, three – three-thirty. If that's all right with you? Then, as an afterthought, I ventured, "By the way, how much is the rent?"

Quick came the retort, "If you have to ask that question, then you can't afford it." Gone was the friendly tone; the voice temperature had dropped a clear ten degrees!

Several similarly futile attempts later, I deemed it best to pursue the apartment on Fifth Avenue even though it had no alluring bathroom features. I foresaw no insurmountable problems in raising a mortgage. "This is the US of A, I can do anything like everybody else," I told myself dialing the number.

"Two months' rent is required as security. Of course, this goes into an interest-bearing account."

An alarm went off in my head. Something was radically wrong. Why was this man talking about rent, about security?

I no longer recall most of what this particular agent said by way of explanation. My ears had taken unscheduled leave; my brain reduced to cornmeal porridge. *TWENTY THOUSAND DOLLARS!* I had difficulty seeing the figure in my mind's eye. *$20,000!* Not the sale price. Not the down payment or deposit. No. This was the monthly rental. I didn't make that much money in six months! The whole of me boggled. I broke out into a cold sweat. This piece of information was just too much for me to digest – that there were people out there who not only made that kind of money, each month; but made so much that they could spend $20,000, per month, on rent alone.

As straw to a drowning man, conventional wisdom sprang to the rescue: *Cut your coat according to your cloth!* came unbidden to my mind.

But the real lesson, the full brunt of the "benevolence" of a government that had painstakingly "sheltered" me, was only then beginning to unfold.

My coat, I saw with brutal clarity, was going to have to be a cheap rental. Very cheap. After a brief search, I found something suitable. Less than a week after we'd moved in, I also learnt why the rent was that low. There is a bit more to looking for accommodation than affordability alone.

The apartment I had rented was located in that part of the Bronx where the film *Fort Apache* was shot.

All around were rotting, burn-blackened buildings; a thick pall of foulness strangled the very air; gaunt, misshapen human frames in tatters aimlessly roamed the streets all day long, and all night through; the whole place displayed ample evidence of total decay, scars from ancient battles.

It is here that the term "danger money" assumed new meaning for us as a family. I insisted on each child carrying, separately, two ten-dollar bills: one, to give to a mugger in the event of being accosted by one; and the other, to hop into a cab if lost or in a threatening situation. This had nothing to do with dating and I gave this sum to the boys as well as to the girls. Never mind, that I discovered later, my gang used the money as extra pocket money for they had made their own discovery: their poor old mother had finally gone soft in the head. Before six months and although we had a one-year lease, we fled that far from cozy nest.

I found a sublet in a co-op building. Two months later, we had to leave. I was paying both rent and storage for my furniture which had not been allowed into the building. What did I know of Board approval? I did not even know there were such things as Co-op Boards.

Our next castle was also a co-op. But, wiser now, I had insisted on, and received, the approval of the board before moving in. The rent was going to be $100 less for the first month because the place badly needed painting. During that time the landlady promised to have that done while I kept my furniture in storage; hence the deduction in rent.

Four months later, the workmen had become permanent fixtures in "my" home. The project had insidiously expanded. The lady was putting lights in the closets, changing the ceiling light fixtures, adding scones to the walls, replastering the walls, and putting new faucets in the bathroom and kitchen sinks. All commendable, no doubt. However, the constant drilling and chirping, hammering and scrapping and the droning of machines furiously at work, drove us all up the wall. The constant assault of foul, acidic smells penetrated every niche, nook and cranny of the apartment and glued themselves into our clothes and our very hair. We could taste them on our teeth, I swear. But above all, the intrusion of the workmen on our lives became an unbearable irritation. In short, this work, necessary, no doubt, should never have been done while the place was occupied. I had a mighty fight with the landlady and withheld part of the rent telling her, "We are taking our clothes to the cleaners with it." You know how it is when you are desperately unhappy about a situation? It is the one topic you cannot leave alone. At work, on the subway, at the office, I talked about nothing else. To total strangers at times. Of course, there is nothing people like better than giving advice. And I became the recipient of many and varied counsel from concerned veterans of real estate battles.

"If you are thinking of moving into a certain neighborhood," said my eager advisors, "go there at different times: weekdays, weekends, early mornings, late at night."

"A place can look fine with the morning rush – school kids and people going to work, you know? But you don't know what comes creeping out during the day."

"Check the public transportation. You don't want to be far from buses and the subway. And you definitely want to watch out you do not end up in a two-fare zone. That adds to your expenses."

"A good indicator is if you find long-term real estate near by: schools and church buildings. Those don't go away and the neighbourhoods where you find them are less likely to go to the dogs in a hurry."

Unfortunately, this sound advice came a little late to save me, beleaguered from many fronts as I was. Moving is expensive in New York; a far cry from home where one calls on friends and neighbours to lend a hand. In New York, movers are hired and they don't come cheap. So, we had to tarry longer than we would have liked at this place because I needed to recuperate, financially, from the previous moves, chasing each other as they did.

Eventually though, we did move. And the younger of my two sons stopped saying "Thugs willing!" in response to my "See you soon" as I left for work or went jogging or food shopping.

Now, we live in a good neighbourhood. I no longer worry about the safety of my children. But that is not to say that everything is honky-dorry now. The children have had quite a hard time adjusting. Of course, they want to be like the other young people here; they don't want to be different. I think it's harder for me, watching them change; seeing the people I knew become others, very different to what I had envisaged.

Remember, when I had these children I had a very different set of beliefs, different expectations, and I was in a different world. I was going to get *lobola* for my daughters, one day. And here I am, getting used to the idea that no young man's family will come and meet with members of my family; enter into negotiations, give us *lobola*; and then, and only then, marry my daughter. No. My daughters' weddings will be individual affairs: between "two consenting adults" and I will be lucky if someone remembers to inform me – not ask for my permission – no. Inform me she is getting married. To a man I might not know from a bar of soap!

I am a mother to daughters who can now bring young men into my house, boyfriends. And I welcome that. Families have lost daughters in this country because the young man simply killed the girl. Just like that. So, for the safety of my daughters, I allow what was an abomination in my youth to take place in my house. A man who has given no *lobola* for my daughter comes into my house; when my people have not set eye on his people. This child whom I bore and nursed at my sweet breast, with whom I sat up long nights when she was ill, this child is now a free gift to some man who promises me nothing, nothing at all. And cares little about me and the people of whom I am part; of whom the young woman he will marry is a part. One day, I will have grandchildren who will not know my language or my customs, whose ways will not be the ways of my people. Truly, it is a never-ending journey that I have undertaken. The children are getting their education in this country. But, so am I. Although mine will not come with any certificates. So am I…getting quite an education.

Ismail Mahomed

> I'm quite interested in what apartheid has done to men and women on an individual level as much as what it has done to them at a societal level. The play deals with somebody who feels neither white nor black but is lost in between; how this woman allows herself to be bounced around like a ball by policies of the old government and now comes back to take advantage of the policies of the new government. Apartheid has not only brutalized her but also her family and all of us who have to be witness to their pain.

Sometimes referred to as the Salman Rushdie of South Africa, playwright, director, and producer Ismail Mahomed was born in Newclare township, outside Johannesburg. His family was later moved to Lenasia, an area reserved for Indians under the Group Areas Act. His involvement in theatre followed a long-term commitment to young people in his community.

> I lived in a community that still does not have a single theatre. Even in the new South Africa none of the schools offer arts education as part of the curriculum. Arts takes second place to science and maths.

Ismail began his career as a maths and science teacher at a state high school. He studied at the Transvaal College of Education, the University of South Africa, and the University of the Witwatersrand. After realizing his lack of interest in a teaching career, he stopped his studies. His teaching years, from 1980 to 1985, were times of high frustration.

> Education at that time was in a major crisis, and almost at a point of breaking down completely. We needed to create alternative programs to engage students during the times they were coming to school and not wanting to take classes. Art became a viable means for the students to express their forms of protest through creative writing, songs, dance, and poetry.

Ismail discovered the excitement of involving students in the arts where they were able to create and research their own history instead of using outdated, inaccurate textbooks. Education became dynamic! With the support of his principal, Ismail became increasingly active in drama.

In 1985, he travelled with fifty-six students to the Grahamstown Festival.

> Those ten days were the most meaningful for me in terms of my teaching career. For the first time, I was able to see my students learning without constraints or force. For almost all fifty-six students, this was the first time in the twelve years of their school lives that they were able to interact with students of colour.

From the Grahamstown experience, Ismail witnessed tremendous growth in the students. Inspired, he resigned from teaching, took his small pension, and launched the Creative Arts Workshop (CAW), which, with thirteen students aged 12–14 years, met on weekends. CAW is community-supported and receives no government funding.

Ismail created his first play, *Mama, They Say I'm Mad*, about a mentally disabled child, based on the experiences of a student's sister. CAW's format is to conduct research and bring real-life experiences into writings. The play was very successful and was performed in various communities. The following year Ismail returned to Grahamstown with a one-woman show, *Koebaai Mary Jane*, which focused on teenage drug abuse. The play's success saw CAW's registration for the following year escalate from thirteen to ninety-eight students. Another play by Ismail, *Hush-a-Bye Baby*, examines back-street abortion – an issue that was taboo in the community. Because of travel costs for five to six people, solo theatre appeared a more viable medium. "You could engage people – it was a cost-effective way of doing theatre and you could tour a production very easily." In 1995, Ismail launched the Just Solo Festival in Johannesburg to encourage solo theatre as a legitimate theatre genre.

Another early one-woman show was *Purdah*, based on the violation of women's rights in fundamentalist Islamic communities. It traces the life of a young woman who murders her abusive husband in order to break the cycle of violence. This play was followed by *Cheaper Than Roses*. People are often surprised to discover a man behind these works.

> I disagree with the argument that men can't write stories about women. We can be sensitive and perceptive about other people. I don't look at people with a gender bias. I'm interested in the stories which they tell me and that's what I put in my scripts. Women have supported my work.

Ismail has been primarily self-taught as a writer, although he has received a lot of exposure at the festival level. In 1989, he was one of five finalists in a national playwriting competition for his script, *The Last White Christmas*. He travelled to the United States in 1995 through the United States Information Services (USIS) to examine training for playwrights. He is concerned about the fact South Africa has no real development program for playwrights.

In 1996, CAW launched a playwrights' development program at the Windybrow Theatre with a small budget from the Foundation for the Creative Arts. The aim of the program was to encourage works by young playwrights. The result was the completion of eleven scripts, which were produced at the Grahamstown Festival.

Ismail served as Vice President of Theatre Management South Africa and reformed the organization's constitution. After a year, however, he resigned because he found that white theatre managers were patronizing in their attitudes, not committed to transformation, and were still not committed to developing black audiences or black theatre. Ismail also served on the education committee of PAWE – a trade union for performing artists and the task group for arts and culture policy formulation in the Gauteng province. Since December, 1996, he has been theatre manager at the Witbank Civic Theatre.

ARTISTIC STATEMENT

In 1991, I was travelling on a train one evening. I'm always fascinated by the dialogue of simple folk. I was listening to the dialogue of this particular woman who had so much angst and fear about what the new South Africa was going to mean to her. There was so much richness in what she was saying; so much pain, so much bitterness, so much humour as well. What I found quite fascinating was that I was being entranced by a woman who kept referring to herself as Coloured but who could easily have passed off as a white. As she continued venting her anger, it slipped that she had actually been playing white in the old South Africa and she was now remorseful that things were going to change for her, and I thought – that's my play!

I went home and thought about this for a while. The position of the Coloured woman in our transitional society fascinated me because here we were dealing with a woman whose status continues to remain undefined. Here we were dealing with a woman who wasn't just presenting a gender problem, but also a race problem, and who continued to remain an unknown element in both cases.

THE ROLE OF THEATRE IN SOUTH AFRICA

I will always believe that theatre has a formidable role to play in the humanizing of our brutalized society. Theatre with a strictly entertainment and escapist value is an elitist activity which can in any event only be afforded by an insignificantly small group of English-speaking white South Africans. During the most crucial years of liberation of our country, we fuelled the struggle with our writings, our poetry, and our various forms of performance expressions.

Theatres in our country will have to continue reflecting the vibrant pulses of our souls. There are stories still to be told which have been stifled for far too long. There are stories to be told of our past denials and our present reconciliations. There are stories to be told of our dreams and aspirations. There are stories to be told which must give a new impetus to our changing society. It is, however, unfortunate that some theatres such as the renowned Market Theatre, which has always been at the forefront of producing South African voice and more so works by black artists, have lost their vision.

I'm not very optimistic about established theatres in South Africa. The pulse of South African theatres is in the communities and the developing festival circuit, where theatre continually gets created despite a lack of resources. Established theatres such as the Market Theatre created wonderful works with no funding. Now, with government funding, they've increased their bureaucracy and haven't created any new exciting works by black writers. They're rehashing old shows, telling black stories from a white person's perspective, and they're bringing in imports to appease their few old white liberal audiences. There is no real vision there anymore for black theatre. The excitement is at the community level and the festival circuit, which will definitely be the life-blood for South African theatre. It is, however, unfortunate that the circles of employment, creativity, and discovery happening at the festival and community circuit are not extending into the established subsidized theatre circuit.

HAVE THINGS IMPROVED IN GENERAL IN THE NEW SOUTH AFRICA?

One ballot hasn't changed our lives. People are going to be bitter and angry for a long time. The tragedy of apartheid is that it didn't just physically separate us from each other but that it attempted to destroy our value system and our humanity. People are going to distrust one another for a long time. Nation-building is going to take a long time and has to start with us finding ourselves first before we can even reach out to others. I'm content that more people are having access to water, sanitation, housing, education, and health services than ever before, but I'm saddened at the same time that a large group of former black revolutionaries have been absorbed into a bureaucracy which is becoming increasingly alienated from the ideals which gave us our first democratic election.

PRODUCTION HISTORY

Cheaper Than Roses premiered at the Standard Bank National Arts Festival in Grahamstown in 1995 with Gabi Murray, and directed by Ismail Mahomed. In 1996, *Cheaper Than Roses* was performed at the same festival by Nicole Krowitz, and directed by Karyn de Abreau.

Interview conducted July 1996 in Grahamstown, and July 1997 in Johannesburg. Photo by Stuart Bush.

4 Cheaper Than Roses

A one-woman play

Ismail Mahomed

Setting

On a railway platform at the Bedaarsdorp Station. It is night. The platform is desolate save for BETTY FOURIE, *a young lady waiting for the train to Johannesburg. Upstage, there is a railway track. On the platform (centre stage) a bench. Right stage, signboard weathered by wind and rain detailing train times. On the signboard there is a huge African National Congress election poster with the image of President Nelson Mandela. The poster also contains a promotional slogan of the Reconstruction and Development Programme (RDP).*

Cast

BETTY FOURIE (a lady in her early thirties): physically she should look white but the nuances and accents in her speech should have traces of being Coloured.

(*Enter* BETTY FOURIE, *dressed in her black outfit and with a suitcase and packets in her hands. She looks around the station with disgust at the filth. Puts her bags down near the bench. Sits down and lights a cigarette. Goes to take a close look at the Nelson Mandela image. As she walks back to the bench, she walks over the shit lying on the floor.*)

BETTY Agh Sies, man! Kleurling kak! *(Removing her shoe and scraping the shit off against the bench)* That's what happens to them...blerrie Coloureds. Give them freedom and that's what they do. Shit all over the place. Shit here. Shit there. Shit on the trains. Shit on the railway station but they won't shit in the blerrie toilets. (*Goes back to sit at the bench, opens a pack to take out a bottle of lotion which she rubs over her knuckles. As she opens the suitcase to put the bottle back, she takes out a wreath.*) Jislaaik! Agh nay man! That's all I blerrie need at a time like this. Not going to the cemetery is one thing but forgetting to send the wreath to the cemetery is a even bigger problem. Besides nobody's going to understand that I didn't go to the cemetery because I didn't have the heart for it. Nobody's going to remember that at least I attended my father's funeral service in church this morning.

(*Takes a puff on her cigarette. Tries to recompose herself. Places the wreath on the bench.*)

Carnations...blerrie carnations! My father loved his white carnations and here...I'm now blerrie sitting with the carnations that was supposed to be his wreath. Is waar! Is the honest truth, you know, what the old people say. The dead...they always come back to haunt you. (*Covers the wreath with her parcels.*) My father always used to tell us that when he dies we mustn't forget to put white carnations in his coffin. Al wat ek nou nodig is for him to come spook me to reclaim his white carnations.

(*Walks to the signboard to read the times of the trains.*)

When last any one cleaned this blerrie notice board...only God knows! The dust on here is so blerrie thick. Hy's lekker gebou om te klou but not this blerrie dust. You can't even read what's written on here and there isn't even a blerrie station conductor here to tell me when the next train is coming. Yah Bedaarsdorp...ons moet maar fokken bedaar! (*She goes back to the bench very carefully not to walk over the shit again.*) Ha! Coloured shit! I don't make the same mistakes twice.

(She sits down and then takes one more look at the signboard.)

BETTY Man! Take your blerrie eyes off me. You're watching me like a blerrie eagle. It's times like this that I always say give me back the blerrie old South Africa. I'd rather sit here waiting for my father to come and spook me to fetch his carnations than to sit here with ou Mandela hanging over my shoulders. Arme old man…I can still remember him say *(mimicking her father)* "I don't care if we don't have bread in this house so long as I have a white carnation in the lapel of my brown corduroy jacket on Sundays." And shame mammie, she mos had to work her poephol off to prepare a bouquet of white carnations for the altar in the church. And if there was a wedding in the church, the bride got a complimentary bouquet of white carnations from us. Agh! I suppose the bonus was that vir daai bos blomme, is ons maar sommer VIP invitations. It's a matter of give and take. Everything in Bedaarsdorp is a matter of give a blerrie little here and take a blerrie little there. Here in Bedaarsdorp, our whole lives went around carnations. *(Fidgets with the wreath.)* Carnations! Fokken carnations! Even this morning at the funeral service in church, every one wore one.

(Scratches through her bags.)

BETTY Trust my luck! I'll smoke all my blerrie cigarettes, finish and the train still won't be here. It's almost three hours since I'm sitting here. Maybe I should just spite myself and have gone to the cemetery. Blerrie hypocrites…my whole family is a bunch of blerrie hypocrites…crying for the whole man now that he's dead. Man! It must be like a blerrie circus at the cemetery. You should have seen them at the church. The whole family was there in the first row.

Tant Sennah and her moffie husband, Oom Gamied. Boeta Freddy and his Moslem wife Rookaya and their children. Huh! Blerrie Moslem rubbish with a black mini-skirt mourning for my father in a blerrie Christian church. Boeta Paul and his vrou and children drove all the way from Hawston for the funeral. Blerrie sophisticated rubbishes! Ek ken hulle so goed…ek kan hulle ruik as hulle aan kom. Boeta Paul and his two sons wore their black jackets and bow-ties. And Rebecca…that's now Boeta Paul's wife…Tant Sennah told me they got married about nine years ago. She says the whole dorpie had a celebration. They wanted to invite me but why they didn't is maar just another long story but anyway…life has to go on whether you are invited or not. Rebecca, as I was telling you, she looked beautiful in a black chiffon dress. For all I care, it's still on appro from Edgars Stores. Huh…chiffon in Bedaarsdorp. It's like putting Winnie Mandela in a boob tube and stove pipes.

(Takes a quick glance to the Mandela image.)

BETTY Yah Mr. Mandela, and you left a sexy woman like that! You think I'm sexy? Ga, old man! I don't know why I'm telling you all this but I suppose it's good to get it off my blerrie chest. *(Opens her handbag. Removes a leather bound Bible. Reads it silently before commencing to speak again.)* Shame! Tant Sennah says that before my father died he asked a lot about his children. At times, he would talk about us in his sleep…and then he would just cry and the tears would roll over his wrinkled cheeks. Man! It was sad and then two weeks ago, Tant Sennah sent us all telegrams to come home urgently. Jislaaik! I've still got my telegram folded in my Bible. I don't know why I put it in the Bible but I suppose some things in life is mos best left unanswered, isn't it? *(Puts the Bible on the bench.)* I've seen many people die in my job so I don't get all emotional about it but somehow it was different when I came back here after all these blerrie years. They were all around his bed. The priest was reading from Genesis…this was my father's favourite chapter…because he always said Coloured people were like Adam and Eve…Adam and Eve made a whole lot of children to fill up a whole chapter in the Bible and the Coloured people sommer made a whole lot of children to fill up a population register. Anyway, like I was telling you, I walk through that door with these same suit-cases and almal is dood verstom. They all just look at me. Yah, just the way you're looking at me, Mr. Mandela, eye to eye, and I'm not sure about whether I should stay or just leave. But me I'm a hardegat so I just stand there. Then my father coughs and the priest…He continues to read from the Bible. Only Tant Sennah came to hug me. She was the only one who over all these years had contact with me. If you can maar put it this way…Tant Sennah was my mother by correspondence. The only problem is that the postal service from Johannesburg to Bedaarsdorp is like a blerrie miscarriage. Even the fokken train service is no better! Anyway, ek gee nie om for all the dirty looks that everyone was beginning to give Tant Sennah because she hugged me and asked me to sit next to my dying father's bedside. Worst still…for the two days that I'm here in Bedaarsdorp, I stayed at her home. If everyone wants to ignore me, shit with them all! I haven't come back for any of them…I've come back to see my father before he dies.

(Walks up to the Mandela image.)

Pap en boontjies…pap en boontjies…and after twenty-seven years you still manage to smile. Experience is the best teacher so you'll understand what I mean when I say that twelve years is a long and painful time to be away from home and then to come back and walk straight into a room to see your father on his deathbed… deurmekaar and unable to recognize you. I took unpaid leave from my hospital job to come here with a purpose and I was going to fulfil it…even if my blerrie family didn't want to see me. *(Picks up the Bible: pages through it.)* You should have seen them sit around his bed and cry Amen every time the priest read a verse from the Bible. Blah blah blah…Blah blah blah…blerrie hypocrites! When I opened my Bible to read silently…all to myself…everyone looked at me and the priest…he stopped reading and he walked out of the room.

(Puts the Bible back into her handbag.)

Really, I don't know what made me take out the Bible. You know, as a nurse in the hospital…you do it all the time so naturally when you know that your patient is going to die any minute from now. Agh but me…I can be a hardegat when I want to be so when the priest walks out of the room…I sommer start to read aloud from the Bible…Nogal van Genesis ook…selfde plek where the priest was reading from. And so waar, just like a miracle…my father…he takes his last sluk of air and as I read all the names from Genesis…my father begins to call out all the names of his family…Wallah! One after the other. Tant Sennah, Oom Gamied, Boeta Freddy…he even called out the names of all his grandchildren…and I waited for him to call out mine…but he took his last sluk of air, dropped the white carnation that I put in his hand and he closed his eyes for the last time…forever! It was all over…just like that…even before you could snap your fingers! *(Agitatedly looking at her wristwatch, scratching through her bags.)* Yah! Everyone hugged each other and cried for the old man. I just sat there met niemand om my te hug nie but I'm not sure if I really wanted to cry. So, I just sat there looking at my father…dead but dignified. It was sad! Somehow my father didn't realize that the voice reading from the Bible was mine…His only daughter. But I suppose that's what life is all about. When you least expect it…a smack in your face and a kick up your blerrie arse! You should have seen them at the funeral service. Boeta Paul and Boeta Freddy at opposite sides of the pews; and the two vrouens next to each other holding hands all the time. One big united Coloured family…huh! Tell me all about it! I sat next to the grandchildren in the fourth row pretending not to notice that the hele dorp hou vir my dop. Staring at me and whispering about me. Then this blerrie cheeky bastard, Boeta Paul's and Rebecca's son…he's about seven years old…hy skud my arm amper af and he asks me…if I'm the white carnation that people say has come home. He says he heard his mum and Boeta Paul say so this morning. Blerrie shits! They're supposed to be religious but they're teaching their children to be Coloured-conscious! Well, in any event…If that's what they thought…I wasn't the only one at the funeral who they were too busy with their grief to take notice of. Man! It's really strange, you know…I tell you, somehow I just know it that at the funeral service this morning, mammie was there. She mos died when I was still about fourteen years old. I'm sure I saw her at the service this morning…especially when we all stood up to sing. Man! I could see her clearly and I could smell her perfume…the Lavender Water that pappie mos bought for her in Cape Town by the Parade. Mammie was there in the front re-arranging the carnations on the altar. She took one out of the arrangement and then something strange began to happen. Mammie kissed the carnation and then as she held it close to her heart, the carnation turned into a beautiful red rose and when mammie tried to smell it again...A huge thorn cut her hand...and mammie's hand began to bleed terribly and even though the people tried to grab the rose away from her, mammie hung tight to it...and then suddenly I heard the congregation shout out amen and when I looked again...mammie was not there but on the floor there was a drop of blood.

(She notices the shit on the floor.)

Fok off man, Coloured shit! You're haunting me. *(Picks up her Bible.)* And I know it wasn't a spook. I mean I won't be so stupid to sit here alone on a Bedaarsdorp station at half past eleven at night and talk about spooks to the president of the country. *(Silently reads through her Bible.)* Tant Sennah always said that when you feel something strange, you must just open your Bible and read from it...aloud. The evil spirits die when they hear you read from the Bible. You know I don't believe in all this gemors but sometimes...it's best not to take chances. Come to think of it maybe there is some truth in all this gemors...maybe that's why the priest left the room when I started to read from the Bible. *(Laughs to herself.)* Jislaaik! Mr. Mandela, if I knew you were such good company I would have given you my vote in the blerrie elections. I don't even know why I'm telling you all this...It's like I know you forever. Hey isn't it Mr. Mandela? Can I call you Nelson? All right Nelson. I'd rather sit here talking to you than be with that lot. When nobody was around, they were like the blerrie security police...asking Oom Gamied about the house papers and about whether the old man left a will before he lost his memory. They've come today to throw carnations in my father's coffin like we all promised to do...and tomorrow morning, they'll start scratching into his wallet...like two dogs fighting over a blerrie bone. As for the two vrouens, their eyes were all ready scanning the curtains, the crockery and mammie's antique furniture and ornaments. And poor Tant Sennah who spent all her time looking after the old man and giving Boeta Paul and Boeta Freddy an education...all this from the day after mammie died...what will she get! I suppose inherit all the blerrie carnations growing in the garden...and those pot-plants all over the blerrie house. After all, somebody has to maar water them. I don't give a damn if I don't get anything from the old man's will. If the old man couldn't give a damn for me before he closed his eyes for good...it's no use trying to keep his spirits alive with a few second hand souvenirs. *(Paces around the station.)* It's times like this that I say to myself...Betty Fourie, be grateful for the choice you made.

(Looks at her wristwatch.)

Two hours...and the train is still not here. Waiting for a train in Bedaarsdorp is like watching your whole life crawl past you. And dammit...nothing's changed on this blerrie station. Bedaarsdorp...come to think of it. I gave this town eighteen years of my childhood and twelve years later...still nothing has blerrie changed. The same old house...the same old curtains and furniture. Look out of the window and you see these blerrie rusting railway lines. Look out of the front door...and the blerrie cemetery is your scenery. The only thing that's ever changed in Bedaarsdorp is the number of graves in the blerrie cemetery. Boeta Paul had a strange way of describing it when we were still children. Another one bites the dust. That's mos the Queen's song, nuh Mr. Mandela. I wonder if ou Freddy Mercury knew he was going to die when he wrote that song.

(Goes back to sit on the bench, picks up her Bible, pages through it.)

Truth is like death, man! Nobody can run away from it. I mean, look at mammie and the old man. She tried to run away from him forever when she committed suicide...and now he goes to party with her in the same graveyard. Now they have to maar lie there...next to each...forever!

It's a miracle, man, how fate works. Tant Sennah says their graves are in line with each other...parallel...just like these railway lines...only four rows difference...one here and the other there. If six feet down under they have to fight the way they did here…they'll probably wake up everyone next to them. You can maar imagine the headlines in the *You* magazine…"Dead resurrected in Bedaarsdorp…town's meisie tells her story". Yah! And I don't have to go and dig up a story…it's all locked up in here. A whole blerrie life story locked up in a blerrie cardboard suitcase. It just get heavier all the time but when you open to look at what's inside…all you find is just a whole lot of shit staring you in the face. Shit from yesterday, shit from last week, shit from last month and the year before. Just a whole lot of shit from the past and nobody's going to pick it up for you. You made it so you must carry it.

(Scratches through her suitcase, takes out a bottle of lotion and rubs the cream into her knuckles.)

Yah Mr. Mandela! That's what I did. Swopped all my dreams for all this blerrie shit in Bedaarsdorp…only to find out that the shit on the other side of the fence is not any more fertile and it all smells the blerrie same…but you don't know until you take a swim through the swamp and learn to separate the shit from the moss. That's what I did!

(Walks up to the signboard.)

Yah, Mr. Mandela, that's exactly what I did! Reconstruction and Development even before it came into your vocabulary…can you spell it? I don't suppose so. Anyway that's what I did. I reconstructed myself and I developed myself. *(Goes back to the bench; sits on the suitcase)* Betty Fourie, a shoemaker's daughter…that's me! Anyone could tell what the future was going to hold for me when half the town was walking kaalvoet. *(Removes her stockings)* Fokken stockings is also ripped from all this blerrie waiting. Here in Bedaarsdorp you only had two choices…to grow up to be a poor Coloured or you could grow up to be a miserable Coloured. I chose to give up being a blerrie Coloured. Just packed my suitcases and threw it all up…just like that! It wasn't easy…you can pass a driving test after two tries…but it wasn't easy passing the test of changing from Betty Fourie, the Coloured girl from Bedaarsdorp to Betty Fourie the Coloured meisie from Joburg.

(Looks at the Mandela image.)

Jy kan maar lag…lag maar lekker! But I wasn't alone I'm telling you walking in Joburg and you look at them! Secretly, we were maar all play-whites with our souls stuck to our roots but it was worth it! Man! You could walk wherever you wanted…jobs…education…clubs…parties…the whole world was yours…and men respected you.

No more were you just a blerrie kleurling meid that they could pass off for a prostitute! That's what I wanted when I decided to get out of here…just a good life…a little bit of decency…not like a dog cramped in a treurige kennel and waiting for the welfare to give you a parcel like somebody throwing a bone to a stray dog. I just wanted a nice life and that wasn't asking for much! I was young…I had dreams…I was tired of seeing mammie spending her whole life watering the carnations and pappie fixing shoes. Both of them gave me something that could change it all. From mammie's side…I got my straight hair…that's the Jewish blood. From pappie's side, I got the light skin…that's the German blood. Yah! History made the Holocaust but our family made the blerrie half-castes. Our family was just the joke of Bedaarsdorp. Boeta Paul was light-skinned. Man, like real Boer but his hair was a blerrie give away! It was curly like popcorn. Boeta Freddy…when we got cross with him, we used to call him Kaffirboetie because he was the darkest of us three children. Yah, Mr. Mandela, and now you are trying to change it all but I suppose you don't know enough about the problems of making Coloured offspring. You just never know what they're going to look like. Ask me…I know…when I went to Joburg…I told myself…Betty Fourie, you're not going to fall in love with the first guy that comes along. I turned down a lot of them…bankers, clerks, teachers…all professional men! Guys who knew how to treat a woman.

(She scratches through her suitcase and takes out a small cuddly teddy bear.)

There was a difference…Phillip, hy was mos so sweet! He worked as a clerk for a lawyer's firm. They were involved in defending your human rights cases…but

Phillip wasn't political at all! We used to go to the movies and clubs...then six months later, he asked me to marry him. Jislaaik! I was so delighted! Then two weeks before the wedding, we go to a restaurant. Nogal at the Carlton Hotel...the same place where you held your elections victory party. So Mr. Mandela, you can see you and I jol at the same place. There it was me and Phillip. Just the two of us by candle-light. Gentle music in the background...and Phillip takes my hands into his strong arms and he says that he wants to tell me a secret. Even a blerrie idiot could guess what he wanted to tell me. Phillip was a blerrie halfnaartjie...just like me...a blerrie reclassified Coloured.

(Walks to the edge of the railway line.)

Talk about a lump in your throat, I could feel the whole blerrie Table Mountain in mine. I wasn't sure if I should just tell Phillip about myself. I was feeling sick...I rush up to the blerrie ladies upstairs...lock myself in a blerrie cubicle for ten minutes solid. God was playing fucking hopscotch with my life! I avoided seeing Phillip for two blerrie solid days...and then I move from one flat to another place and it was like starting the running game all over again. It's all God's fault! He just made my life blerrie deurmekaar! Imagine getting married...and then have a baby that's got Boeta Paul's popcorn hair and Boeta Freddy dark skin...and then your whole blerrie secret is out of the bag. *(Goes to the image of Mandela.)* Yah Mr. Mandela, look at me. I feel blerrie. kalgat in front of you telling you my whole blerrie life story. It's not easy trying to run away from my blerrie Robben Island so what do I do? I just blerrie pull myself together...and I say to myself...Betty Fourie, life goes forward and not backwards and so...you must move with it so if you got it, flaunt it! Yah Mr. Mandela, not all of us wanted to be saints and martyrs. Some of us just didn't want to be like Nelson the sea-gull who couldn't even fly out of Robben Island. We all dealt with apartheid in our own blerrie ways. If I looked white and if I got the opportunity to be reclassified...I took it!

(Goes to sit at the bench, scratches through her handbag, takes out a cosmetic pouch and powders her face white.)

The social worker who used to come here to Bedaarsdorp...she told me about it. So, when I turned eighteen, I decided that's what I wanted to do. Betty Fourie is not going to sit here and grow carnations like her mother. Betty Fourie is going to be white! I can still remember it all. A Wednesday morning...I sat with the social worker on this same railway station...me over here by the Coloured benches and she over there by the white benches because in that time that's how the benches were made. We waited for the train to Cape Town and only that time Mr. Mandela, the trains used to be on time. The only trains that are on time now are the blerrie gravy trains. Every now and then, the social worker would put cream on my knuckles and fingers. She would rub it deep in till my fingers were sore. I didn't know why. At the government offices, there was a big lady and she looked really cheeky. We all sat in rows...then one by one...the government lady would call us and give us forms to fill in. Just before I went up...there was a light skinned lady who went to fill in the form. The government lady smiled and then as the woman filled in the form, the government lady hit her on the knuckles with a ruler and shouted, "look at the spot on your knuckles...anyone can tell jy is a blerrie kleurling!" I again began to rub the cream deep into my knuckles. I still got a habit of doing it. Jislaaik! I can still remember all the measurements and the jokes that the officials were making. It was funny, man! The one ou still asked the other ou...if you can fit two combis into a Bantu's nostrils...what can you fit into a Coloured's brains? Also two combis...but only if the tyres are punctured and the combis are loaded with beers. It was crazy...they examined you but they also made lots of jokes with you. I filled in the form and then they took me to a room... another government lady put a pencil through my hair...like this...the pencil fell right through and the government lady smiled. Then, with a ruler she measured my nostrils and my lips...she wrote down all the measurements.

(Mockingly she measures Mandela's lips with her fingers.)

Yo! With those Dunlops, you would never have made it. You needed roller-blades like mine. Then I thought they were going to take me to a doctor when they asked me to take off my clothes. All they did was examine the skin around my anus...what a fancy name for a poephol. They said it was light enough for me to pass as a white. Imagine showing your poephol to get an examination result. Even passing exams at school wasn't so easy and Mr. Mandela, you should have seen the rows of poephols waiting to do the test. Yah! And the poephol examiners in their white safari suits and khakhi vellies...they failed Sub A but they all had a B. Arse degree. You should have seen them Mr. Mandela. *(She mimics the poephol examiner.)* "Poephol in die lug...goed...too tight, you must be Chinese. Next. Ah...too loose, you must be a moffie. Next. Oh...samoosas, you must be Indian. Ah. Pink poephol, you must be Betty Fourie."

Yah, Mr. Mandela, it was a dream come true. My new life...all because my poephol was pink enough. On the way back in the train that's all I could think about...my new life as a white woman with a God-given pink poephol. I couldn't sleep that night but I told myself...Betty Fourie, you're not going to tell anyone until you get your new ID book. Yah Mr. Mandela, race reclassification, it's a moerse big word! If you made it, you got a passport to opportunity but then of course you had to pay the price. I did and I'm still recovering from the debt! It's like buying a Volvo voetstoets...a nice ride until you get up the hill and then you find the engine is bedonnerd. It was two weeks before I got my new ID...the social worker brought it home. She did it because she wanted to give me a better life. That's what she told my father. He didn't say a word and he couldn't get cross with the social worker because in any way the welfare was supporting us from the time mammie died. Shame! Oom Gamied looked at Tant Sennah and then Tant Sennah walked out of the room with tears in her eyes. Boeta Freddy was about eleven years old at the time. He didn't really seem to understand the fuss. Boeta Paul sat one side trying to force a pencil through his popcorn hair. Later that evening, Tant Sennah and I were having coffee in the kitchen. Boeta Freddy was in the bath when he shouted to me..."nou sis, hoe't jy gesë n mens se poephol moet lyk?"

(She pages through the Bible with a poignant smile on her face.)

Boeta Paul gave me this Bible...this same one...as a present. He said I must keep it with me wherever I go and God will always be with me. Tant Sennah took me to the station the next morning and my father went to the cemetery to put carnations on mammie's grave. Man! He was behaving strangely. I never saw him cry but that morning, he did! Boeta Paul and Boeta Freddy came with us to the station. Boeta Freddy bought me a bouquet of red carnations from the flower seller. Asked him why he didn't just take white carnations out of the garden and agh shame...he told me that he wanted to buy me red roses but he didn't have enough money so he bought me red carnations because they were cheaper than roses. When the train came, Tant Sennah held my hand tightly and she told me...Betty, you're going...don't ever come back again. Before I could say anything more, she showed me a photo which she took out from her purse. It was Simon...her son. In Bedaarsdorp, everyone told us that Simon was dead but Tant Sennah told me the truth. Simon also went away to be reclassified and to find a better life.

(She walks on the railway tracks.)

The train pulled away. I saw Tant Sennah holding Boeta Paul and Boeta Freddy's hands and walk back home. It was quiet...only them walking on the railway lines...and Tant Sennah's voice still echoing in my mind..."Betty...loop en soek uit jou eie lewe maar in hierdie dorp is jy nou dood." *(Picks up pebbles from the railway tracks.)* And I suppose the dead don't rise from their graves. *(As she throws the pebbles back on to the tracks.)* Or do they?

(She sits on the tracks.)

To think of it now, it's strange. When we were children, Boeta Paul and I used to play on these same railway lines. We always wanted to know where the railway lines ended. We would walk along them trying to find out where they would lead to. We didn't know whether we should walk this way to the African locations or that way to the white dorpies. Well, that's what happened to our lives...I found my way to the white dorpies. Boeta Paul stayed behind until he got angry with all the pain...And he held Boeta Freddy's hands and they both walked on the railway line until they got to the other end of it.

(Goes back to sit at the bench.)

Tant Sennah says that before my father became ill, he too would sit here at the railway station with a basket full of white carnations and every time a young girl stepped off the train, he would walk up to her and give her a carnation. *(Holds the wreath.)* I don't understand...I really don't understand! If my father did that because he was longing for me then why did he lose his memory before I came home? And why didn't he recognize my voice when I was reading from the Bible? Or, why didn't he call out my name when he called out the names of all his offsprings?

(Places the wreath back on the bench.)

I suppose...that's why he even dropped the white carnation that I put in his hand before he died. I suppose its only mammie from this family who still holds her hand out to me from heaven...and maybe, that's why I suppose nobody else could see the drop of blood in church this morning. *(Scratches through her bags and finds her ID book.)* And all these blerrie problems in my life just because of a blerrie ID book. Betty Fourie, armoedige meisie van Bedaarsdorp who went through all this shit to be reclassified white...And now with all this blerrie new South Africa bullshit it doesn't even matter anymore. Yah! Mr. Mandela! Dis al jou blerrie skuld! *(Mimicking the president.)* "In our Reconstruction and Development Programme even Coloureds will be considered for affirmative action." Jou blerrie moer, man! First we were not too white...now we're not too black. We are just the blerrie filling in the middle of the blerrie sandwich. Gam se kinders...that's who we are.

(Walks up to the Mandela image with her ID book.)

I did it once so why not again? *(Kisses the ID book and throws it on to the railway tracks)* Goodbye ID...tomorrow I can apply for a new one. *(Goes to pick up all her luggage.)* One that says I'm just a South African and not a Coloured, White, African or an Indian. En ek BETTY FOURIE kan vir myself decide what I want to be...Mondays, a white...Tuesdays, a Jew...Wednesdays, a Coloured,...Thursdays, an exile and on Fridays, dronk en deurmekaar just like Betty Fourie. *(With all her luggage in her hand and the wreath still resting on the bench she starts to walk away.)* En jy trein in Bedaarsdorp...dit is mos die nuwe Suid-Afrika, so jy kan maar jou ma se tyd neem om te kom. Life waits for nobody and especially not for Betty Fourie. So, I'm going to walk on and you Mr. Mandela, maybe we'll meet again in the next town under better conditions. *(She walks a few steps and then turns to look at the wreath. She walks backs, picks it up and throws in on to the railway tracks.)* Bye bye Bedaarsdorp...the flowers are for you...I would have bought you roses but times are tough and money is scarce...so I suppose you'll understand...carnations are cheaper than roses.

(She rips off the Mandela picture from the signboard, puts it into her suitcase and walks off quietly.)

Maishe Maponya

> The atmosphere and political climate became my inspiration and mentor because I wrote simply about those conditions that existed.

Maishe Maponya is recognized as one of the most prominent voices of anti-apartheid theatre. His plays include *The Cry*, *Peace and Forgiveness*, *The Hungry Earth*, *Gangsters*, *Jika*, and *Umongikazi/The Nurse*. A writer, activist, director, actor, and teacher, Maishe was born in Alexandra township, Johannesburg, but grew up in Diepkloof, Soweto.

Maishe's interest in theatre began as a youth when he attended performances by writers such as Gibson Kente and Sermona Gwani. Says Maishe, "I didn't understand it as theatre, but developed an interest as I saw more plays and became inquisitive in terms of performance styles and what actors had to go through." Because he also noticed that many of the plays were commenting and taking stands on social and political issues, Maishe realized the power of theatre to reach people.

Maishe's writing career began in 1975 when he joined the Medupi Writers Association, during the height of the Black Consciousness Movement. The movement also included the South African Student Organization (SASO) headed by the late Steven Bantu Biko, and seventeen other groups. In October 1977, these organizations were banned by the government. When he began to write, Maishe had as his only mentor the guiding philosophy of Pan Africanism. He always wanted to make a statement about his condition as an oppressed black person in South Africa.

Maishe's first play, *The Cry* (1976), was inspired by the inferior Bantu education system. During this period, he formed his own ensemble, The Bahumutsi Drama Group, which means "comforters". The group was committed to "comforting those who weep bitter tears of oppression." The group operated from 1976 through the early 1990s, performing poetry, dance, and music, and touring the townships.

Maishe's most prominent play, *The Hungry Earth* (1978), is based on the migrant labor system and the effect of apartheid on blacks. In 1983, he wrote *Umongikazi/The Nurse*, which examines the day-to-day effects of racism on health-care services in the country. When the play prepared to travel to Europe, Maishe and his key actress, Gcina Mhlophe, had their passports withdrawn, and were detained and prevented from leaving the country until later (and then only for a short period). His plays *Dirty Work* and *Gangsters*, written in the mid-1980s, both deal with the South African security system. The plays were written and performed during a period of detention, banning, harassment, and murder by the national security forces.

During his early years as a playwright, Maishe produced his own shows because he didn't have the name or track record for others to consider producing them, nor were any publishers interested in his plays. Many of his shows were funded from his salary as a clerk with a major insurance company from 1974 to the early 1980s. By the time he resigned to pursue theatre full time, he was one of only two black supervisors in the company. During the late 1970s he received his M.A. in Theatre Studies from Leeds University in Britain, and he did further studies in directing and playwriting at St. Mary's College and Hebden Bridge, both in England.

Maishe has traveled internationally as a director, performer, and lecturer. His awards include the Standard Bank Young Artist Award 1985; Best Diepkloof Poet 1985, and the 1994–1995 South African Faculty Fellowship Award from Northwestern University in Evanston, Illinois. He served for several years as a lecturer at the University of Witwatersrand in Johannesburg. He is currently Executive Officer for Libraries, Arts, and Culture for the Southern Metropolitan Local Council of Johannesburg.

A collection of his plays have been published in *Doing Plays for a Change: A Selection of Five Plays* (Wits University Press, 1995). According to historian Ian Steadman, writing in the introduction, "Maponya's career is central to a survey of black South African theatre. He is a product of the formative years of Black Consciousness, and also a precursor of the new voice of South African Theatre."

ARTISTIC STATEMENT

I wrote the play after spending an evening with some nurses. We were at a party and these women were talking about their experiences at Baragwanath (now Chris Hani Hospital in Soweto, which is the biggest hospital in the western hemisphere. I found their discussions quite fascinating. I kept saying to them, why don't we know about all of these things. They said you'd never hear about them because no one is allowed to talk about them because they have what is called the Codes of Conduct and they cannot discuss them. You'll pick up phrases like "the Codes of Conduct" in the play, and those phrases and words are what I got from the actual experiences from the nurses. My research was interviewing these women, talking about their experiences. I told them I wanted to write a play so people can know more about their situation. As I was writing the play, I kept going back to them with questions and subsequently I met up with some doctors to whom I submitted the script and had them make comments. I made friends with them. On Saturdays I traveled to do voluntary work in various communities in the squatter camps to help the doctors. The doctors also ended up being organizers for my show at the various clinics.

The trade union movement in South Africa was beginning to be established – this was the early 1980s – and the nurses and some of the doctors had established the Health Workers Association (HWA). This was more like a union as opposed to what already existed, which was the South African Nursing Association (SANA). SANA was a structure formed by the system. The HWA was seen as being illegal and, therefore, for me it became something I identified with because it was not recognized by the system. It became much more interesting because we aimed to perform productions at clinics and hospitals throughout the country so we could make sense to the general nurses. Nurses came out in large numbers and pledged support and were very amazed at the correctness of the information in the play.

[Maishe was eventually interrogated by the security branch for his play. They invited him to come down for a "friendly chat" with his script and passport, and told him not to bring a lawyer, but he did. In his introduction to *Doing Plays for a Change*, he notes: "I was asked why I had written the play, where I got the material, and about my relationship with the Health Workers Association (HWA – now NEHAWU), its leadership, and why we had organized performances at various hospitals and clinics. I was also asked what I hoped to achieve through the play."]

THE ROLE OF THEATRE IN SOUTH AFRICA

It is important that theatre continues to exist, to be a catalyst in some sense to raise the level of consciousness, to be able to challenge, to be able to resist certain impositions on communities either by government or the corporate world and even challenge practices in their own communities. Theatre should address the issue of whether there is moral decline within the community, and the plays need to be sensitive to these issues. The theatre needs to be more responsible in addressing the imbalance that exists between the urban life and the privileged class, and the rural life and the disprivileged majority. Theatre still has a major role to play. It needs to continue to be the eyes and ears of the people and continue to challenge. It should delve into other aspects of life, not only politics.

HAVE THINGS IMPROVED IN GENERAL IN THE NEW SOUTH AFRICA?

In general, yes, things have changed. They have changed, obviously, but not for everybody. You don't fight the same system, but you still fight a particular system. We're fighting budget cuts. I work for the local government, and the cuts are the worst I've ever seen. You're left with a budget that you can't do much with, and this comes from the politicians. I'm in a position that was previously occupied by whites or that didn't exist. Now I'm in a position to address the issues of the arts from my perspective. I aim to address the ills and disadvantages of my people.

To a large extent, things have changed. We have black parliamentarians that we never had who are doing their best to change their communities. In other instances things haven't changed. We still have the squatter camps, and the crime level has gone up to some extent.

PRODUCTION HISTORY

Umongikazi/The Nurse premiered at the Donaldson Orlando Community Centre in Soweto, in 1983. The cast included Gcina Mhlophe, Fumane Kokome, Bennette Tlouana, and Maishe Maponya, who directed his play.

It later opened at the Market Theatre for three weeks and then performed to packed houses at Glynn Thomas (Baragwanath Hospital). The performers were Gcina Mhlophe, Sidwell Yola, Maishe Maponya, and Bennette Tlouana.

The play later toured Germany, Switzerland, and the United Kingdom, initially without the two leading performers, Gcina Mhlophe and Maishe Maponya, who were refused permission to travel for security reasons.

Interview conducted July 1996 and 1997.

Photo by Kathy A. Perkins.

5 Umongikazi/The Nurse

Maishe Maponya

Setting

Stage right takes only a third of the stage and serves as FEZILE*'s home. It is sometimes used as an exit area from stage left. Stage left takes two-thirds of the whole stage as the Hospital. When action moves from one to the other the Transition is indicated by a switch of lighting. Some scenes and episodes are flashbacks; these all take place in the Hospital.*

Props and costumes

Two garden chairs and a small round table for stage right. A normal size table and a chair for stage left. A typical hospital screen, four chairs.

Nurses' white uniforms, matron's uniform, theatre overalls and caps, khaki watchman's uniform and a big-headed stick, men's blue overalls, hedge-cutter, shirt, white shoes, doctor's uniforms and overalls, stethoscope, surgical scissors, incubator, four pairs of spectacles (different kinds), two brown wigs, one Afro wig, newspapers (*Nursing News*), a big yo-yo, a brown file, small board with words "CHEMIST" and two sticks at the edges to hold it, telephone, two white masks (different kinds), a hair brush, bucket containing water, soap, a washing rag, a walking stick, floral dress and a cap (for old woman), hospital pyjamas.

Characters

The main characters in the play are:
FEZILE in his early thirties
NYAMEZO a nurse; twenty-eight years old; FEZILE's wife
MARIA a nurse; in her mid-thirties
ACTOR FOUR portrays several characters indicated in the text

Other characters

MAHLALELA, DR. LUMUMBA, BLACK DOCTOR, MALE NURSE, LOCAL SECURITY They are all played by the actor who plays FEZILE.
PAEDIATRICIAN, PATIENTS (Scene 6), 1ST NURSE (Scene 6), 2ND NURSE (Scene 6), 3RD NURSE (Scene 6). They are all played by the actress who plays NYAMEZO.
OLD WOMAN, NURSE (Scene 1), NURSE (Scene 4), MATRON, THEATRE MATRON, NURSE (Scene 5), MAGOGO, 3RD NURSE (Scene 7). They are played by the actress who plays MARIA.
WHITE DOCTOR, DR. OWEN, PREGNANT WOMAN, QUEUE MARSHALL, PHARMACIST, 2ND MALE NURSE, POLICE OFFICIAL. These are all played by the ACTOR FOUR.

Scene 1

(Blackout. Spotlight comes on an OLD WOMAN *singing an overture; a background to the struggle. The song is entitled "Ntsikana" and is sung in Xhosa.)*

Wayetshilo uNtsikana
Wayetshilo umfo kaGabha
Ukuth' umzomnyama uyophalala
Ngenene wa phalala njengamanzi
Wayetshilo wathi nothengisana
Nithegisane nge qosh'elingenamxunya
Amadoda ahlele ezinjwaleni
Abafazi base marabini
Kwenze njani na mzi kaphalo
Wovuswa ngubani xa ulelenje
Ahambile 'amaqhawe amahle
Ahambile ngenxa yo Mzomnyama
Abanye bakufele wena Afrika
Banye base mazweni bangamabanjwa
Uzo vuka nini
Uzo vuka nini we Afrika

Zayaphin' inkokheli zo mzomnyama
Ndi hlab'umkhosi
Ndi hlab'umkhosi ndithi vukani kusile
Vukani kusile magwala ndini
Ndiyalila ndilel' umzomnyama
Ndithi ziphi inkokhelizawo
Hlobanizikhali iyohlasela
Vukani kusile magwala ndini!

[Translation]

Ntsikana said
The son of Gabha said
That the black home will be spilled
And truly it was spilled like water
He had said that you will sell each other
Sell each other for the button without holes [money]
Men are now in the drinking places
The women are with the marabi
What's wrong home of Phalo?
Who'll wake you up as you sleep
The beautiful heroes have gone
They have gone for the sake of the black home
Others have died for you Afrika
Others are prisoners in foreign lands.
When will you wake up?
When will you wake up Afrika?
Where have the leadership of the black home gone?
I am making a call
I make a call to say wake up it's dawn
Wake up it's dawn you cowards
I mourn the black home
Where is its leadership?
Arm yourself and attack
Wake up it's dawn you cowards! (End)

(The lights come up slowly stage left on the patients at the rear. The DOCTOR *is visiting the patients in the ward. He goes from one bed to the other with Sister* NYAMEZO *assisting in translations and other regular duties. Sister* NYAMEZO *is delayed at the back talking to one patient.)*

DOCTOR *(Calls out at* NYAMEZO*)* Sister Nyamezo please come and help here.

NYAMEZO I'm coming Doctor...

DOCTOR *(Goes to the next patient)*...And who is this one?

NYAMEZO Mandla, doctor.

DOCTOR I see...Breathe in, Mandla... Again...Okay. Open your mouth wider,...say ahhh! Ahhh! *(Examines him. Turns to* NYAMEZO*)* I think he's right.

DOCTOR *(They move away from the patients)* Good sister...I am satisfied with the progress of all the patients. As you heard, I may discharge about three of them tomorrow if their condition stays good. But, there is one patient I haven't seen in a long time...what on earth is happening to him?

NYAMEZO Mahlalela, doctor?

DOCTOR ...That's right sister.

NYAMEZO He's always here at night. The sister I relieved this morning tells me he sleeps all night; but as soon as she knocks off and I take over, he disappears. He was given his medication last night...here, look at his report...

DOCTOR Remember sister, the patients are your sole responsibility. I want to see that patient tomorrow. Just imagine, I've had this ward for the past three weeks, yet I haven't seen all my patients. Make sure that I see Mahl – Mahl...

NYAMEZO Mahlalela, doctor...

DOCTOR Never mind about the name, sister...I want to see him! *(He rushes out.)*

(Transition.)

(Very early in the morning. NYAMEZO *bursts into the hospital ward only to bump against* MAHLALELA *who is already preparing to sneak out.* MAHLALELA *is dressed in hospital pyjamas, he has his personal clothes in his hands.)*

NYAMEZO Ja, and where are you off to?

MAHLALELA To the toilet sister – out of my way I'm pressed, I'm in a hurry...Nurse kha undiyeke torho! [Nurse just leave me alone please!] *(Tries to push past)*

(Enter on-duty NURSE*)*

NURSE What on earth is happening here? What's wrong sister? Why are you so early today?

NYAMEZO I want to see a certain patient. I miss him every day because as soon as you knock off he disappears. The doctor wants to know what he is up to...

NURSE Which patient is that?

NYAMEZO Mahlalela.

NURSE Mos nank'uMahlalela. [But here is Mahlalela.]

MAHLALELA Leave me alone women, you are wasting your time, I want to go...

NURSES Where to?

MAHLALELA Toilet!...Since when do you stop patients from going to the toilet? Watch out...I'll report you to the doctor!

NURSE But the toilet is on the other end Mahlalela!

MAHLALELA *(Louder)* I want to take some fresh air first before I go to the toilet.

NURSE *(Angry)* That's madness! What air? Go straight to the toilet or go back to sleep!

MAHLALELA No one is going to tell me what to do. I do what I like here, I warn you women, get out of my way!

NYAMEZO Remember you are a patient here and we are in charge of all patients. We tell the patients what to do.

MAHLALELA Not me!

NURSE You included!

MAHLALELA If I lose my job because of late-coming you will lose yours the next day. Get out of my way I'm late. *(Pushes them aside)* I am going to work...

NYAMEZO He is mad! We must report him to the Superintendent.

NURSE No sister, it is dangerous.

NYAMEZO *(Puzzled)* Why?

NURSE Mahlalela stayed on in hospital after he was discharged, that was three weeks ago.... And every morning when he wakes up he goes straight to work...

CHORUS OF PATIENTS Fifteen thousand people have been on the waiting list fifteen years. No houses! Where do you expect him to live!

(Exit all except NURSE*)*

NURSE *(Recalls as she laughs)* And...I know of a certain patient who apparently had an agreement with the doctor. This one was never discharged from the hospital because he had to clean the doctor's car every morning!

(Exit NURSE *laughing)*
(End of scene)

Scene 2

*(*FEZILE*'s home. Enter* NYAMEZO *still dressed in her white hospital uniform – from work. On the small garden table are several copies of* Nursing News*. Her attention is drawn to the very first paper with headlines which she reads out loudly to herself.)*

NYAMEZO "Be positive, despite problems." *(Throws it away and takes a look at another)* "Call on SANA members. Before you raise your voice to criticize the South African Nursing Association along with other uninformed people, make the effort to find out what the association does for its members; particularly in the area of salaries." *(Disappointed at yet another)* "A Christmas message from our President"; very interesting. *(Stands up to read it carefully)* "As the year draws to a close, my thoughts go out to all the nurses of South Africa, who in this exceptionally difficult year have served the nation with dignity, devotion and distinction. Have faith in your future – a better deal for nurses is just around the corner." Shit!

(Enter FEZILE *in a happy mood)*

FEZILE *(With both hands clutched together, hiding something. He sings.)* I've got the world in my hands...I've got the world on my fingertips...

NYAMEZO *(Getting more irritated)* And what is that supposed to mean?

FEZILE It's a song...

NYAMEZO I know that, but what are you doing?

FEZILE The conquest of nature by Fezile – a discovery. I am yo-yoing...First I yo; and then yo again...Thus producing a familiar repetitive motion known as yo-yoing...*(Parting his hands to reveal long string with a yo-yo at the tip)*...One of these days my name will go down in the history books of the world. How would you feel about it? Obviously great! And what is that supposed to mean? *(Gesturing at the papers with his head)*

NYAMEZO What?

FEZILE Papers on the floor!

NYAMEZO Rubbish! Rubbish! I can't stand reading this paper these days. I often wonder why we have to pay subscription fees each year. It is as if the black nurse does not exist. Nothing is said about us and the progress we make.

FEZILE *(Ignoring her)* Well I'm conquering gravity. Proving that what goes down must come up.

NYAMEZO Will you stop that and start clearing this mess, if you don't want to listen – go and trim the hedge!

FEZILE *(Continues with his yo-yo tricks)*...I thought as much – look – look I told you. I'm conquering nature! *(Sings)* I've got the world spinning and spinning at my command...

NYAMEZO You are wasting time! Will you clear up this mess?

FEZILE I'll clear it up after I've done this my dear.

NYAMEZO I know you won't.

FEZILE I will. Look at that skill! Makes me feel like a god. A movement of my hand and the world spins my way. *(Sings)* Give it a twist, just a flick of the wrist.

NYAMEZO *(Peering at something she has missed as she went through the papers. Pulls the whole page out.)* Yes, this is where it all began, the whole story of the nursing council – all in one phrase...

FEZILE Shoo! Ain't funny? Keeps on going down and up again – I can't stop it...

NYAMEZO I sometimes think you don't live in the same world as the rest of us. The only thing you are concerned about is that daft toy. Does nothing get through to you? Does your mind drift through your head like foggy smoke with no direction, no purpose?

(FEZILE *continues to yo-yo.)*

FEZILE You should relax my darling...

NYAMEZO *(Irritated)* You don't understand, just put that thing away?

FEZILE It is a cord. An umbilical cord between me and peace...

NYAMEZO Some shit cord!

FEZILE Well it keeps me alive... *(Still yo-yoing)*

(NYAMEZO *moves out angrily. She comes back with a pair of hedge-cutters and in a split second cuts the string of the yo-yo leaving* FEZILE *with his mouth open in disbelief. Silence)*

NYAMEZO With that out of the way you will probably listen to me!

FEZILE Damn it! I have no spare thing...

NYAMEZO Thank God for that.

FEZILE I shall mend it. Though it will never be the same again because the knot will make it jerk...

NYAMEZO At least you will now have to listen to me!

FEZILE *(Getting a new idea)* Wait a minute. I am going to devise a new trick. This time I won't have to use the string. And you know what? Some mad-caps around the world will be identifying it as an unidentified flying object...I'm going to do it, I'm telling you... *(He wants to leave.)*

NYAMEZO All I'm telling you now is to go and trim the hedge! What kind of husband are you. It's toys, toys...an old man like you. You should be ashamed of yourself!

(FEZILE *picks up the cutters and reluctantly starts to trim the hedge.* NYAMEZO *picks up another* Nursing Times *and begins to read.* FEZILE *continues to trim the hedge.)*

NYAMEZO Fezile! Fezile! Do you know that Dr. Lumumba has resigned?

FEZILE What?

NYAMEZO Yes, he is leaving at the end of this month. Apparently he is leaving the country too.

FEZILE Rubbish! I can't believe it.

NYAMEZO "Rubbish! I can't believe it." It's here in this useless paper. I understand his reasons though...how can they expect him to drive all the way from Benoni to Attridgeville in that old "Skodonk" every day, that's wrong! They should give him transport allowance. Not only that...

(Flashback. Enter a white DOCTOR *giving information to trainees.)*

DOCTOR Look, working in this place you've got all the advantages on earth. A good salary – a really good salary, you attend to only a few patients like of course in the white hospitals. Granted there is congestion everywhere in the black hospitals, but you have all those sisters who have done primary health care to assist you. They are always around. You will get travelling allowance no matter where you come from. We don't expect you to come all the way from Cape Town for work. And another advantage is that you are a white-doctor-in-a-black hospital...Ever thought of that! Yes, "tolerance fee"! I presume that we are serving a different community group...that is our compensation..."Tolerance fee"!

(End of flashback)

NYAMEZO Yes but these are precisely the reasons for his resignation. You see, apartheid is rooted in the hospitals too. Dr. Lumumba was the first to realize this and he made us aware of it. Oh how I'm going to miss those moments when Dr. Lumumba would call us like a father to his children.

(Exit FEZILE. NYAMEZO *moves to stage left. Flashback. Enter* FEZILE *as* DR. LUMUMBA*)*

DR. LUMUMBA *(Calling out to* NYAMEZO*)* Sister! Sister! Nyamezo!

NYAMEZO Yes doctor.

DR. LUMUMBA Listen. Whether you accept it or not, the truth is right in front of you. Whilst we appreciate the progress you as nurses are making, we are not blind to the fact that this move is not only to alleviate the pressure in the clinics. No! It's also an economic strategy by the Department of Health. None of us is getting what the white doctors get and we examine the patients just as well as they do.

NYAMEZO But Dr. Lumumba, it's an opportunity we have to grab. At the end of we'll know what every doctor knows...

DR. LUMUMBA *(Raises his voice)* That doesn't make you a doctor. Why train a lot of health workers instead of educating people. It's ridiculous – out of 23 million black people how many qualified black doctors have we got in the country – less than 4000. And out of five million whites how many qualified white doctors are there? More than 12,000! The education system is rotten! And once you've come to this conclusion – you must start suspecting the teacher, suspect the book he reads from, suspect the school principal, the regional inspector and the whole bloody education system!

NYAMEZO *(Shocked)* Dr. Lumumba! *(Exits to reappear stage right)*

DR. LUMUMBA *(Softer and slower)* Yes, frustration of the black mother frustrates the black child and the result is a social breakdown of black life – that's why we have what they call in our schools "drop-outs"!

(Exit DR. LUMUMBA. *End of flashback)*

NYAMEZO That was the man – Dr. Lumumba. To think that he is no longer with us...He used to smart every nurse's ear with wisdom. He would say this in front of everyone. He would even say it to the officials...

FEZILE *(Still backstage)* Hai! hai! hai! Would he have said it in the presence of whites?

NYAMEZO What whites? Aren't whites officials?...Oh how we used to admire his convictions. And now to think that he's gone; what a loss!

*(*FEZILE *now comes out with a bucket full of water and soap all over his head and face.)*

FEZILE Now I see Dr. Lumumba has chosen a wrong profession.

NYAMEZO That is the man who has given me the right education...

FEZILE Wrong education. That man is not supposed to be a doctor.

NYAMEZO His education was spiritually uplifting...

FEZILE Wrong education...

NYAMEZO Right education!

FEZILE I'm telling you that kind of education is wrong...

NYAMEZO That's the right education!

(Enter MARIA *as they continue to scream at each other.)*

(End of scene)

Scene 3

MARIA Hi Nyamezo! Hi Fezile!

NYAMEZO AND FEZILE *(Surprised)* Hi Maria hi!

NYAMEZO Long time no see Maria. Where have you been, what's up?

MARIA Nyamezo, I am the most disillusioned nurse in the country. Things are bad for me, I'm out of work again.

NYAMEZO Come now Maria, we are busy discussing something serious about Dr. Lumumba and here you come with one of your silly jokes.

MARIA Serious, I've lost my job.

FEZILE Come on Maria, not so long ago you were telling us how nice it was to be working in the white hospitals...and so what's gone wrong?

MARIA Yes Fezi, but remember greener pastures are always full of snakes. Terrible snakes! The other nurses are still there but it's going to become very difficult for them there. Nowadays, the black nurses are put at the mercy of people we never thought mattered a lot in the hospitals.

NYAMEZO Like?

MARIA Like the white cook of course. *(*NYAMEZO *and* FEZILE *burst out laughing.)* Just imagine a fat white woman who has no inkling of what it is like to be a nurse, exercising her unprofessional status on a black qualified nurse. "I will fire you! I will fire you my girl! If you don't know how to behave in front of your seniors, this is not the place to learn that! I'm your senior and I will bloody fire you!"

NYAMEZO *(Laughing)* Is that what happens?

MARIA For God's sake! To think she's got an apron and I've got epaulettes and bars to show status, but to her status is this *(Indicating her cheeks)*, and the thing that makes me mad is that we are barred from attending to some patients because there is a general complaint from the patients that they don't feel safe when they are attended to by black nurses...

FEZILE Ja Maria, to expect to work harmoniously with the white nurses is impossible. It won't work. Just won't work! You see we come from different places, different homes and different cultures and apartheid has damaged the minds of the white people. The only thing that puts them together is the iron hand!

NYAMEZO Exactly!

MARIA To rub salt into the wound; black nurses at Wenela Hospital are now being instructed to leave their uniforms behind when they knock off.

NYAMEZO Why, so they are not seen to be working there?

MARIA Precisely. You know we are treated like assistant nurses in the white hospitals. When the white hospital nurses are scrubbing...

FEZILE Come on Maria, do you want to tell us white nurses scrub floors too? No we can't believe this one.

MARIA No Fezi...I don't mean that. What I mean is that when they are in the middle of an operation...

FEZILE Oh I see, that's hospital terminology...

MARIA Yes Fezi. This is not a layman's language. What I mean is that when they are in the middle of an operation, I, qualified as I am, have to wait on the sidelines and take instructions from them...And the other thing that really made me mad was when I discovered their "skinder-hoekie" [gossip corner]!

NYAMEZO A what?

MARIA Yes a skinder-hoekie. You know, they keep a "skinder-boek" [gossip-log].

FEZILE Maria tell us why they call it a "skinder-boek". What a name?

MARIA Because that's where they sharpen their scalpels!

FEZILE *(Shocked)* Scalpels shoo! That's a dangerous weapon. Hai, white people in this country are a "disaster" to black people.

(He exits with the bucket and comes back with a hair brush in his hand.)

MARIA Sister Nyamezo, I think I am going to rejoin the black hospitals. I will learn to tolerate the attitudes of other black nurses and black patients, after all they are my people and I understand them.

NYAMEZO It's high time you did.

MARIA I think I have to go now. Bye!

(Exit MARIA. FEZILE *continues to brush his hair whilst looking himself up and down in the mirror.)*

NYAMEZO Poor Maria...To think she was so excited when she was going to this white hospital of hers. And now she's back. Just imagine the white cook...

FEZILE Alright, alright let's forget about Maria for the time being...

NYAMEZO Yes.

FEZILE I've some business to talk to you about.

NYAMEZO Some business? Aren't we getting serious these days...

FEZILE Yes we are getting serious.

NYAMEZO Come, tell me what's the business about?

NYAMEZO *(Quickly)* Remember the project I told you about?

NYAMEZO A project? I can't remember talking to you about a project.

FEZILE Damn it, can't you remember the other day when you asked me to trim the hedge?

NYAMEZO Yes I remember asking you to trim the hedge.

FEZILE Ja, that very same day I told you about the project.

NYAMEZO What kind of project is that? In fact I can't even imagine you involved in a project.

FEZILE Well you had better start imagining it now.

NYAMEZO Alright tell me, what kind of project is it?

FEZILE *(Getting irritated)* It's a project!

NYAMEZO Ja, I know it's a project but what kind of project is it?

FEZILE I need some cash.
NYAMEZO What for?
FEZILE For the project.
NYAMEZO I know but what is the project?
FEZILE I need to buy some machinery. It's actually a fuel injection carburettor. Do you know what it is...?
NYAMEZO Fuel injection carburettor, what a beautiful name for a project...but you still haven't told me what the project is. Isn't it boring for me to keep asking what is the project, what is the project, and still I can't get an answer.
FEZILE *(Doubtful)* Well...you know that I am inventing a new...Hmm...yo-yo.
NYAMEZO What? A yo-yo. Do you seriously mean you expect me to give you money for a yo-yo! A toy! That'll be the day! Andi soze! [I won't!] *(Walks out of the house)*
FEZILE *(Angrily)* Hei wena mfazi [Hey woman] give me some money! If you don't want to give me the money, bring back my whole pay-packet I gave you last Friday – I want my money! *(Follows her)*

(End of scene)

Scene 4

(In the theatre – casualty theatre for minor cases like circumcision, skin graft or tooth extraction; a screen. A FLOOR NURSE *peeps through the screen.)*

NURSE *(To the audience)* We were left only with five minutes to finish the case.

(The FLOOR NURSE *comes out from the screen with some utensils, she bumps into* DR. OWEN*, they fall.* DR. OWEN *instructs her to pick the utensils up.)*

DR. OWEN *(Puzzled)*... And now, what's going on in my theatre?
NURSE We are busy on a case, doctor.
DR. OWEN I want an answer from the surgeon.
NURSE That won't help. All cases must be booked.
DR. OWEN *(angry)*But I always get preference you small banana!
NURSE *(Fuming)* Not this time you big orange!
DR. OWEN You don't call me a big orange, you stupid!
NYAMEZO *(Peeping from the screen and interrupting)*...And I never realised there were oranges and bananas working here!
NURSE Neither did I, but I've been trying to tell Dr. Owen that we are busy on a case!
NYAMEZO And how does he react to that?
NURSE You know this silly doctor has a bad tendency of bullying us around here in the theatre. He even goes to the extent of beating up the patients. He is really getting on my nerves...
DR. OWEN *(Pulls out a gun)* I'll shoot you!!
NYAMEZO *(Bravely)* That'll be the day...
DR. OWEN I'll shoot you too!
NURSE Do it now!

(Exit DR. OWEN *to call the* MATRON*)*

NYAMEZO *(Agitated)*...A whole doctor pointing a gun at us! I'm going to report this matter to the nursing council!

(The NURSE *rushes out. She returns as the* MATRON*, closely followed by* DR. OWEN*, to confront* NYAMEZO*.)*

MATRON *(Not even waiting for her side of the story)* Sister! It's indecent to talk so arrogantly to the doctor. Remember that he has sacrificed years of his life for this hospital.
NYAMEZO If you talk to me in that attitude I will not waste my breath!
DR. OWEN Hear, I told you. This is the kind of people the hospitals employ these days, cheeky!! I will report this matter to the chief matron! You are not solving my problem either! *(Pulling the matron by the hand)*
MATRON Don't pull me so hard doctor!

(The MATRON *exits and returns as* THEATRE MATRON*. She has hardly opened her mouth to speak when* DR. OWEN *starts.)*

DR. OWEN *(Still angry)*...These little bananas have a tendency of calling me names!
NYAMEZO There he goes again calling us...
DR. OWEN Shut up!
THEATRE MATRON *(Questions* NYAMEZO*)* Sister, where were you in1976?
NYAMEZO Don't crack your skull...I had already begun working here!
THEATRE MATRON Well, here we don't behave like the 1976 children!
DR. OWEN Bloody terrorists!
THEATRE MATRON ...And remember sister...I am going to write a report about your unprofessional behaviour...I'm going to do it!

DR. OWEN I like your attitude matron...these nurses need discipline.
THEATRE MATRON Thank you doctor...

(Exit DR. OWEN *and* THEATRE MATRON*)*
End of scene

Scene 5

*(*FEZILE*'s home. Once more he is seen with a yo-yo in his hands. He seems quite happy with life while something is seriously bothering* NYAMEZO.*)*

FEZILE Lovie wee!
NYAMEZO Hee—
FEZILE I have trimmed the hedge...
NYAMEZO Ja I saw that...
FEZILE And did you see where I planted the lilac flowers. It makes the view better, doesn't it? Lovie you know what?
NYAMEZO Ja...
FEZILE You don't look too good today.
NYAMEZO I know.
FEZILE But you didn't tell me why?
NYAMEZO How can I talk sense to you when that daft toy still occupies your mind.
FEZILE Okay then dear I'm listening.
NYAMEZO I think I'm going to quit!
FEZILE Quit what now!
NYAMEZO Just this morning I had a terrible experience at the hospital...

(Transition. A wordless song while the actors change clothes. A delivery room at the hospital; NYAMEZO *offstage as a* WHITE SENIOR PAEDIATRICIAN*; a* WOMAN *giving birth. The* WOMAN *lies on the table and goes through the process of birth-giving.)*

NURSE *(To woman)* C'ammon sisi, push – push – again – push! Alright, alright hold it *(Taking scissors to cut umbilical cord)* Let's see how much it weighs, no! 850 grammes but it has life – it will live. *(Puts the child in an incubator and goes out shouting)* Let me rush for the paediatrician. Doctor! Paediatrician!...
PAEDIATRICIAN Yes what is it?
NURSE We have a premature baby weighing only 850 grammes...but it's alive!
PAEDIATRICIAN *(Peeps out the half-open door)* Ag!...let it die man, it's got no chance anyway. Take that thing to the sluice room.
NURSE But doctor, can't we save it?

(The PAEDIATRICIAN *ignores her. A pause)*

NURSE *(To audience)* One hour later I went to clean the sluice room only to find it gasping for air. *(Speaks to herself)* It's alive! Let me rush for the paediatrician! *(Runs)* Paediatrician! Paediatrician! You've got to resuscitate please!!
PAEDIATRICIAN *(Reluctantly)* Right! I-am-giving-life-to-this-thing and tomorrow it'll be the one that will snatch my bag!

(The devastated NURSE *sings.)*

Senze ntoni na? [What have we done?]
Senze ntoni na?
Senze ntoni na?
Ho-ho-ho
Ho-ho-ho
Senze ntoni na?
Ho-ho-ho-ho-ho-ho

(Transition – FEZILE*'s home)*

FEZILE And what happened?
NYAMEZO The child had already developed hypothermia and it died!
FEZILE *(Shattered)* Hayi man!
NYAMEZO There were no questions. No investigation and nobody will be taken to task.
FEZILE What do the nurses say about it?
NYAMEZO The nurses fear victimization, all they can do is lament. It is, in fact, against the Codes of Conduct for me to give you this information.
FEZILE *(Contemptuously)* Rubbish! Codes of Conduct! The nurses must stand up! The nurses must be organized! All those racists must be pulled out of our hospitals. To hell with codes of racist conduct!
NYAMEZO It's just such a pity...
FEZILE What is a pity?
NYAMEZO Dr. Lumumba has left.
FEZILE But you are there and every dedicated nurse is there! You should shout in one voice!
NYAMEZO We cannot, because we do not have a union. The South African Nursing Association would be against it.
FEZILE That very association consists of racist mentality – how can they take action against their own brothers? You should form your own union, go for it!! DON'T BE AFRAID.
NYAMEZO I won't be. I will go for it!
FEZILE *(Encouragingly)* If you do that, I will be right next to you. And you know what my next step is going to be?

NYAMEZO Yes, buy another yo-yo!
FEZILE No-ways my dear...I will give up my yo-yo adventures...(NYAMEZO *looks surprised.)* Can't believe it? It's true. I will give up my yo-yo adventures! *(Grabbing the yo-yo to throw it away, while shouting with* NYAMEZO *close behind him)*
FEZILE AND NYAMEZO Away with the yo-yo! Away with the yo-yo. Away! *(They continue to make noise backstage.)*

(End of scene)

Scene 6

(The hospital. A QUEUE MARSHALL; PATIENTS*)*

QUEUE MARSHALL *(Angry at patients)* Msindo! *(Looks down)* And now whose card is this! Kha u bheke! [Just look!] *(Calls out the name out loud)* Jonas Magugane! Jonas Magugane c'ammon come for your card. Hurry up! Give him way, let him pass – take! Damn it! You are even in the wrong queue. Don't argue with me ngi zaku phihlizajong! [I will clobber you!] *(Threatens to hit her)* And remember this is not an old age home. Hamba! [Go!]

(Enter a NURSE *to confront a* PATIENT. *The* PATIENT *is imaginary.)*

NURSE *(To patient)* Yes?...You come all the way from the gate to ask me questions? Who told you I'm the information officer? You must go back to the enquiries and there, you can ask them as many questions as you want. That's what they are there for. *(Turns and freezes with back towards audience)*

(Enter MAGOGO, *an old woman)*

MAGOGO We phoyisa [policeman], do you mean I must stand in that long queue?
QUEUE MARSHALL I can't help it salugazi, you must wake up. Do you think this is the pass office where there is a lot of bribery?

(Phone rings. NYAMEZO *still plays* NURSE*)*

2ND NURSE *(Rushing to answer)* Hallo, hallo! Yes. Can I help you? *(Pause)* Hi Joey! *(Excitedly)* How are you my lover-boy? Oh I'm, fine as usual. What? Pardon I can't hear you. Just hold on a minute. *(Turns around to scream at a patient)* You are making noise! I say you are making noise! An old man like you crying from pain? Look at the blood! Are you trying to paint this place red? Rubbish! You must have been drunk when you had that accident! C'ammon move it! *(Back to phone)* I'm sorry Joey, you know these patients can really drive you up the wall sometimes. Yes. When? Where? Irene's place? Good! We can even go to Mosoja's joint. You know I love these two shebeens, they've got a touch of class...Yes for people like us. That's why all the visiting superstars are taken there for entertainment...the Champion Jack Duprees, the Millie Jacksons and some football team directors enjoy themselves there. Even well-known playwrights like Maishe Maponya and Matsemela Manaka also go there for entertainment. Can't we fall under the same class? Good! You are a darling, what do you think I love you for? *(A bit disappointed)* C'ammon Joey you must pick me up. Please Joey fetch me, fetch me Joey? *(Excited again)* I knew you were joking. Now tell me, which car will you be driving? My favourite one? The red Colt Gallant? I love that one...Love? I must go now to that boring job you know – come give me a kiss – mba! Mncpwa! *(Drops the phone and still excited)* Just imagine, Masoja's joint! Lets go dancing oolalaaah! *(She dances a bit and she freezes with her back to the audience.)*
MAGOGO Haaibo! This can't be. Does this suggest that I must queue again just to pay? Why didn't that man take the money the same time he gave me the file?
QUEUE MARSHALL Hey salugazi! You wake up and stop complaining! U ya kompleya, kompleya! Ag man! [You are complaining, complaint!]

(NYAMEZO *plays another* NURSE.*)*

3RD NURSE *(To another* PATIENT*)* Yebo buti, can I help you? O you want to go to Ward Fourteen. No problem I can help you. You don't need enquiries. You go straight, turn to your right, you will see red footmarks and they'll lead you to Ward Fourteen...Tell me are you sick? I mean with a tie and a suit on, you don't look sick to me. What? This necklace? My grandmother gave it to me *(Giggle)* Who me? Thank you, Thank you! *(Giggle)* I live in Soweto – Chiawela. I work in this ward. Yes you can visit me at anytime...Just follow my directions and you won't get lost. Okay, bye-bye. Hope to see you again! *(Freezes)*

MAGOGO *(To audience)* After another hour, I was told to go to the nurse. I tried to protest. A ngizanga ku nesi apha, ngifuna udokotela! [I've not come to the nurse, I want the doctor.]

QUEUE MARSHALL Salugazi are you still here? Awu guli wena mos! You are not sick! Uzo cheka la! You've come for your boyfriends! Fuck off! *(Exit* QUEUE MARSHALL*)*

MAGOGO *(To audience)* I lost the battle and I queued.

(NYAMEZO *plays herself and attends to* MAGOGO*. A* BLACK DOCTOR *played by* FEZILE *comes in.)*

NYAMEZO *(After looking at* MAGOGO*'s file)* I'm sorry Gogo I can't handle your case. I will refer you to the doctor.

MAGOGO *(Exploding)* I told you I wanted to see a doctor!

NYAMEZO Gogo this is the procedure here…

MAGOGO Rubbish procedure. It's procedure! Procedure everywhere you go. Orderless procedure. *(To audience)* I was now running mad.

BLACK DOCTOR *(To* MAGOGO*)* Next please *(Remembers)* Ah it's you again Gogo? And what's wrong this time? Pain? Let's see your card. Alright, I will prescribe some very good medicine for you. Good. You must go to the chemist and collect your medicine but make sure that you come back here next Monday.

MAGOGO Doctor you mean I must go and queue again here?

BLACK DOCTOR No Gogo. This time of day there are not a lot of patients around here. *(She moves out.)* No Gogo the chemist is on your right. Next please!

(The BLACK DOCTOR *holds the "chemist" board and freezes whilst* MAGOGO *comes to the counter for her medication. A white pharmacist appears behind the counter.)*

PHARMACIST Come Magogo, let's see, *(Scrutinizes the card)* No, no Magogo go back to your doctor for motivation!

MAGOGO *(Confused)* Usukhuluma ngani manje mntanami? [What are you talking about now my child?]

PHARMACIST I said motivation, motivation Magogo!

(She goes to NYAMEZO *for help.)*

MAGOGO Angiyitholanga imithi futhi angiyizwa nale ndoda ekhuluma ngokungishawuda; wozongisiza ntombazana yami. [I didn't get the medicine, also I can't understand this man who talks to me in a shouting tone; come and help me my girl.]

(NYAMEZO *takes her to the chemist.)*

PHARMACIST *(To* NURSE*)* I told her to go for motivation! Motivation Magogo!

NYAMEZO But Doctor I can't understand this, this is the third patient you sent back for motivation…

PHARMACIST And the first two were changed. What's wrong in changing the prescription for this one?

NYAMEZO Yes, but what I don't understand is that the doctor has actually examined the patient and has prescribed exactly what he knows will cure the patient.

PHARMACIST I don't dispute that when the patient is young. The old people just waste medicine – they don't take it regularly. Hypertension tablets are very expensive, sister – and you know there is a very low compliance. The follow-up on patients is poor, so why waste expensive medicine? Next please!

(Song, led by NYAMEZO*)*

Wozani Manesi
Wezw'e simnyama
Wozani silweni lomkhuba

Ngqu – Ngqu – Ngqu

Kwaf'a bantwana
Imith'ikhona
Wozani silweni lomkhuba

Ngqu – Ngqu – Ngqu

[Translation]

Come nurses
Of the black nation
Come let's fight these strange goings on

Children die
While medication is there
Come let's fight these strange goings on

NYAMEZO *(To audience)*…A few months later

I was called to the local hospital security where I was told that...

(Flashback)

LOCAL SECURITY NYAMEZO, you are organising misconduct amongst the nurses! You are stirring them up! You behaviour is intolerable and unprofessional. You will be dealt with severely...

(End of flashback)

NYAMEZO *(To audience)* And then came the security branch to "take me for a drive". I was blindfolded and put at the back of the van. And during the honeymoon with the Security Branch I was told in no uncertain terms that...

(Transition. The two male actors put the white masks and march to confront NYAMEZO *standing on her sides and singing.)*

SECURITY BRANCH

We will panel beat you kaffir
We will panel beat you goed.

Take you to Protea station

Panel beat you
Take you to Modderbee
Leave you naked
Take you to John Vorster Square
Los jou morsdood...

We will panel beat you kaffir
We will panel beat you goed.

NYAMEZO I was told to bring the Health Workers Association constitution, which I promised to bring for I have seen cars being panel-beaten. But when I realized I was being turned into an informer, I discussed it with my husband. He was angry with me for offering to assist the police.

CHORUS INSTATE SECURITY!

NYAMEZO So I never complied; instead I became brave. We cannot go into battle when we do not expect casualties...*(A continuation of the song "Wozani Manesi")*

Hey wena vuka
Wesaba bani
Vukani silweni lomkhuba...
Ngqu – Ngqu – Ngqu

[Translation]

Hey you wake up
Who do you fear
Wake up let's fight these strange goings on...

(End of scene)

Scene 7

(A gathering of the South African Nursing Association [SANA] members. A WHITE OFFICIAL *is making some points.* NYAMEZO *is present. Only the last bits of her speech can be heard.)*

OFFICIAL ...The South African Nursing Association needs your full support. To bring this body closer to you we will take another look at the constitution to change it. So far we are very happy with the way things have gone. Our critics have also acknowledged this point...And for this reason we must give ourselves a standing ovation! *(Some of the other* NURSES *give the speaker a standing ovation.* NYAMEZO *starts ululating and addresses the audience. The other actors take their seats.)*

NYAMEZO Liiiiiiwu! liiiiwu! Ngcanda Kwedini agcwal'amancgwaba Umongikazi ebhekile! Ngcanda kwedini agcwal'amancgwaba Umongikazi ebhekile!

Mongikazi wase Afrika!

Have you forgotten the day you took your vow?

Did you vow to let your people die in front of you?

Or are you scared to follow your convictions?

Two patients in a bed for one;

Overcrowding!

And where do our children get malnutrition in a rich country like ours? No! No!

That's nonsense! That's nonsense! We must form our own union. Nurses of Afrika, you are the light you are the life, you are the light you are the life, you are the light you are the life!

Mongikazi omnyama ongubozimhlophe!
Floors, floors are beds for dying millions of your people!

Au wena Owavela nokukhanya Kwelanga!

There is life in your hands, resuscitate them to life because you can! It is inevitable that we must now form our own union! The situation here is being reinforced and aggravated by the poorly-qualified so-called doctors – the Taiwanese, the Polish, the Israelis, the Germans and all those chance takers who could not make it in their countries. This is their Canaan. There is manna here for them. Yes, the authoritarian type of institution is showing its true colours...

(A MALE NURSE *has raised his hand. He gets the approval of the meeting to speak.)*

1ST MALE NURSE To add to that...recently a great number of qualified nurses have been refused permission to practise in the cities. The reason is that it is alleged that they come from the homelands. Ridiculous that this is done at a hospital level!

2ND MALE NURSE *(Interrupting)* Who cares where a nurse comes from?

1ST MALE NURSE Now, what I fail to understand is that the hospital also practise influx control! I agree to the formation of a union of the nurses, the doctors, the porters, and all other people who are employed in the hospitals. We are a trade! The hospital is a factory where broken bodies are being mended, you know! Yes, I support the formation of a union...!

(Applause. 2ND MALE NURSE *stands up.)*

2ND MALE NURSE Sister Nyamezo, since we are all off-duty, I move that we take off these hospital uniforms so that we are not caught off-guard by the "Codes of Conduct".

(All-out excitement as everybody starts to undress. Amid the pandemonium. They sing...)

Ndithi nyuka nxai ndini
Ndithi nyuka nxai ndini
Ndithi nyuka nxai ndini!

[Translation]

I say rise up you lazy ones
I say rise up you lazy ones
I say rise up you lazy ones!

(End of the play)

Gcina Mhlophe

> Storytelling is the mother of all the other creative art forms. Whether you want to write songs or drama, storytelling is the mother of them all.

Gcina Mhlophe is an internationally celebrated poet, actress, storyteller, writer, and director. She was born in Hammersdale in KwaZulu-Natal, but her teenage years were spent in the Transkei. A lover of language, Gcina grew up in a home where education was embraced and reading was important: "Reading became a very strong pillar for me. It was something that I held on to."

At the age of 17, Gcina decided to become a poet after being mesmerized from hearing her first praise poet.

> A praise poet is one who sings the praises of the people, the praises of the community, the good and the bad, and the experiences they've gone through. It's like oral history in poetry – wonderful delicious language. If you ever wanted to taste good language, listen to a praise poet…I had never heard one speak before. I went back to boarding school and my life was changed dramatically! The following week I wrote my first poem and read it out loud and just fell in love with my voice.

Gcina is a self-taught writer. During the late 1970s she published short stories, including "The Toilet", and "Dear Madame", an autobiographical piece about her work as a domestic. In 1979 she moved to Johannesburg and had a wonderful opportunity to work with *Learn & Teach*, an adult literacy magazine. During her two years there, she was the only black on the staff, where she grew tremendously as a writer. Gcina considers herself a writer: "I write poetry, songs, short stories and plays. If something comes and I feel a shape, I let it be born that way. Since my daughter's birth, I've been writing lullabies."

Her first play, *Have You Seen Zandile?* was written in 1985. For the 1989–1990 season, Gcina was the in-house director at the Market Theatre in Johannesburg, where she wrote and directed *Somdaka*.

Somdaka, which means "proud to be dark-skinned", is a play about a man who refuses to work in the gold mines. With co-author Janet Suzman, Gcina wrote *The Good Woman of*

Sharksville, an adaptation of Brecht's *The Good Person of Setzuan*, for the Market Theatre in 1995. Her latest play is *Love Child*, a biographical work about a love relationship between a Zulu and Xhosa.

In 1992, Gcina founded Zanendaba Storytellers. *Zanendaba*, which means "tell us a story", is an organization of about eight members, committed to promoting, and including into the school curriculum, the ancient art form of storytelling. The group performs and runs workshops for schools, church groups, and other organizations. They also develop books for children and produce tapes of their stories. Gcina has elevated storytelling to a national art form. She believes that as a storyteller you can change people's views of life and themselves. Through storytelling she feels you can take people on a journey: "*Zandile* is very much like a story and it's natural that I wrote it. After all, I am a storyteller. As a storyteller I can have so many flexibilities. Yes, it's still theatre."

Gcina has travelled extensively as a visiting lecturer nationally, to the United States, Japan, and Europe. In May of 1994 Gcina was awarded an Honorary Doctorate by the Open University in England. Other awards include a 1987 Obie Award (New York) for Best Actress in *Born in the R.S.A.* She is also a recipient of a 1988 Joseph Jefferson Award (Chicago) for Best Actress in *Have You Seen Zandile?* In collaboration with Ladysmith Black Mambazo, she released an album of children's songs and stories in 1994.

Gcina is the author of numerous publications ranging from children's stories to poetry. Her books include *The Snake with Seven Heads*, *Queen of the Tortoises*, *The Singing Dog*, *Hi! Zoleka*, and *Ma Zanendaba*.

ARTISTIC STATEMENT

While I was working at *Learn & Teach* magazine, I was offered an acting job with Maishe Maponya to do a role in his play, *Umongikazi/The Nurse* in 1983. I thought that I would do just one piece in theatre and continue with my journalism, since I was happy as a writer working for the magazine. I did the play and didn't realize it was the beginning of my theatre career.

In the meantime, my short story, "Nokulunga's Wedding" got published. When it was published, I received a lot of letters from people suggesting I make a movie, a play, and even a musical out of the story. I didn't know how to write a play. Then Maralyn Van Reenen, a director, suggested we get together, fund-raise, and do "Nokulunga's Wedding" as a play. By this time, I had just returned from a six-month tour with Maishe's play *Umongikazi/The Nurse*, and had also been performing at the Market Theatre in Barney Simon's play *The Black Dog*. Before we even began rehearsals for *Nokulunga's Wedding*, my mother passed away – December, 1984. Something hit me like nothing I could have imagined. I just went under with my mother's death. I was mourning for at least five months. I didn't want to go out, I didn't want to do anything. I was just sitting alone crying a lot. The only outlet I had was writing. So I wrote many of the things that were welling up inside of me. Especially because my mother had passed away without the two of us having made peace and becoming friends. I had a dream that one day my mother would be my friend. We had a hard time with my mother. We had a very difficult relationship. So I was dealing with all these emotions and things were just spilling out. So Maralyn had been talking to me about fund-raising for the play and getting a cast. We didn't get the money. A lot of difficulties arose. So out of not having enough money to produce *Nokulunga's Wedding*, we decided on something smaller. So I told Maralyn what I had been writing concerning my life and she suggested I write the material as a play. So I just began writing one act after another, and that's how it happened. It was a two-hander. I used the name Zandile because it's the name of my sister who is two years older than I am. I admire her a lot. It was a name that came first to me. The name is also symbolic. When you say the number of girls are growing, it could be translated to mean that the contribution of women in the arts is growing. This was really my first play.

THE ROLE OF THEATRE IN SOUTH AFRICA

Theatre has played a very important role in the past. Theatre has allowed us to speak about things we were not allowed to speak about. It gave us a voice. Theatre brought people together who wouldn't necessarily meet in the street and say, "hey, what do you think about this?" So you got together and rehearsed a play that expressed your innermost feelings. Now as South Africa is changing, there's been a kind of dip in the production of theatre pieces. How do I analyze that? One of the reasons is that perhaps South Africans dwelt too much on writing plays dealing only with apartheid. I often say that I'm not a writer because of apartheid. I'm a writer because I'm a writer. Whether I was born under apartheid or after apartheid, I was destined to be a writer. So I wouldn't give the apartheid architects such credit that they could claim they made me. South Africa is going through a very strange period now because we started exporting too much, and when you start exporting things, you tailor-make things for a particular audience. And so there was a lot of *amandla*, *viva*, *toyi-toyi*, and throwing of the stones. When I did *Zandile*, I was criticized a lot by political-minded people asking why was a powerful woman like me writing a play like *Zandile?* If I can write about the masses, I can write about me. I'm one of the masses.

HAVE SITUATIONS IMPROVED FOR BLACK WOMEN IN THEATRE IN THE NEW SOUTH AFRICA?

I think we've got a big job ahead. I don't see a lot of young black women playwrights coming up. I don't know why we're not seeing a surge of young women. I'm nervous about that. I wish I knew why. From time to time I may run a workshop and somebody comes and says, "I've been writing," and your hope rises, thinking, the next time I'm going to see an opening of someone's work I've never seen before. But then it doesn't happen. Perhaps we need to resuscitate workshop theatre. Go and work with someone who's writing. There's no real network for black women, or real training unless you go to a university.

HAVE THINGS IMPROVED IN GENERAL IN THE NEW SOUTH AFRICA?

Yes, some things have really changed. But then some things have changed for the worse, like the escalation of child abuse. It is terrifying. I'm amazed by the kindness of the law toward rapists. They get bail easily and are out on the streets raping again. The victims can be one year old, women, and even young boys. Some of these people [rapists] are respected members of the community. So this worries me.

I'd also like to see some miracle that will bring back the culture of learning in the schools.

PRODUCTION HISTORY

Have You Seen Zandile? premiered at the Market Theatre, Johannesburg in February 1986. The cast included Gcina Mhlophe as Zandile and Thembi Mtshali as the other characters. The production was directed by Maralyn Van Reenen.

Interview conducted July 1997, in Johannesburg.

Photo by Ruphin Coudyzer.

6 Have You Seen Zandile?

A play originated by Gcina Mhlophe, based on her childhood

Gcina Mhlophe, Maralyn van Reenen, and Thembi Mtshali

Scenes

1: Zandile and Bongi
2: Grandmother (Gogo) at home
3: Zandile's life with Gogo
4a: Zandile teaches flowers
4b: Zandile with Gogo in the garden
5: The white car comes for Zandile
6: Gogo discovers Zandile is gone
7: Gogo searches for Zandile and Zandile's letter to Gogo
8: Zandile with mother in the field
9: Zandi and Lindiwe swim in the river
10: Zandile gets to know her mother
11: Lindiwe goes to Johannesburg
12: Praise poetry and Gogo's entrance
13: Zandile and Lindiwe prepare for the farewell party
14: Zandile finds Gogo's suitcase

Scene 1: Zandile and Bongi

(ZANDILE *is heard offstage saying goodbye to her school friends, who are going in the opposite direction. There is a lot of talking and laughing and the hubbub of taking leave.*)

ZANDILE Umbonile ke lowa mfana ukuthi ushaywe kanjani esathi wenza lokuhlakanipha kwakhe kanti kade eseboniwe… washaywa ezinqeni vumphu vumphu! Wabaleka. Zamhleka-ke ezinye izingane. Hahahaha! Nihambe kahle ngizonibona kusasa, heyi Nomusa, ungakhohlwa phela ukuphatha iskipping rope mina ngizoza namacryons – I'll bring my crayons…Nomusa you promised hawu…mpff, kanti udlala ngami…bye bye…bye bye.

(ZANDILE *now enters the acting area. She is quite subdued and she looks a bit sad and apprehensive as she faces the rest of her journey homeward on her own. She starts singing about mothers who will be coming home bringing their children sweets, rice and meat. At first she sings the song to herself, but it grows more confident as she winds her way around the acting area as if it were her path home. She notices some pretty stones on her path and stops to pick them up. She continues, now playing a hop-scotch game with the stones. She slows down as she sings…*)

ZANDILE

Nabaya omame, bethwel' imithwalo
Nabaya omame, bethwel' imithwalo
Ngcingci bo, ngcingci bo, nabaya omame
Sabona ngoricey, sabona ngonyama
Sabona ngokhekhe, sabona ngoswitie

Mhhhm swities! I wonder if my grandmother will bring me some sweets today…lucky if she does because she will bring me my favourite icemints! That's what I like. I could be standing here like this and my Gogo would say to me – Zandi, I have a surprise for you. Close your eyes, open your mouth…

(*She closes her eyes and opens her mouth for* GOGO *to put something in it. Her eyes grow bigger with the thought of the sweets and she pops a stone into her mouth. She imagines that it has become her favourite sweet.*)

ZANDILE Mmmm icemints. (*She succeeds in her fantasy for one moment, but once again the sweet becomes a stone, and she spits it out.*) Ag phu! Ngiyisilirna kanti akunaswidi la, it's just a stone!

(*Suddenly in her imagination she hears a little girl*

laughing at her. She turns around and focuses her attention where the imaginary child is seated.)

ZANDILE What are you laughing at wena? Uthini? I know it was just a stone. I am not stupid. And I am not talking to myself! Maybe you have got lots of friends to play with, but I don't... You also don't have anybody to play with? You can play with me. You could be my friend. What's your name? *(Pause)* Bongi – that's a nice name.

Mina nginguZandile... I'm so glad I found you Bongi, you are going to be my own friend and you will play with me everyday when I come back from school.

Where do you stay? *(Pauses and listens as if the child is answering her)* At our house? Ooh Bongi, but how come I've never seen you before? *(Pause)* Yes, we are wearing the same shoes *(Laughs)*. I like your dress though. Jo! Those goats! They are beautiful Bongi. I wish I had a dress like that too. And who plaits your hair for you? *(*ZANDI *is wide-eyed with shock and envy.)* You plait your own hair... everyday before you go to school! Hayi uclever wena.

Which school do you go to? *(Pauses and listens as if the child is answering her)* Why do you go to a school like that? That is a bad school. My father would never let me go there. You must change and come to my school now that you are my friend. *(Pause as if Bongi is arguing for her school)* I know somebody there... you know what they did? This girl, she was only sick, she stays next door to me, and they beat her up *(Demonstrating)* and they beat her up until her hands were so swollen... they thought she was dodging school but she wasn't, she was sick. I'll never go there where they beat you so much. Ngeke!

*(*ZANDI *has been talking so much she doesn't see* BONGI *take out some sweets.)*

ZANDILE Bongi? Who bought you those sweets? *(Pause)* I wish I had one. You won't give me? *(Pause as she goes to get one from* BONGI*)* Thank you Bongi, and the thing is nobody is going to see you, I'm the only one who's going to see you, only when I want to see you. It's just the two of us. *(They hold hands.)*

*(*ZANDILE *draws some circles on the floor to prepare for a game.)*

ZANDILE Come, let's play amagendo. You don't know how to play it? But how old are you? *(Excitement)* Eight! I'm also eight. *(Pause)* I am eight Bongi. I know people think I'm ten because I'm so tall. *(Pause)* I am tall, I'm taller than you. Come, let's stand back to back. *(She backs up and starts measuring with the flat of her hand against her head and* BONGI'S.*)* Bongi, don't stand on tip toe, he-e uyarobha wena, I'm not playing with you anymore, I am not pla – yi – ngi! *(*BONGI *apologizes and promises not to cheat anymore.)*

Look at my feet, let's stand like this – you see, I am taller! One day, I'm going to be a tall teacher, like Miss Dlamini, and walk like this *(Demonstrates)* hee ngiqhenye habe... What will you become when you grow up? *(Pause)* Jo! A white lady! That is nice Bongi, we can still be friends. I'll be a tall teacher and you will be a white lady with long hair like that, and you will have nice clothes and nice shoes with high heels... and, and you can put rouge on your lips njengalomlungu wakaWebber... but I don't like it so much... And Bongi, we can speak English – Ismasdat lapetelez for you? And I can say – Was da meta be you? *(Stops and thinks)* Bongi, you can also have a car! Unginike ilift sihambe sobabili sigqoke kahle abantu basibuke bathi... hish mame, qhaks baby. We can go anywhere together! Come Bongi, let's sing.

Nabaya omame, bethwel' imithwalo
Nabaya omame, bethwel' imithwalo
Ngcingi bo, ngcingci bo, nabaya omame
Sabona ngoswidi, sabona ngokhekhe
Sabona ngoricey, sabona ngonyama
Ngcingi bo, ngcingci bo, nabaya omame...

(Carried away by the excitement of the moment, BONGI *and* ZANDI *sing their way off the stage.)*

Scene 2: Grandmother (Gogo) at home

*(*GOGO *returns from shopping in town with* ZANDILE. *She puts down the packets and goes out to*

the stoep to greet her neighbour. The neighbour is a little distance away, so GOGO *calls to her.)*

GOGO Sawubona weMaGumede! *(Laughs)* Ninjani? Sisaphila. No I have just arrived...You mean from the weekend? Oh! I came back last night. I really had a good time. Dundee is a beautiful little town. Hayi *(Looking at her dress)*, me? Looking good? No, I'm getting too old now *(Laughs)* but not too old to travel. I really had a good time. Bye bye. *(Half to herself)* It's always nice to come-back home.

(Humming a church song, GOGO *looks through the window and sees* ZANDILE *playing with other children. She turns and starts unpacking the shopping bags. A new doll falls out.* GOGO *picks it up and chuckles to herself as she looks at the doll, remembering...)*

GOGO Oh, my grandchild. What did she say to me the other day when I bought this doll? Hawu Gogo, I love this doll but why do they always make them pink? *(She laughs)*

I hope Zandile is happy living with me. Oh, I could not bear to see the child playing all by herself looking so subdued. And there I was, with all the time in the world. Why could my grandchild be lonely? And yes, I have been lonely too since my husband died and my son Tom moved out with his family.

I would not talk badly about Tom, but he is the one who should take care of Zandile. His wife's hands are full – she has to take care of their six children. Zandile's own mother lives in the Transkei with her husband and four children. So Zandile is nobody's responsibility it seems. Well, she's welcome to be my responsibility. Oh, she's such a delight to cook for. *(Pauses, thinking)*

And is she clever! You should see her at the shops. She reads that shopping list so well. She is really a clever little girl. She could become a doctor, or a lawyer or an accountant. *(Excited)* She could be anything. And I'm here to help her with her homework, and tell her stories. Her father used to love my stories.

Am I glad I work! With Tom's two boys ready to go to college, I could smell trouble. I asked him to let Zandile come and stay with me because I thought if he ran short of money, Zandile would be the first to be taken out of school.

Tom thinks education is not important for a girl. Ha! Even if I have to die doing it, I'm keeping Zandile at school.

Scene 3: Zandile's life with Gogo

(We see ZANDILE *and her* GRANDMOTHER*'s lives together. They each thrive on this relationship.* GRANDMOTHER *gives the child the great gift of stories and the magic to tell them, and the child gives the* GRANDMOTHER *a purpose.*
ZANDILE *and her* GRANDMOTHER *enter stage left, down the passage. They have just returned from West Street, where* GRANDMOTHER *had taken* ZANDILE *shopping. It is* ZANDILE*'s first time in the big city.)*

ZANDILE Kungeve kumnandi edrobheni Gogo, and I had nice ice-cream.
GOGO You had three ice-creams!
ZANDILE Futhi ngadla nobhanana omude ongaka, I like banana, and Gogo, do you remember when we got a lift korisho? I thought I was going to fall at the back when he started to run with us. Gogo, wena awuzisabi izimpondo zakhe ezinkulu kangaka?
GOGO Oh, I know you are so excited...Come, sit down now. I must get you something to drink.
ZANDILE Sizophuzani weGogo?
GOGO Milk.
ZANDILE Can I have lemonade weGogo?
GOGO No no no no, you must have milk. Do you know what's going to happen if you don't drink milk? Your teeth will fall out. Your bones will be so weak, you won't be able to walk. I don't want my grandchild to be like that. Milk for you. *(She exits centre as if to go to the kitchen.)*
ZANDILE WeGogo?
GOGO *(Off)* Yebo.
ZANDILE When are we going to the beach?
GOGO No, no, I am too old to swim now.
ZANDILE I know Gogo, but you can take me and you can sit at the beach and you can put your feet in the water and I will do all the swimming. *(*GOGO *returns with* ZANDILE*'s milk in a cup and a glass of sherry on a tray.)*
GOGO Okay, we'll go to the beach, but first drink up your milk now. And Granny's going to have a little sherry.
ZANDILE Gogo, are you drinking lemonade?
GOGO Yes.
ZANDILE Can I have some?

GOGO When you've finished your milk you can drink lemonade.

ZANDILE Gogo, amakhekhe?

GOGO I nearly forgot, I have some cakes. Would you like some? *(*GOGO *leaves stage.* ZANDILE *takes a quick gulp of "lemonade", chokes and returns to her seat, drinking all her milk.* GOGO *re-enters with a tin of Mazawatee tea filled with Eet-sum-more biscuits.)* Good girl, you are drinking your milk. Do you want some lemonade?

ZANDILE Gogo I don't want lemonade. I like my milk. *(She imitates the pose on the biscuit tin of "Happy Family".)* Angithi Gogo yithi sobabili laba?

GOGO Yes, just the two of us. *(Laughs)* These biscuits...do you like them? *(*ZANDILE *nods.)* Do you know what they are called? Eet-sum-more. Do you know what that means?

ZANDILE Does it mean you can eat one and another and another and another and the tin never goes empty?

GOGO Ake uveze izincwadi phyla ngibone. Show me your books. What were you doing this week at school?

ZANDILE Kade senza izibalo i-arithmetic mina ngathola ten out of ten. Ngisayolanda incwadi yami ngikubonise. Buka ke, I got correct, correct, correct, and my teacher wrote good. And you know what else we did, we said poems and played some nice games we know.

GOGO And what did you do?

ZANDILE I played this game: "Ngake ngahamba, ngahamba wema". Wena-ke Gogo uzothi "Two Sheleni". Asenze-ke.

GOGO O...O.

ZANDILE Ngake ngahamba, ngahamba wema.

GOGO Two Sheleni.

ZANDILE Ngahlangana nezinsizw' ezimbili.

GOGO Three Sheleni.

ZANDILE *(*GOGO *has made a mistake.)* Eh-eh Gogo. Two Sheleni njalo, njalo.

GOGO O...O. Njalo, njalo?

ZANDILE *(Starts again)* Ngake ngahamba, ngahamba wema.

GOGO Two Sheleni.

ZANDILE Ngahlangana nezinsizw' ezimbili.

GOGO Two Sheleni.

ZANDILE Zangimisa zangibingelela.

GOGO Two Sheleni.

ZANDILE Zangibuz' igama lami wema.

GOGO Two Sheleni.

ZANDILE Ngazitshela ngathi ngingu.

GOGO Two Sheleni.

ZANDILE Zangibuza zathi ntomb' ungowaphi.

GOGO Two Sheleni.

ZANDILE Ngazitshela ngathi ngingowakaMthembu, kaQhudeni kaMvelase, kaMpofane, owawel' uThukela ngobindlala iwile.

GOGO Two Sheleni. *(She starts clapping enthusiastically.)* O...!

ZANDILE Eh-eh Gogo, I'm not finished!

GOGO I'm sorry.

ZANDILE Zangibuza zathi ntomb' uqomephi.

GOGO Two Sheleni.

ZANDILE Ngazitshela ngathi angikakaqomi ngiseyingane, yesikole, yesikole, yesikole!

GOGO Hawu! And you say you learnt this song about boyfriends from your teacher?

ZANDILE No Gogo. Sis Kate did it at the wedding last month. I can't do it as good as she, but I'm going to be good. Angithi Gogo?

GOGO Mntanomntanami you are very, very good, and now I have a little surprise for you, for being so good at school.

ZANDILE Oh, Gogo, I'm going to stay with you forever because you always have surprises. *(*GOGO *takes a small packet of sweets called Zulu Mottos out of her handbag.)*

GOGO You make me so happy! Here, Zulu Mottos.

ZANDILE Gogo, I like Zulu Mottos. *(She puts the sweet straight into her mouth.)*

GOGO Eh-eh, read it first!

ZANDILE Yebo Gogo...*(She reads.)*

GOGO What does it say?

ZANDILE Elami libhalwe ukuthi ene, "Ndlebenkulu". Hawu Gogo, does that mean I'm going to have big ears after eating it?

GOGO Bakithi no no no, it's just a playful writing! Give me one too, please.

ZANDILE Yebo, Gogo...what does yours say?

GOGO Uyisithandwa somphefumulo wami – you are the love of my heart.

ZANDILE Asho mina angithi Gogo? WeGogo, is it true that there is somebody on the moon?

GOGO Yes, there is someone on the moon.

ZANDILE Are you going to tell me a story? *(Excited)*

GOGO In fact, I do have a little story about that. You see there was this woman. She always woke up early in the morning just after the cock crowed for the third time.

ZANDILE *(Imitates a cock crowing)* Lithi kukulukugu.

GOGO Yes, she would go to the river to fetch some water for her family.

ZANDILE Why did she go to the river? Did they have no water taps in the house?
GOGO Mntanomntanami, in those times nobody had any water taps. And they also had to make a fire to warm the water so they could wash. The woman got up early one winter morning, it was freezing cold, and saw that there was no firewood to make fire. It was a Sunday and she knew that she was not allowed to chop wood or do any work on a Sunday.
ZANDILE Gogo, they also told us that at Sunday school.
GOGO But she had a baby and she could not wash that small baby in cold water. Again the husband and the baby would need some food as well. So she thought she would quickly get some firewood before anyone could see her. She took the baby and tied it to her back, took some ropes and set off, walking very fast. Their dog followed them.
ZANDILE Gogo, what was the dog's name?
GOGO Baxakile...
ZANDILE And what colour was it, Gogo?
GOGO Green...with pink spots and a red nose and a purple tail and big green eyes.
ZANDILE Gogo, I wish I was living in the olden days.
GOGO Why?
ZANDILE So that I could have a dog like that.
GOGO Oh, Mntanomntanami, it's a pity because they don't make them like that anymore.
ZANDILE If I had a dog like that, I could take it to town and to school with me and I could...
GOGO Can I go on with my story now?
ZANDILE Yebo, Gogo.
GOGO So she collected quite a bit of firewood and made a bundle. She carried it on her head and went back home. She was still on her way when she felt dizzy like she was walking in a dream. But she did not know what was happening. So people say she was punished and sent up to the moon with her baby on her back, the bundle of wood on her head and the dog behind her.
ZANDILE *(Very sleepy now)* I wonder what happened to the father and the grandmother and the other people.
GOGO It was a shame because they never saw her again and the father and the grandmother never had the pleasure of watching the baby grow into a beautiful, clever little girl like you! That is why when the moon is full you can see a woman on the moon...so that people can see and learn.

(GOGO now looks down at ZANDILE, who has rested her head on her grandmother's lap. ZANDILE has fallen asleep.)

GOGO Sleepy...sleepy. Come Mntanomntanami, you must go to bed now. *(She gently wakes up ZANDILE.)*
ZANDILE Is the story finished now, Gogo?
GOGO Yes, I even started another one. Come, you can go to bed now.
ZANDILE Goodnight Gogo. *(Offstage)* Gogo.
GOGO Okay, your pyjamas are under your pillow.
ZANDILE Gogo are you coming to sleep with me? *(Pause)* Gogo, when are you coming to bed? *(Sounding very sleepy)*
GOGO As soon as I finish tidying up here.
ZANDILE Gogo, can I start praying now?
GOGO *(She starts the prayer while tidying up.)* Yebo, UJehova unguMalusi wami...
ZANDILE *(Even more sleepy)* UJehova unguMalusi wami...
GOGO Angiyikweswela...
ZANDILE Angiyikweswela...
GOGO Ungilalisa emadlelweni aluhlaza
ZANDILE Ungilalisa emadlelweni aluhla. *(Her voice fades away. She has fallen asleep.)*

Scene 4a: Zandile teaches flowers

(ZANDILE enters in her new dress. She addresses the grandmother's flowerbeds as if the flowers are a class of children and she is the teacher. She has a small stick in her hand.)

ZANDILE Ho ho ho ho! Good morning class! Good morning, Miss Zandile. And what was all that noise I was hearing down the passage? Poor Miss Bongi could hardly teach her Standard Twos. She teaches Nature Study, you know, she's very clever. But do you know what happens to naughty children? The white car will come for you and you won't even know it's coming. It's going to be standing there and it will be too late to run. Nobody can hear you scream because its engine makes such a loud noise. They're going to take out your eyes and take you to a far away place and nobody's going to see you ever again. *(She pauses as if she is listening to something.)* And what is that I'm hearing...is that the white car? Ho ho ho ho! No, you are lucky this time. But I'm going to send you straight to the principal's office and he is going to give you this. *(She demonstrates a hiding with her stick.)*

Wena, and you are chewing gum in class. *(She holds out her hand.)* Give it to me. I am going to put it on your naughty, naughty little face. Teach you! And the rest of you must listen to me! And how do you like my new dress? This is a new dress, and my grandmother bought it for me and she let me choose it all by myself. I chose it because of all the goats and the giraffes and the elephants. It is very important for you to be clean, and look at you, you've got grass on your hair. Don't you know what day it is today? It is the 21st of September 1966 and the inspector is coming here today. You know the inspector does not understand our language *(She starts giggling)* and we don't want to embarrass him. *(Puts her hand over her mouth and laughs)* He cannot say our real names so we must all use white names in class today. Hands up those of you who don't have white names. We'll just have to give them to you. Wena you can be Violet. *(She points to different sections of the audience each time she mentions a different flower.)* Petunia. Daisy. Sunflower and Innocentia...I don't know what that means...Do you know what name the inspector gave me in class today? Elsie. And I don't even look like an Elsie! Don't laugh! At least you are flowers. And do you know what he called Bongi? Moses! He couldn't even tell that she is a girl.

Now where was I? Good morning class. Good morning Miss Zandile. What can we do today? We could sing! This could be a singing class...if we get it right we can sing for the inspector, but if we get it wrong, then the white car will come for us. Now where are you noise makers, you Violets, because you are always shrieking – you can sing soprano – mmhh! *(Humming a note for them to sing)* And you my lovely Daisies, are my favourites! You never make any noise – just like me, you will sing alto, because I'm alto too. *(Hums a note)* And my little Petunias, those compositions you wrote were top class, you can sing tenor...mhhhmm! *(Hums a note. Each time she hums the notes get lower.)* Good! And you Sunflowers, you are such a disappointment, so tall and you are still in Sub A. Honestly, this is because your voices are broken already – Booaah! *(She struggles getting a deep bass note, and starts walking like Miss Dlamini. She has a problem climbing the big box where she stands to conduct her choir, but as soon as she succeeds she pulls herself together.)*

The song is called Hamba kahle Vuyelwa. *(She enunciates the title again)* Hamba – kahle – Vuyelwa

1, 2, 3, 4
Hamba Kahle Vuyelwa
Usikhonzele emzini
Kwandonga ziyaduma
Inkos' isikelele
Inkos' ithamsanqele
Hamba Vuyelwa!

Very good, let's do it again. *(She is very pleased. She starts singing, but the song breaks down.)* You don't want to sing nina, he? You think I'm a fool opening my mouth like this ha ha ha nx! Let's do it again...*(Tearfully)* Hamba kahle Vuyelwa...*(This time the Sunflowers make a mistake and she cannot take it anymore, she climbs down to give them all a hiding, breaking the flowers in the process.)*

You children don't want to sing. I'll teach you. *(Beats the ground with her stick)* He-e man, I'm not your friend, you are not my friends anymore. I'm going to call the white car for you...

Scene 4b: Zandile with Gogo in the garden

(The GRANDMOTHER *enters, having heard all the noise.)*

GOGO Hawu hawu Zandile! What are you doing breaking my flowers?

ZANDILE But Gogo, these children don't want to sing the way I tell them to.

GOGO Zandile, you can teach them if you like, but don't beat them. How will they grow? Hawu Zandile!

ZANDILE I'm sorry, Gogo, ngiyacela ungangishayi...

GOGO Okay, okay, nobody is going to hit you. You must sing as well, so that they can learn from you. How would you like it, if I hit you with a stick, as hard as you were hitting them?

ZANDILE I'm sorry. I didn't know that they could feel, Gogo...

GOGO You must remember one thing, everything that grows has feelings. Now sing to them, the way you would like them to sing.

ZANDILE Eh-eh. Angifuni. I've been teaching them the whole day.

GOGO Then Gogo's going to teach them a new song. *(She starts singing.)* Vuka vuka Zola sesifikile – Ah…*(She notices that* ZANDILE *has moved closer to her, and seems to want to sing the song.)* Oh, so you also want to sing now?

ZANDILE Yebo Gogo!

GOGO Alright, let me teach you. *(She sings very slowly, emphasizing the words and melody, so that* ZANDILE *can learn the song.)* Vuka – Vuka – Zola – Sesifikile – Ah – Ulele na – Ulele na *(*ZANDILE *joins in on the odd words when she feels confident with a note or word.)* Sogibel' ibhasi – Zola – Sig eThekwini – Ah – Ulele na – Ulele na – Sobon' ulwandle – Zola – Lugubh' amagagasi – Ah – Ulele na – Ulele na.

GOGO Very good. Now let's try.

ZANDILE Yebo Gogo.

TOGETHER

Vuka Vuka Zola Sesifikile ah
Ulele na ulele na
Sogibel' ibhasi Zola
Siy' eThekwini ah
Ulele na ulele na
Sobon' ulwandle Zola
Lugubh' amagagasi ah
Ulele na ulele…

*(*GOGO *gestures to* ZANDILE *that she should sing a higher harmony.)*

Ah ulele na
Ulele ah
Ulele na
Ulele ah…

GOGO *(As they finish)* You see, we can all sing together.

ZANDILE WeGogo, I want to sing again.

GOGO No, no. I think that's enough for today. It's a special day tomorrow. Go and polish your shoes now.

ZANDILE And shine them until I see my face on them!

GOGO Do you know that tomorrow is a special day?

ZANDILE What Gogo? I'm going to the beach – ngci ngci!

GOGO It's the end of the term and…

ZANDILE It's a surprise!

GOGO Yes Gogo Mthwalo is going on holiday to Port Shepstone.

ZANDILE Is your overcoat coming with you? Ibhantshi lakho liyakulandela, angithi Gogo?

GOGO Of course my little overcoat is coming with me.

ZANDILE I want to start packing now!

GOGO Why do you think they call me "Gogo Mthwalo Uboshiwe"?

ZANDILE Because your bags are already ready. Are we going now?

GOGO No, you still have one more day at school.

ZANDILE My new dress is not packed, can I wear it to school tomorrow?

GOGO Are you going to pass tomorrow?

ZANDILE Yebo, I did work hard!

GOGO Alright, you can wear your dress!

ZANDILE And can I wear my neckless to school?

GOGO Neckless? Okay!

ZANDILE And my earrings and my bangles, Gogo?

GOGO Okay!

ZANDILE And my hairpins, Gogo?

GOGO Okay! And can you do something for Gogo?

ZANDILE Yebo Gogo.

GOGO Go and polish your shoes!

*(*ZANDILE *exits, laughing while the* GRANDMOTHER *remains on stage to tidy up.)*

GOGO Oh! My grandchild I can even see my little Zandile, wearing a white dress, walking slowly out of church with her husband and smiling with those dimples that I like. And I can see the neighbours watching with envy. Then I'll come out, sweeping the whole yard with a new broom – lilili! Kwakuhle kwethu, uthini wemfazi ongazalanga, halala!

(She sweeps her way out of the stage.)

Scene 5: The white car comes for Zandile

*(*GOGO*'s ululation can still be heard in the background.* ZANDILE *enters singing happily on her way back from school. It's the last day and she has passed her exams. She knows that* GOGO *will give her a present.)*

ZANDILE
Khilikithi
Khilikithi khilikithi
Zandile uphasile
Uzothol' ipresenti
Khilikithi khilikithi
Zandile uphasile
Uzohamba noGogo
Baye ePort Shepstone
Khilikithi khilikithi.

(She sings until she gets home, where she leaves her books and goes out to play. She notices a white car idling towards her. She stops singing abruptly. As if somebody has come out of the car and is advancing towards her, she retreats accordingly.)

ZANDILE Bongi, stay next to me. It's the white car. I'm scared. Sawubona...No, I've got my own sweets from Gogo...No! I don't want to go with you. Gogo's taking me on holiday to Port Shepstone. Gogo wouldn't want me to go with people I don't know. *(Pause)* No, you're not! *(She is trapped against the back wall.)* Bongi, go and tell my grandmother the white car has come for me, go tell my brother Paul, please Bongi, run! *(She screams.)*

(Then as if she is being pulled into the car she lunges forward, screaming as she reaches the end of the stage.)

Scene 6: Gogo discovers that Zandile is gone

(The GRANDMOTHER enters. She is humming happily to herself and is carrying a beautifully wrapped present. She has been shopping.)

GOGO Zandi, I'm home...Zandile, I'm home my little one and I have a present for you. Ntombizandile! Usebuyile uMthwalo Uboshiwe. UMthwalo Uzethule. Siyahamba namhlanje we are going to Port Shepstone today – where is my little overcoat? If you don't come I'm cancelling the trip. I'm so tired, come and give Granny a big hug...Zandile! I'm not playing hide and seek today I'm tired, just come out. Zandi! Zandile! *(She notices the school satchel on the ground.)*

Zandi! Just because we are going on holiday she is throwing things around. *(She picks up the satchel, sits down, opens the satchel and finds ZANDILE's report card and reads it.)* Oooo! She passed. Three gold stars! Bakithi! *(She reads)* Zandile is quiet and well mannered in class. With a little more effort she is capable of producing work of a very high standard. Ooo! My grandchild!... Zandile, how can I give you your present if you don't come out? Little feet under the bed, game is over now. *(She is getting really worried.)* This is strange...wait, let me ask MaGumede. *(She calls her neighbour.)*

MaGumede!...Have you seen Zandile?...Yes...Who?...Where? A white car? No, I didn't ask anyone to take her! Oh my God. *(Crying)* What am I going to do now? I never instructed anyone to take her...What am I going to say to her father? Oh Zandile!

(Towards the end of this speech a police siren and a radio announcement are heard.)

ANNOUNCER Attention! We interrupt this programme with an important news flash. A little girl has gone missing from her grand-mother's home in Hammersdale. She was last seen at about 2.30 this afternoon, getting into a white car, type and registration not known. The child is eight years old, she speaks Zulu, her name is Zandile and she was wearing a yellow dress, with animal and flower patterns on it. Anyone who may have any information at all as to her whereabouts, is requested to contact the nearest police station or the child's grandmother Mrs Zwide, at the Hammersdale Police Station.

(The voices of ZANDILE and GOGO fade in singing "Vuka Vuka" on a pre-recorded tape.)

Vuka Vuka Zola
Sesifikile ah
Ulele na
Sogibel' ibhasi
ola sit eThekwini ah
Ulele na
Sobon' ulwandle Zola
Lugubha amagagasi ah
Ulele na
Ulele na ulele na ulele na.

(During the radio announcement GOGO leaves the stage to fetch a large, well travelled suitcase. She re-enters, and into it, she lovingly packs the brightly

gift-wrapped presents that she had bought for ZANDILE, *but can now no longer give her. By now the tape recording of the song "Vuka Vuka" is playing. She slowly and sadly leaves the stage.)*

Scene 7: Gogo searches for Zandile and Zandile's letter to Gogo

*(*ZANDILE *is writing letters to her grandmother on the sand with a large stick Her hope is that the birds, that fly so far, will take the words she has written to her grandmother. In this way her need to communicate with her grandmother is expressed, and to a degree satisfied, particularly when she goes to check the next day and finds that the words have gone.)*

ZANDILE Dear Gogo. How are you? I'm still not happy in this place. You must come and fetch me now. Always when I write to you, they tear the letters, now I hope if I write like this, on the sand, the birds will see this letter and bring it to you. They are my friends and talk to me all the time. Maybe if you can talk with them, they will bring me a message from you. I don't get time to play anymore, there are so many chores to do.

Maybe it's good for me, maybe it can make me strong.

And you know what? Yesterday I had to chop wood before I went to school, and I got a splinter in my hand, and blisters. When I told my mother, she said I was making excuses for being lazy. During lunch break at school my teacher saw me crying and she took the splinter out for me. She put Zambuk on my blisters, and that reminded me of you. They don't have Zambuk here. *(*ZANDILE *becomes quite enthusiastic now.)*

My teacher, I like her. Her name is Miss Maduma. She is very clever. I always come first in all my subjects. I am very lucky because she takes all my classes. I will show you my report and test books. *(*ZANDILE *lies down as if to rest.)*

(The GRANDMOTHER *re-enters, with a photograph of* ZANDILE *in her hand She asks members of the audience):*

GOGO Have you seen this child? *(Showing the photograph)* Have you seen her? Her name is Zandile. *(She moves to others.)* She is eight years old, she disappeared on the 14th December 1966. She was wearing a little dress with animals on it. *(She moves on.)* Have you seen Zandile?

(Just as she begins to leave the auditorium...)

ZANDILE But soon now, I must go and cut grass for thatch for the roof. And it's very far to walk to fetch the grass. And Gogo, when you come please can you bring me some shoes. They won't let me wear them here. They only wear shoes when they go to church. Do you think that God can see their shoes under the benches? I must still wear the ones you bought me and they are too small now and old and the children always laugh at the way these shoes make me walk.

They also laughed at me when I didn't know how to put cow dung on the floor. They said I was making funny faces when I did not like the smell. But I can do it much better now and I always help them when it's their turn. And Gogo, when we are in the fields with other children, and the parents are far away, I always tell them stories. I told them all the stories you told me. And they say I am very lucky to have someone like you. Gogo, I can make up my own stories now, but I miss you very very very much Gogo, but I know that you love me and you'll come and fetch me.

Obebhala
Zandile

Scene 8: Zandile with mother in the field

(LULAMA *enters centre stage.*)

LULAMA Uphi Zandile? Where are you? What are you doing? It's getting late and you must still cut more grass.

ZANDILE Hawu Mama, I'm afraid of the mice.

LULAMA What are they going to do? Are they going to eat you up? *(Sees the letter)* And what is this...this child is full of dreams. *(She rubs the letter out with her feet.* ZANDILE *and* LULAMA *mime cutting grass with sickles.* LULAMA *looks up at* ZANDILE.*)* Zandile bend lower. You must cut the grass at the bottom.

ZANDILE The grass is cutting my hands Mama.

LULAMA I don't know what to do with this child now.

ZANDILE And you don't know what to do with me.

LULAMA I want you to grow up and be a strong woman and...

ZANDILE I'm going to be a teacher.

LULAMA Not here. You have to work outside here, where the men can see you.

ZANDILE Men can still see me if I teach.

LULAMA Where are you going to teach here? Are you going to teach the goats? Sit down. I want to talk to you. What are you doing?

ZANDILE *(Mumbles, scratching her left leg)* The grass is itchy Mama.

LULAMA Sukugoza! *(*ZANDILE *gets up as if to leave the stage.)* Where are you going?

ZANDILE You told me to go and wash.

LULAMA Tyhini bethuna! I didn't say go and wash. I only said don't be silly. You are not good for me if you are doing this. In a few years you have to be married. Who do you think you are going to marry if you can't do a woman's work?

ZANDILE I'm not going to get married. I am very good at school.

LULAMA What are you going to do with this education? All you have to be is a good wife and have good children. That's what I want from you.

ZANDILE I don't want to.

LULAMA This is not Durban, this is the Transkei. Here you must stop arguing with me. You must shut up when I speak. Zandile, listen to me. I was talking to Matshezi the other day. Do you know her son?

ZANDILE Yebo Mama.

LULAMA His family wants you.

ZANDILE But I don't want him.

LULAMA What do you mean you don't want him? His uncle has the richest family in this village. He could have any girl in the village and he chose you. That's how I got married as well. You must have your own house.

ZANDILE But I don't like him. He's got all these ugly scars on his face.

LULAMA But that's our tradition! *(She notices* ZANDILE *scratching her back.)*

LULAMA What's wrong with you now?

ZANDILE My back is so sore from the bending.

LULAMA Why are you so lazy? First your hands get cut by grass and then your legs are itchy – now it's your back! How do you think you will build your own house if you don't let your hands get used to it? Look at mine. I've been cutting grass every winter – ever since I was your age. I cut the grass for every roof in this house.

ZANDILE I don't like thatch roofs anyway. I like the roof my grandmother had in Durban.

LULAMA Life is different here. No time for rest – just work. If you learn that then you will make a good wife for Matshezi's son.

ZANDILE I don't know why you took me from Gogo, if you are just going to give me away to Matshezi's son.

LULAMA Zandile I took you because you are my child.

ZANDILE But you don't even let me visit my grandmother.

LULAMA I can't because if I let you go there, you will never come back again. I know you were happy there, I saw you that night.

ZANDILE You saw me Mama?

LULAMA Yes, when I went to visit your grandmother in Durban. *(Sits)* I wanted to take you then, but I knew Gogo would never let you go, after all those years you had become her child.

ZANDILE But you shouldn't have stolen me.

LULAMA How else was I going to get you? Wait till you have a child, you'll know what I've been going through all the years. How do you think it feels, to know that your child doesn't even know you exist?

ZANDILE But Ma, I'm only 12, why are you in such a hurry to give me away, if you missed me so much?

LULAMA But it's our tradition. It was the same when I got married. By the time I was 22, I already had four children.

ZANDILE But I don't even like him.

LULAMA You don't have to like him, he has to like you. Do you think I was happy with my husband? But he chose me. I had to stay married to him.

ZANDILE But he left you.

LULAMA It's easy for men to go.

ZANDILE And you also left me all those years.

LULAMA I left you because I had to. Do you think my husband would have accepted you? He would have killed me if I had come to his home with another man's child. My going to find work in Durban was bad enough – even though he knew I was forced to because he was not bringing us any money. He would beat me if I asked for money. My mother said I must go and find work while she was still able to look after my children. So I went to Durban and because my papers were not in order, it was hard to find work. And when I did get work they could pay me anything they liked. I got two pounds a month. Even in those days it was nothing.

ZANDILE Was that before I was born?

LULAMA Yes, 1958...*(Pause)* That was a difficult year for me. Then something happened, I bumped into an old friend that I grew up with here. Dudu looked so happy and beautiful and I could see that she had a good job.

ZANDILE She was a teacher?

LULAMA No, she was a singer with a successful group called "Mtateni Queens", and one of their singers had just left the band, so Dudu asked me if I would like to join so I joined the group.

ZANDILE *(Holding back laughter)* Haai bo wena!

LULAMA Yes, before Dudu left here we used to sing together for all the weddings, we were quite famous around here. There would never be a wedding without us singing. *(Does a bit of a wedding song)*

ZANDILE I wish I could have seen that.

LULAMA I thought I could earn better money, but it was hard work.

ZANDILE Harder work than here?

LULAMA *(Laughs)* Oho! Much harder and I had to send my money back to the Transkei for the children.

ZANDILE Why did you stay then?

LULAMA I stayed, hoping for better things to come, but they didn't. That is why I have learnt not to live on hopes, that is why I am teaching you to work. The sun is going down, it's time to cook supper. Run and start the fire. I'll call you back when the bundles are ready.

(As LULAMA *mimes gathering the bundles, she starts to sing "Mgewundini", a song she used to sing when she was on the cabaret circuit. As she picks up the last bundle, she stands and arches her back, and tries to rub away the pain.)*

Scene 9: Zandi and Lindiwe swim in the river

*(*ZANDI *runs on to the stage, jumps on to part of the set, as if it were a river bank. She looks down, as if into the water. She's very excited.)*

ZANDILE Oops! I got here first. *(She turns as if she expects to see* LINDIWE *behind her. There is no* LINDIWE.*)* Khawuleza man Lindi! Utsho ngokuba mde ngathi ngumntu endimthandayo. *(Laughs)* I got here first, you said you could run faster than I, but where are you now? I can run faster than you Lindiwe. I can't wait man. I wonder if Thekwane is here. Last week when I was here I found this bird, Thekwane, looking at himself in the water. Ndimhle ngapha ndimbi ngapha, ndoniwa yilendawo. *(As she imitates the bird and turns around,* LINDIWE *jumps on to the stage, as if into the water, behind* ZANDILE *and gives her a big fright.)*

LINDIWE I got here first! Pe!

(Both in the water, they laugh and feel the water, splashing, holding their breath and noses. Still holding her nose, ZANDILE *jumps as if into the water. They sit on the stage floor, with boxes around them so that all you can see of them are their heads and shoulders, to create the illusion that they are submerged in the river. Then* ZANDILE *starts to scream.)*

ZANDILE Iyo, Iyo! Inyoka! It's the snake, it's bitten me.

LINDIWE What?

ZANDILE I thought I felt a snake at my feet.

LINDIWE No, it's my feet kicking the water.

ZANDILE I'm sure it was a snake.

LINDIWE Hayi suka eligwala, inyoka yakwabani? There's no snake here.

ZANDILE You know that snake scares me, nyani nyani. The other day, we were swimming here, you remember Nomthandazo, she was swimming with us, now she doesn't swim with us anymore.

LINDIWE Why?

ZANDILE Because the snake bit her, here in the water.

LINDIWE He-ena wena, are you sure?

ZANDILE I don't know, but...

LINDIWE But I've never seen a snake here! I suspect it's something else.

ZANDILE Lindiwe it is the snake because she was swimming here with us, when she got out of the water we saw blood running down her legs. She told us Izilenzi bit her.

LINDIWE Uyazi yintoni Zandi? *(Whispering confidently)* I suspect she could be sleeping with boys!

ZANDILE *(Shocked)* Lindiwe! How do you know?

LINDIWE I know because the other day in class she had blood coming out of her and she had to put a book under the skirt. She was so embarrassed. You should have seen her!

ZANDILE What did the teacher say?

LINDIWE He told her to go out of class. The teacher also knows that she is sleeping with boys. What would you do if you see blood?

ZANDILE I'd just wipe it.

LINDIWE O Yehova, andifuni nokuyicinga loo nto! I'd kill myself, what would they say at home?

ZANDILE Why do they think if you sleep with boys then you have blood?

LINDIWE I don't know, but I think it's true.

ZANDILE I wonder if the boys can also get it?

LINDIWE I want to ask my mother but I'm scared.

ZANDILE You can't! It's rude, tyhini unantoni kakade!

LINDIWE Why rude? Then how are we going to know for sure if we don't ask?

ZANDILE I just wish they would tell us those things.

LINDIWE I wonder where it comes from – you know umama kaGugu? Gugu told me that her mother is going to hospital.

ZANDILE Is she sick?

LINDIWE No, to get a baby.

ZANDILE They make babies esibhedlele?

LINDIWE Yes.

ZANDILE You know, my mother told me that babies come from the aeroplane.

LINDIWE Ha ha! When we want our babies we can get them from the hospital.

ZANDILE We can play with real babies.

LINDIWE And when we get tired…

TOGETHER We take them back. *(They laugh and dip under the water.)*

LINDIWE Let's go now, it's getting cold. Let's sit in the sun.

ZANDILE I hope my mother doesn't bring that Mama Matshezi to our house for tea.

LINDIWE Ha ha! Makoti kaMatshezi.

ZANDILE Just because his family has a lot of cattle! The boy is so ugly, if they ever send me to be his wife, I will have to run away.

LINDIWE I wish I could get married to somebody nice, but I hate the very long dresses married women wear, vhu-vhu-vhu – when they walk.

ZANDILE The other day when we took bundles of firewood to Matshezi's house, my mother was so happy and she made me dress up nicely so that that stupid boy could see me. I was so shy all the time and I had to work hard doing this, preparing that, so that the family could see how hard I can work.

LINDIWE Does the boy ever talk to you? Maybe he is a nice person even if he's ugly. You know what they say about a man – "ubuhle bendoda".

ZANDILE I find that very stupid. A man doesn't have to be good-looking but a girl has to be pretty. The ugliest man wants the most beautiful girl. Why?

LINDIWE I like to look pretty. I'm glad I'm a girl.

ZANDILE But when you are getting married you have to work even harder to look very special on that day, like Sis' Lulu at the wedding.

LINDIWE Oh! *(She closes her eyes with her hands.)* Zandile I've never seen anybody looking so beautiful, and she's got this round face and her teeth are snow white and a little mouth like a bird.

ZANDILE I know, I could never look like that even if I were to get married. I wonder what they did to her face.

LINDIWE They mix all kinds of herbs and I think the yellow of an egg and smear it all over the bride's face. Raw egg, lots of things and she has to stay inside. She hardly sees the sun. They prepare special food for her so that when she comes out–

ZANDILE Aqhakaze axele ikhwezi lomso. I think the morning star that shines brightest at dawn is the most beautiful thing I've ever seen.

LINDIWE I know, but I hate waking up early in the morning, especially when it's winter.

ZANDILE Winter – hayi hayi my feet get so cold and they crack on the sides.

LINDIWE Zandile! Iminkenke? You must make ntyolantyola.

ZANDILE I don't know how to make it.

LINDIWE I know. You keep all the old pieces of candle, take out the twine inside and chop them to small pieces, put them in a tin on red-hot coals. When it's melted take it off and add some paraffin, stir it till it's cold, then you can just put it on your feet everyday when you finish washing them.

ZANDILE But it smells!

LINDIWE Not for long, it dries quickly.

ZANDILE I will try, I hate cracked feet.

LINDIWE Let's go now, it's getting cold!

ZANDILE Let's get back into the water!

(ZANDILE *jumps back into the water. The resultant*

spray catches LINDIWE *unawares. She screams and then also jumps into the water.)*

ZANDILE How come you've got bigger...Your bells are bigger than mine. Sewunamabele amakhulu.

LINDIWE What? You know, I think I'm getting fat!

ZANDILE But you are getting big bells like your sister.

LINDIWE I don't know, and it's sore here.

ZANDILE Is it sore?

LINDIWE Yes *(Rubbing them gently)*.

ZANDILE I wonder what happened? But why there?

LINDIWE I don't know, and I must stop eating chocolate because they say chocolate makes you fat.

ZANDILE But I eat all these things and my bells are not getting any bigger.

LINDIWE You'll always be skinny. Anyway I am bigger than you, that's why.

ZANDILE Have you slept with the boys?

LINDIWE No!

ZANDILE Is that why your bells are bigger than mine?

LINDIWE No! Who says if you sleep with boys you get fat? My mother checks me all the time and she knows I'm alright. (LINDIWE *sulks,* ZANDILE *touches her on the arm.)*

ZANDILE Lindiwe...(LINDIWE *pushes her away.)* I am your friend. I know you have not slept with boys.

LINDIWE I'm just fat.

ZANDILE Yes, you're just fat. *(Uncomfortable silence, until* ZANDILE *changes the subject)* Lindiwe, you know what we can do? We can read books, we can read *Bona* and *Drum* and discover everything.

LINDIWE What do they say?

ZANDILE Lindiwe, I don't know. I haven't read them, but I've seen them.

LINDIWE I can steal some from my sister. And I can take them to school tomorrow.

ZANDILE The history class.

LINDIWE But...but...we can't...the teacher will see them. I saw...the other day, another girl was reading eeh...*True Love* in class and the teacher beat and beat her.

ZANDILE But she should have put it inside the history book, man.

LINDIWE Oh, and she won't see it?

ZANDILE Ya.

LINDIWE Why the history book?

ZANDILE Because I hate history! The great trek, great trek, every year it is the same, the great trek. Nothing else ever happened here or anywhere, just the great trek. Yes, and so we put it in the history book, and we read, looking very serious.

LINDIWE Yes, I'll bring some tomorrow. *(Laughs)*

ZANDILE We are going to read, discover everything. We are going to be grown ups. *(She sneaks away.)*

LINDIWE *(Dives under the water, leaps up and screams, terrified)* Yo! Snake! *(She looks around, and under her breath...)* Blood! Yo! Snake!

(Blackout)

Scene 10: Zandile gets to know her mother

(ZANDILE *enters centre stage with goatskin, candle, notebook and pencil. She is singing "Vuka Vuka" softly to herself.)*

LULAMA *(Offstage)* Did you lock up the kitchen? Don't leave the candle burning.

ZANDILE Ewe Ma. *(Lays out her goatskin, then looks over her shoulder to make sure that her mother isn't around. She hides the notebook and pencil under the goatskin. She lies down and sleeps. In her sleep...)* Gogo, Gogo, Gogo. (LULAMA *enters.)*

LULAMA Zandile, wake up! You are dreaming.

ZANDILE Gogo?

LULAMA This is your mother here.

ZANDILE I thought I heard Gogo calling me.

LULAMA There is no Gogo here, Zandile! Try to go back to sleep. (ZANDILE *gets up and moves away.)*

LULAMA Where are you going?

ZANDILE I just want to sit here for a while.

LULAMA Zandile, is there something troubling you?

ZANDILE No, Ma.

LULAMA Well, just come here and sit with me. *(Pats bed, discovers it is wet)* Oh, Zandile, not again.

ZANDILE I don't know what else to do. Already I have stopped drinking anything from after lunch.

LULAMA What do you dream? Do you dream you want to go to the toilet and then you dream you are on the toilet? You must wake up just before...

ZANDILE But Ma, I don't have these dreams.

LULAMA Are you sure you're not just being lazy to wake up?

ZANDILE No Ma, I also hate this thing – it embarrasses me.

LULAMA You must really try. In two years' time, everybody is expecting you to get married. And how am I going to give you to any man if you are wetting your bed? Oh Zandile *(Lifting mat)* you'll have to remake your bed. What's this *(Seeing the notebook and pencil she picks up the notebook and flips the pages)*...another letter, you still write when you know that your Gogo will never get them?

ZANDILE But they are my letters, and I know one day Gogo will come and fetch me.

LULAMA Fetch you where? She doesn't...does she know where you are? Maybe if you forget your Gogo, you will stop wetting your bed!

ZANDILE I never used to wet my bed with Gogo, Gogo would have...

LULAMA Gogo, Gogo, Gogo! Zandile. I'm not going to argue with you. I'm tired. *(As if she's leaving)* I'm tired.

ZANDILE People say if we slaughter a goat the ancestors will help me.

LULAMA *(She stops and turns.)* I know...I have been thinking about that but you know that's impossible. Your father must be the one to do the ceremony. Even if I did it, it wouldn't help.

ZANDILE Then Mama, maybe we must go to Durban.

LULAMA With what money?

ZANDILE We can write to my father to send us money.

LULAMA And if he sends it do you think I would let you go alone? I can't go with you.

ZANDILE This means I'll never go to Durban. Oh, why didn't you stay with my father because now I would have my mother and my father and my Gogo would be here with us, not like this here now.

LULAMA Who says things will ever be like you want them to be? Who knows, one day you might see your father again.

ZANDILE But Ma, I miss my father. You never talk about him.

LULAMA Yes, I do think about him.

ZANDILE He was a good man, andithi Ma?

LULAMA Yes, I knew that from the first time I met him.

ZANDILE Kuphi Ma?

LULAMA In Durban.

ZANDILE He was in your band?

LULAMA No. I remember when I first met him. It was a Friday night and we were singing in one of the biggest shebeens eMkhumbane. It was packed full with people and our audience was really pleased. Then suddenly there was dead silence. Everybody looked towards the door – five men had just come in. They were all wearing oversized black suits and their shoes were shining. They had hats on, and people moved away nervously. I just wondered who they were but I kept on singing. People seemed to know there was going to be trouble – first a few people left then a few more followed and then the gang ordered us to sing "Mgewundini" over and over. *(She sings a bit of it.)* Do you know that song?

ZANDILE Haai Mama.

LULAMA You wouldn't know it. It was one of the popular songs those days.

ZANDILE But Mama, was my father one of these men?

LULAMA No! There was this tall well-dressed man who had been watching us since we started singing and he had been smiling at me all the time. I was looking at him when one of the gang came up on stage and grabbed me. I tried to fight him off but before I knew it, he was on the floor. That tall well-dressed man had knocked him down...that was your father.

ZANDILE He was brave, Mama!

LULAMA And that's not all. He talked to the gang to let us go and they did. I couldn't believe it, a miracle. Tom became the friend of the group. I loved him. He was so different from my husband and kind *(She is immediately embarrassed by her statement, and in the background, a cock crows.)* Hamba Zandile, I've been talking for the whole night. The sun is already coming up...*(ZANDILE exits, taking her goatskin with her.)*

I nearly made it. We were going to Johannesburg to cut a record and the people there were organizing a tour for us. We were going to sing in Cape Town, PE, East London and all the other lovely places. But then we had to tell them that I was four months pregnant. Intoni, they wouldn't hear of it. They wanted me replaced. My friends stood for me but the organizers said they wouldn't have a pregnant woman on stage – as if it was such a disgrace, or as if I had made myself pregnant.

You know, at times I so wish that men

could get pregnant too. All my hopes of improving my life and the lives of my children were finished. Tom and I agreed that I should stay in Durban until our child was born. I had a baby girl and we called her Zandile, Ntombi Zandile, which means "the number of girls has grown".

(She blows out the candle.)

Scene 11: Lindiwe goes to Johannesburg

(ZANDILE *enters. Letta Mbuli's "I'll Never be the Same" is playing on the house radio.* ZANDILE *dances and sings with the music while she moves the "furniture". She then picks up* Bona *magazine and proceeds to read out loud one of the letters from the problems page. Letta Mbuli fades out.)*

ZANDILE *(Reading)* Do you have a personal problem? Don't let it embarrass or worry you. Whether it be about love, sex, bad dreams, divorced parents or an unexpected pregnancy. Help is in sight. Dear Dolly, I am in love with a girl who loves me dearly, but I keep hearing that her father was a thief until he went to the Holy Land. He has since changed but I don't know if she will follow in his footsteps. Confused. Port Elizabeth.

(To herself) I wonder what Dolly will say to this.

Dear Confused. You can test your girl to see if she steals through various methods. If she does steal, things must be missing from your place. In most cases you can't judge a child by her father's behaviour, so don't let his reputation affect your decision about the daughter.

LINDIWE Zandile, uphi uZandile? Where are you?

ZANDILE Ngapha.

LINDIWE Zandile, usekhitshini, are you in the kitchen? What are you doing *(Giggling)* here?

ZANDILE I'm reading.

LINDIWE You are always reading. What are you reading now? *(*ZANDILE *hides the magazine behind her back.)*

ZANDILE Guess. Just *Bona*.

LINDIWE *(Laughs)* I remember when we used to hide those in our biology books.

ZANDILE History books.

LINDIWE Hey listen tshomam, I've got serious news to tell you. My mother told me she received a letter from my aunt and they want me to go to Jo'burg.

ZANDILE Jo'burg? The big city.

LINDIWE Hey wena, my cousin's getting married and they want me to be a bridesmaid.

ZANDILE You are lucky Lindiwe, but I wish you were going to Durban man.

LINDIWE Why? Jo'burg is better.

ZANDILE You could find my grandmother in Durban.

LINDIWE ZANDILE, how will I know which is your grandmother? I'll have to ask all the grandmothers. *(Laughs)*. I can't wait to sing those wedding songs. *(They both start singing a wedding song and end up laughing excitedly on the floor.)*

ZANDILE When are you leaving man?

LINDIWE Next Saturday, ha ha!

ZANDILE Saturday...hawu, Lindi, you are going to miss my performance if you leave on Saturday.

LINDIWE What?

ZANDILE I'm doing a praise poem for Mr Hlatshwayo, you know he is going on pension.

LINDIWE Hawu tshomam, I'm so sorry but ooh, the wedding in Jo'burg.

ZANDILE But can't I at least show you my new dress?

LINDIWE Yes, let me see the dress. *(*ZANDILE *exits to fetch her praise poetry costume.)*

LINDIWE Ooh, but I'm so excited. I can't wait to get to Johannesburg. *(*ZANDILE *re-enters.)*

ZANDILE I'm so nervous. What do you think? I'm not sure about the colour?

LINDIWE *(Half interested as* ZANDILE *turns round to be seen.)* It's nice, but I hear that Jo'burg is a big city. And I'm taking a train by myself.

ZANDILE You are going to enjoy yourself Lindiwe!

LINDIWE And there are going to be some...

TOGETHER Nice boys!

ZANDILE Shhh, keep your voice down! Who's meeting you wena?

LINDIWE And I've never been in a train by myself before.

ZANDILE You must be careful ne? All those boys from town are dangerous.

LINDIWE Hayi! They're putting me in second class. They say it's safe. Hey man, I want you to see me off at the station.

ZANDILE I'll ask my mother, but Lindi man, what will Mzwakhe say?

LINDIWE Hawu, Mzwakhe is just a schoolboy.

ZANDILE But he likes you.
LINDIWE But I'm going to Jo'burg now, I'm going to meet sophisticated men! Maybe bring one for you?
ZANDILE I don't know.
LINDIWE Yes!
ZANDILE Hayi suka, I've got enough problems with Matshezi's son.
LINDIWE Ha! But that one is not getting anywhere!
ZANDILE *(Changing subject)* Lindiwe, what time are you leaving on Saturday?
LINDIWE At 3 o'clock in the afternoon.
ZANDILE And what are you going to wear?
LINDIWE I'm going to be wearing my red mini-skirt.
ZANDILE Jo, the red one?
LINDIWE Yes.
ZANDILE My God.
LINDIWE My platform shoes and my red beret and I have a new white blouse.
ZANDILE Jo! You are going to look beautiful.
LINDIWE Yes, red and white.
ZANDILE Red and white, ishaft iyasifakazela! *(Laughs)*
LINDIWE What are you going to wear to the station?
ZANDILE Aaa...I don't know.
LINDIWE Don't wear your terylene skirt please.
ZANDILE But it's nice, Lindiwe.
LINDIWE Terylene skirts are too old fashioned now. It's 1976, you must look sharp!
ZANDILE But my mother won't let me wear my other clothes just to go out to the station.
LINDIWE You can sneak them out.
ZANDILE Yes, I could take them on Friday and hide them at your place.
LINDIWE Yes. Then I'll keep them with me and you can just wear your terylene skirt when you come and when you get there you...
TOGETHER Change!
ZANDILE Lindiwe, ufuna i-orange squash?
LINDIWE No, but now I must go, I still have to cook supper and start packing and organize.
ZANDILE Awusandiqhosheli. Okay. I'll see you, if not before, Friday night. We are going to look...
TOGETHER Sharp!

(Blackout!)

Scene 12: Praise poetry and Gogo's entrance

(ZANDILE *walks into the light as if on to a school stage, dressed in her kaftan. She addresses the audience a little shyly.)*

ZANDILE Good afternoon. I feel very honoured to have been chosen to do this praise poem for Mr Hlatshwayo. This is the kind of thing I learnt from my grandmother. She was a very good storyteller.

Hlatshwayo, Ngwane, Mhayisa, Ncam Ncam. Mfazindini onamabele amade nangaphesheya komfula uyamunyisa. Untlamvu azimshayi ziyamthantalaza. Usikhumba sehlula abeshuki. Dondolo lamaNgisi namaNkelemane. Mhayisa!

(ZANDILE *completes the first part of Mr Hlatshwayo's family praise name, which every African family has. These names outline each family's history. She then starts a song.)*

ZANDILE Mayidibane bafazi balelali. Mayidibane bafunde abantabethu [Let's get together women of this village. Let's get together so our children can learn.]

(While ZANDILE *sings this song on one side of the stage, on the other side the spotlight shines on* GOGO, *who comes in with some presents for* ZANDILE, *wrapped in colourful paper and she thoughtfully packs them in a suitcase. As she exits, the song gets louder and* ZANDILE *resumes the poetry. Now she focuses on the praises of Mr Hlatshwayo himself – what he has achieved and done for his people.)*

ZANDILE Mde ngeentonga. Nkcuba buchopho eyavumbuka emanzini iphethe ulwazi. Nzulu Iwazi eyavumbuka emanzini iphethe ukuzinikela. Nkunzi ndini emandla. Wena owagila ngophondo. Zathi iziphazamiso zaqikileka phantsi. Zaxela unkunzana ziphethwe ngumbendeni. Wathi ukugawulela phantsi intsasana emile endleleni yakho. Seva ngo khenkce! khenkce! Seva ngo khenkce! khenkce! Seva ngo khenkce! Yathi imikhenkce yasebusika yanyibilika ngaphantsi kwefutha lenyawo zakho. Kuba kalokhu wena wawuxhabashele ukuza kupha thina imfundo. Wawuxhabashele ukuza kupha thina ukhanyo.

Sasisiva sixakeka xa kuthethwa ngemfundo. Sasisiva sixhatshelwe zingqondo xa kuthethwa ngenkqubela phambili. Suka wena – wawelela ngeneno. Ubuso bakho bumamatheka.Wabulisa savuma. Wabalisa samamela.Wafundisa saphulaphula. Wancokola – tyhini sahleka!

Kanti ngokwenze njalo wena uyazi ukuba uyatyala. Nathi namhlanje siyazidla. Ngenxa yakho siyavuna Mhayisa!

Scene 13: Zandile and Lindiwe prepare for the farewell party

(LINDIWE *comes to visit after the examinations.)*

LINDIWE Zandi!
ZANDILE Yebo.
TOGETHER We did it! *(Laugh)*
LINDIWE No more books.
ZANDILE No more swotting.
LINDIWE Matric is done forever. What if we don't pass?
ZANDILE Of course we'll pass, Lindiwe.
LINDIWE Anyway we can worry about that when the results come out next month.
ZANDILE But tomorrow...
TOGETHER It's a party *(Laugh excitedly and start singing)*. Oh what a night! Hey! Late December 1963. What a very special time for me...what a lady, what a night! *(They collapse with laughter.)*
LINDIWE I have been waiting for this day!
ZANDILE But you are glad you came back, aren't you?
LINDIWE Aah, I had no choice, my parents forced me to come back.
ZANDILE They were right, you know, six months wasn't such a long time.
LINDIWE It's been too long for me because I want to see my Paul again.
ZANDILE Ever since you came back from that wedding, it's just Paul...Paul...Paul.
LINDIWE Because you don't know what happened to me the first time I saw Paul at the wedding ha!
ZANDILE Lindiwe, I have heard this a few million times now, I know your heart stopped and you started sweating just like in the Barbara Cartland books.
LINDIWE I can tell you this over and over.
ZANDILE Let me tell you what's going to make my heart stop...I'm worried...what are we presenting at the party tomorrow?
LINDIWE *(Laughs)* Do you remember last year's party?
ZANDILE We were attending on last year's matrics. And were they boring!
LINDIWE And you with the tray!
ZANDILE Don't remind me please.
LINDIWE You were walking along with the big tray.
ZANDILE Yes. There were twenty-four plastic cups filled with Coca-Cola.
LINDIWE For the twelve prefects and their partners.
ZANDILE I remember the tune that was playing: "Papa was a Rolling Stone". As I was walking nicely along to the music with the tray then that stupid clumsy Zola danced right into me!
LINDIWE Nonsense! You tripped. Those shoes you had on were too tight. Why is it your shoes were always too small for you?
ZANDILE This boy danced right into me and over I went, on to the headboy's lap and his girlfriend, I forget her name now...
LINDIWE Caroline.
ZANDILE *(Imitating Caroline in Zulu)* "I always knew you had your eyes on Sipho."
LINDIWE As if you were so desperate.
ZANDILE Meanwhile my eyes were on the floor.
LINDIWE And there was Coca-Cola everywhere, all over the pretty pink and blue and...
ZANDILE Yellow.
LINDIWE Dresses were ruined. I laughed. You! Your face was blushing.
ZANDILE Everybody was so sticky and so cross.
LINDIWE Ah, but at least it woke them up.
ZANDILE Let's stop laughing at other people. What are we going to do tomorrow?
LINDIWE Maybe we can do a song Paul taught me.
ZANDILE Paul again. Lindiwe, this Paul is haunting us now. Who invented telephones? Paul. Who discovered the sea route to India? Paul...Paul. *(Mocking)*
LINDIWE You are jealous.
ZANDILE Okay, let's do his song. What is it?
LINDIWE "Sugar Sugar."
ZANDILE Does that mean I'm going to be your sugar sugar tomorrow? *(Laughs)*
LINDIWE Haai suka wena! *(She starts singing and dancing.)* Sugar Sugar...
ZANDILE And what do I sing?
LINDIWE Pa pum pa pum...
ZANDILE Pa pum pa pum...Okay let's try.

LINDIWE Sugar Sugar…
ZANDILE Pa pum pa pum…
LINDIWE Oh, honey honey…
ZANDILE Pa pa pum *(Lindiwe stares at the way Zandile is dancing and stops singing in horror.)*
LINDIWE You can't dance like this. Oh, they will laugh at you – you must shake like this! *(She shows* ZANDILE.*)*
ZANDILE Well, you must teach me, Lindiwe.
LINDIWE Sugar Sugar…*(Shaking)*
ZANDILE Pa pum pa pum…
LINDIWE Oh honey honey…
ZANDILE Pa pum pa pum…
LINDIWE *(Stops again)* Zandile…haai haai…your shoulders! Ezase Jo'burg!
ZANDILE Alright – siyafunda eJo'burg!
LINDIWE Sugar Sugar…
ZANDILE Pa pum pa pum…
LINDIWE Oh, honey honey…
ZANDILE Pa pum pa pum…
LINDIWE Your knees…go down! Sugar Sugar…
ZANDILE Pa pum pa pum…
LINDIWE Your knees…Sugar Sugar…
ZANDILE Pa pum pa pum…
LINDIWE Oh, honey honey…*(*ZANDILE *is concentrating on her knees and forgets to sing.)* And sing at the same time! You are my candy girl…
ZANDILE Hey?
TOGETHER And you got me wanting you! *(They laugh and exclaim in Xhosa: "We'll show them.")*
ZANDILE I like this, but is this all your Paul does? He doesn't work he just sings "Sugar Sugar" to you all day long? That's marriage material.
LINDIWE Suka! He does work.
ZANDILE What does he do?
LINDIWE He plays drums.
ZANDILE You call that work?
LINDIWE It's hard work drumming.
ZANDILE What does his family say, a grown-up man playing drums? *(She imitates a drummer.)*
LINDIWE They like it. His sisters always come to watch him, Thandi and Phumzile.
ZANDILE Are they our age?
LINDIWE No, they are old, about 27 and 28, and they like me!
ZANDILE Did you see his parents?
LINDIWE No, the parents are in Durban, but Paul says he has already told them about me.
ZANDILE Mmmm! It looks quite serious Lindiwe.
LINDIWE Yes. Mrs Zwide any day now!
ZANDILE Zwide?
LINDIWE Yes.
ZANDILE You say Paul has two sisters Thandi and Phumzile? And that they are older than him and that the family is in Durban and that their surname is Zwide? Please give me your Paul's address.
LINDIWE But why?
ZANDILE Because I need to write to him. It's very important.
LINDIWE But what's the connection? *(Stands up, getting suspicious and jealous)*
ZANDILE Because Zwide, that's my family name.
LINDIWE Sigwili?
ZANDILE Is my mother's name. Zandile Zwide is my real name. Zwide is my father's name.
LINDIWE Zandi, are you trying to tell me that Paul might be your brother?
ZANDILE He could be my half brother from Durban. Your Paul plays drums? I remember I was about seven years old, my half brother in Durban, Paul, used to take the old cake tins, put them down, play drums with them, and my father could never stop him. And the sisters' names connect with my half sisters in Durban. I want to know where my grandmother is.
LINDIWE Gogo *(Thinks)*. Zandile, there is an old woman living there where Paul stays with his uncle. It could be your grandmother.
ZANDILE Oh, Gogo. Nkosiyami!
LINDIWE Let me go now. I will run home to get Paul's number and then go straight to the Post Office to phone him.
ZANDILE Lindiwe, I am coming with you.
LINDIWE No, I'm phoning Paul at work. Even if it is your grandmother you won't talk to her!
ZANDILE Lindiwe, just run and come straight back, Okay?
LINDIWE For sure, Sister-in-law!
ZANDILE Oh God let it be him. Let it be the right Paul and…so I can see Gogo. Please God don't let anything happen to her. Where is Lindiwe? Please, please. I want to go and stay with her again. It will be so nice to stay with her. My own grandmother. Now I can do things for her. I can cook for her, like she used to cook for me. Shame she must be old now. I will cook amadombolo, bake nice cakes for her. Where is Lindiwe?…Make tea for her and bring it to her bed. Every morning – oh I wish I could fly! *(She becomes impatient and moves towards the passage in*

pursuit of LINDIWE.*)* Lindi, Lindiwe, where are you? Come on now, Lindiwe. I want to know. *(She exits end of passage.)*

Scene 14: Zandile find's Gogo's suitcase

(An OLD WOMAN *enters carrying a Bible and leaning on a walking stick.)*

ZANDILE Nkqo! Nkqo! Nkqo! *(*ZANDILE *is knocking offstage.)*

OLD WOMAN Ubani? Who is it?

ZANDILE Yimina uZandile. Gogo sengibuyile. I've come back.

OLD WOMAN Ngena. *(*ZANDILE *enters and sees the* OLD WOMAN *and for a split second thinks it's her grandmother.)*

ZANDILE Gogo, yimina uZandile. *(She stops.)* Sanibonani.

OLD WOMAN Sawubona Zandile.

ZANDILE Is my grandmother here?

OLD WOMAN Hlala phansi Mntanomntanami. You don't know me, but you know uncle Phillip's wife – I'm her mother.

ZANDILE Has Gogo gone to fetch me from the station?

OLD WOMAN No Mntanomntanami – she has left us.

ZANDILE Has she gone…has she moved?

OLD WOMAN No, no – she always knew you would come back. She told me so many stories about you. Oh, she wanted to see you…right until the end she was asking for you.

ZANDILE But where is she?

OLD WOMAN Oh, Mntanomntanami…she passed away.

ZANDILE Aw, no, not my grandmother.

OLD WOMAN I'm so sorry. UGogo Mthwalo, she was visiting here with us when she got sick. We were great friends. Uncle Phillip organized doctors. They did everything they could. We did our best to make her comfortable.

ZANDILE I wish I could have been here.

OLD WOMAN Zandile, it was her time to go.

ZANDILE Did she ever know what happened to me, that I went to the Transkei?

OLD WOMAN Yes, and she knew that your mother took you and that it was not your will to go.

ZANDILE But why didn't she come and fetch me? I waited for her.

OLD WOMAN She did try but they would never tell her exactly where you were.

ZANDILE I wish she had waited for me.

OLD WOMAN She must have known you'd find her. She said to me – if ever my child comes back or if they trace her, give her this photo. *(She takes a photograph out of her Bible.)* And she left a suitcase for you. She said I must give it to you. *(She goes to fetch it.)*

ZANDILE Oh, uGogo nkosi yami!

OLD WOMAN She would have been proud to see you, so tall and beautiful. How old are you now Mntanomntanami?

ZANDILE 18.

OLD WOMAN 18!

ZANDILE Did she say I must take the suitcase?

OLD WOMAN *(Nods)* She said it was yours, and she asked me to give you the key…here. I will leave you now. *(Exits)*

*(*ZANDILE *is on her own in a pool of light, very quiet, very separated from her surroundings. She opens the suitcase and takes out all the little parcels her grandmother has been putting away for her through all the years.* ZANDILE *holds each of them for a moment, before laying them gently to one side. At the bottom of the suitcase she finds a dress, takes it out and holds it up against herself. It is a little girl's dress, which barely reaches beyond her waist. She puts it down, reaches for a second dress and repeats the action. She picks up a third dress and also holds it against her body. She then holds all three dresses closely to her, hugging them and sobbing. The lights slowly fade to black…)*

Thulani S. Mtshali

> I realized as a young man that you come to hate that situation [abuse] or you come to adopt that situation. For me, it became more of a hatred of the situation. This shouldn't happen.

Thulani S. Mtshali, poet, director, producer, and writer, was born in the province of KwaZulu-Natal, but spent most of his childhood in Soweto. He has written and cowritten nine plays which include *Memories*, *Prisons*, *Burning Ambers* (1986 Edinburgh Festival), *Top Down*, *Target*, *Devil's Den*, *Golden Gloves* (1993 Grahamstown Festival's Best of the Fringe Award), *Sekoto*, and *WEEMEN*.

His interest in theatre developed during anti-apartheid school uprisings in the mid-1970s, when one of his teachers brought the students together to do a traditional play about the war with the Boers. As he became politically conscious, he began an active participation in male groups reciting praise poetry, a traditional way of honoring African ancestors and kings. Thulani sometimes travelled with his grandfather's musical group, and this also influenced his decision to pursue theatre. While at boarding school in the later 1970s he became involved in acting, poetry, and writing plays, which he performed at school. He continued training as an actor in Durban from 1980–1981.

Thulani's first play, *Memories* (1981), is about elderly men in the township of Soweto whose sons had gone into exile. From 1984 to 1986 Thulani trained at the Centre for Research and Training in African Theatre under Bhekizizwe Peterson and Benjy Frances, acquiring skills in improvisation, scriptwriting, poetry, movement, and research. In 1987 Thulani cofounded Bachaki Theatre, which means "visitors". They wanted a group that could go to the community, since at that time there were "very few strong black groups". According to Thulani, "we wanted to break away from the sloganing-type theatre and do something authentic." They produced *Top Down* in 1988, which looked at the dilemma of black teachers in the educational system. After *Top Down* played in the townships for several performances, the production opened at the Market Theatre during the state of emergency, later that year. In 1990 *Top Down* toured Europe.

Thulani's plays draw on his own life's experiences and those of others, hinging on social and political issues. He enjoys working with young people, who comprise a large percentage of Bachaki. In recent years Bachaki Theatre has been performing in the growing number of theatre festivals throughout South Africa. In addition to his work as a playwright and director, Thulani has conducted workshops throughout South Africa and Britain, on community development theatre skills, collective playmaking, and praise poetry.

ARTISTIC STATEMENT

This was an experience of someone close to the family. This was an experience of an aunt who was in that kind of situation. The play is basically based on her experience, although I've taken experiences of other people that I know and have seen; but mainly her experience because the husband used to be ruthless to her. He would hack her with the axe and she would have all sorts of scars and blue-and-black eyes. At night the guy would come in drunk, and sometimes sleep outside and stuff like that. As time went on and she started to do these secret jobs and she grew in the business, the husband was deteriorating. When he discovered she was running a dry-cleaning business, the guy was down and out. At first he was begging to her when he found out about the business. She wanted to put him out, but in this African society divorce shouldn't happen. But because there are elders when you have problems, you turn to them. In the 1970s it struck me that this abuse wasn't only happening with my relatives, but also in many other families.

Now because I am an artist, everything is expressed through theatre and poetry. I realized this was something that I must write. After seeing the show, many people were surprised that a man had written this play – some were even suspicious. African men responded favorably to the piece.

THE ROLE OF THEATRE IN SOUTH AFRICA

I still think we need more plays that reflect, educate, and develop the people. We need theatre that will challenge people to think. In the new South Africa, we're [blacks] being taken for a ride by mainstream theatres. They say people have to start writing "real theatre" but they're really talking about themselves, and include "us" in this statement. Our work is very strong. Unfortunately, we lack the administrative expertise. In our situation we are often the director, playwright, producer, and everything. I have learned a lot from this experience, but more training is needed to really carry on a company.

HAVE THINGS IMPROVED IN GENERAL IN THE NEW SOUTH AFRICA?

Things have not changed really. What has changed is just the management of the government. It's now a substitution of black people instead of having white people, but the power is still in the white hands – the economy and everything. So really for me, in my understanding, nothing has changed.

PRODUCTION HISTORY

WEEMEN premiered in July 1996 at the Grahamstown Festival. The production was directed by Thulani Mtshali and featured Thabo Mabe, Zandile Tlale, and Doreen Mphethwane.

Taken from interviews conducted July 1996 and July 1997, in Johannesburg.

Photo by Kathy A. Perkins.

7 WEEMEN

Thulani S. Mtshali

Characters

All characters are from the lower African class, except MRS JOHNSON who is white.
MLITSHE husband
TSOARELO wife
MRS JOHNSON Mlitshe's employer
BRA WILLIE Mlitshe's friend
SANGOMA fortune teller
CHILD Tsoarelo's customer

Set

A shack made of zinc, one room which is kitchen cum bedroom. A bed on one side, a rail to hang clothes; A cupboard with some cups, plates, etc. A table on the side cum cupboard, always covered with a plastic cloth, wherein there's popcorn.

Office symbolized by the chair.

SANGOMA*'s place symbolised by an open space.*

Scene 1

(A young woman sits panicking in her nightdress. The room is sparsely furnished, she gets up and paces up and down from the bedside to the cooking space. Her fists clutched to the towel over her shoulders...A loud knock...It's her husband MLITSHE.*)*

MLITSHE Open up!...Vula!! Vula!!!

TSOARELO *(Jumping to the door)* Just a minute!

MLITSHE Votsek, bloody woman! why take your time?...Vula man! *(She opens, he can't even stand.)* This is my house woman, and you are my wife...when I knock you must not take more than an hour to open up!...why are you staring at me like that?...Bring the bloody plate!

TSOARELO Baba, there is only pap and tea left. There is no money to buy anything else.

MLITSHE What? No food, no money?

TSOARELO Yes no money...

MLITSHE Last week I gave you R100, where is all that money gone to?...you think I am Barclays Bank neh?...

TSOARELO On Saturday you demanded R20, on Sunday you demanded another R20...I mean you nearly killed me for trying to refuse...

MLITSHE Votsek! Shut up! You are lying...you are supporting your family with my money pretending you are supporting my children, you think I am a fool neh?

TSOARELO But the children must go to school, they must eat...my God.

MLITSHE Hey!...Don't argue with me woman...You think a man of my standing should eat plain pap and tea?

TSOARELO But the children...

MLITSHE Hey!...I was not eating at school, they must go and have lunch at home...did I not tell you that?

TSOARELO But the school is far...

MLITSHE *(Throwing things at her.)* Woman ngiyalibeka! uyalibeka! I say one you say two!...*(He takes an axe wanting to chop her.)*...Is that what they taught you when I married you?...Yimi indoda la...I am the only man here...this mouth says the final word here...you, you are just like this furniture!...bloody damn shit. *(Checking pots.)*

TSOARELO Kodwa Baba – do you care to know how much is a bag of mealie mealie, potatoes, sugar...?

MLITSHE Why should I care?...Ha ha ha!!! That is not my department.

TSOARELO But this is unfair...you stopped me from working...

MLITSHE No wife of mine is going to work, because one: I support you, two: next time you will be having a lot of friends and many lunch boyfriends.

TSOARELO How could you not trust me? I am your wife…

MLITSHE Listen here, I know you women. Don't forget that we are working with women, we see what they do…how they flirt around behind their husbands, so don't pretend to be better, you women are all bitches man! *(She starts sobbing.)*…

TSOARELO *(Aloud)* What have I done to deserve this? I have given you all my life and my love…

MLITSHE Oho! you not crying blood but just salty water…I don't know what I saw in you…you are so ugly…Mina I have beautiful girlfriends, so beautiful you could mistake them for white women…and they all love me, and you I don't know what I saw in you really, all you want is my money…Hey! Hey! Mfazi! I want food here and now!…I am going to close my eyes and count up to twenty……if the plate is not here when I open my eyes, you will see my true colours…*(She panics not knowing what to do, he puts his head on the table, closes his eyes and starts counting.)* One!…Two!…Three…

(By the time he reaches to nine, he is fast asleep and snoring, and the panga/axe is near him, she is in tears trying to convince him…On realizing he is asleep she slowly takes the axe into her hands, looks at him snoring…Slowly raises the axe to chop him…But she cannot do it…She breaks down into tears…She packs her clothes to leave the place…After some thought she decides not to…and then goes and lifts him up on her shoulders and drags him to bed, takes off his shoes, socks and shirt, and joins him.)

(Fadeout)

Scene 2

(In the morning. She wakes up, boils water, brings out her washing cloth, towel, toothbrush, toothpaste, water in a cup and gets ready to wash. Meantime, MLITSHE *is snoring loudly on the bed.)*

TSOARELO Baba!…Mlitshe…Mlitshe Vuka! Wake up…*(He turns to the other side.)* Time is up or you will be late…

MLITSHE What time is it?…

TSOARELO It's six o'clock…

MLITSHE Alright…*(Going back to sleep, snoring again.)*

TSOARELO Don't say I didn't wake you up!

MLITSHE Give me another five minutes.

TSOARELO *(Prepares tea and leaves it on the table.)* Five minutes over…Now you are late…*(No answer…)*

MLITSHE Heyi wena! I am not going to work! I don't feel well…

TSOARELO You will be fired, don't do this!

MLITSHE *(Waking up and pointing a finger at her.)* Hey! you are not my boss, shut your stinking mouth…I am sick and not going to work…I will see them on Monday…I know how to play my game. *(When he wakes up, he goes to wash himself.)* Tsoarelo! *(Shouting.)* Give me my silk shirt and mashwabana trouser!…*(She runs, taking the clothes to him.)*…Polish my brown shoes!…*(She brings.)*…Socks!…*(She brings.)*…Coming back soon…*(Off he goes smartly dressed.)*.

TSOARELO Ja! Banna! Amadoda! Men!…as you see him leave now as it is a Saturday, he will only come back on Monday or Tuesday…If I knew that getting married was like this, I would not have dared even to consider it…Funny before we got married he used to be such a loving and caring man, but now…

(There is a gentle knock at the door.)

VOICE Amakipkip [children's popcorn]…

TSOARELO Emalini my child?

VOICE Two packets and amaswidi e20c… *(Behind the cupboard she draws a plastic bag, extracts a larger plastic bag of kipkip and sweets and hands them over to the child.)*

TSOARELO Thank you, come again…
Ah, so you thought I am stuck and depended on him? Sorry, I have my secret, small and private business – otherwise my children would starve in the rural areas, there in Qwa Qwa…But he must not know, and will never know, he is hardly here, or else he can skin me alive…He is fully content with me depending on him.

(Fadeout)

Scene 3

(At work, the Boss MRS JOHNSON *is busy at the computer when in enters* MLITSHE *staggering, trying to pass unseen…)*

JOHNSON Hey you Mlitshe!...Come here...
MLITSHE *(Brushing his head.)* Yes, Madam...
JOHNSON What day is today?
MLITSHE Tuesday...
JOHNSON Tuesday?
MLITSHE Maybe Wednesday...
JOHNSON Tuesday! Wednesday! Which one is it?
MLITSHE I am not sure, Mrs...
JOHNSON What time is it?
MLITSHE ...Half past eleven...
JOHNSON And what time are you supposed to start working?
MLITSHE Seven o'clock, Mrs Johnson...
JOHNSON And what time did you arrive here?
MLITSHE Awu Mrs Johnson, you mean you did not see me when you were parking your car?
JOHNSON You are a blatant liar Mlitshe, I am tired of your lies, of your lateness and ever absenteeism...
MLITSHE I am sorry Mrs...The truth is that my wife is sick, very sick...Please believe you me Mrs...
JOHNSON You are fired...right now!
MLITSHE Mrs Johnson, how can you do this to me?...Okay I swear I won't do it again...You know I am the bread winner, please think of my children...*(Bringing his mouth close to her face.)*
JOHNSON Take your stinking face away from me...Your mouth stinks, you think I am a fool? You are drunk and think I am your stupid my boy?...*(She puts his wages in an envelope.)*

I have been counting for you all this time, you come to work on Wednesdays, Thursdays and Fridays. On Saturdays and Mondays you don't come to work!...What do you think you are?...A shareholder I suppose...My boy I want production...My child is sick...my wife is sick...my father's sister is dead...and yet you are always drunk...*(He is crying real tears.)*

Here is your money, pack your things and go, I don't want to see your face anymore... Out!!

(Fadeout)

Scene 4

*(*TSOARELO *is busy selling her stuff, all neatly packed (mini-store like). Then she sees him approaching from afar. She quickly packs to hide her business from him.)*

TSOARELO Why so early today? *(No answer.)* Baba!...Mlitshe!

(A knock at the door.)

VOICE Amaswidi namachapisi.

(Some noise.)

TSOARELO Sh!!! my children, he is here. *(Cautiously she serves them.)*

But why so early today? This one will be fired one day.

(Blackout)

Scene 5

(A SANGOMA *is singing and dancing, drum beat heard...*MLITSHE *is kneeling and clapping hands...vigorous dance, kneels down, shakes a bag of bones and throws them out...)*

SANGOMA Fuhah!...*(He blows and she throws them again and reads.)* You must thank your ancestors that you are not mad...A pitch black cloud is following you like a shadow, your shadow...Hoyi! Makhosi!!!
MLITSHE Yizwa Mngoma! Siyavuma!...
SANGOMA If you don't wake up, you will lose all you have...You hardly visit your ancestors now,...You must thank your great grandfather that you still have a wife...Hoyi! hoyi!...Makhosi!
MLITSHE Makhosi! Yizwa Mngoma!
SANGOMA The bones says you have lost your job and you want me to help you find another?
MLITSHE Please Mngoma, agemate of our forefathers...Help me...I have tried everywhere but nothing...
SANGOMA The bones say you drink to your brains and not to your belly. I see your wife's heart is bleeding from inside...Your ancestors will turn against you for that.
MLITSHE I don't want to lose my wife Mngoma, what must I do now I am afraid?
SANGOMA Take this...Mix it with water when you take a bath in the morning...I can't give you anything for phalaza [vomit] you fool of alcohol...Take this put it under your tongue when you ask for a job from white people...Hoyi! hoyi!...You will place my cow right here...R250.00...Hoyi...and don't say goodbye when you leave...and

don't look back until you are home…*(She sings.)*

(Fadeout)

Scene 6

(TSOARELO *is sitting next to her stock far in thought.)*

TSOARELO Besides that, I am married to Mlitshe, what is it that I get from him? Constant abuse…harassment, insults and beatings…But why?…Am I doing something wrong?…What?…Nothing!…It is not because he drinks too much, otherwise he would be fighting other men as well!…But just because I am a woman and I am his wife…But why is it that most women suffer one way or another?…He stopped me from working and he gives me pittance, what is R100 a month?…He calls me all sorts of names…I know no happiness, even my business is secret…Will this curse over women ever end?…Maybe I should just pack my bags and leave this man…And then he goes to harass my mother demanding his lobola back!…Maybe I should just kill myself!…Oh no! What will happen to my children?…But until then am I going to live like this?…Yes…why not…Kill the bastard once and for all and live in peace!…Even God will forgive me!…I must and will end this…Never never again!

(She continues to be busy. A knock at the door…enter MLITSHE*…*TSOARELO *jumps with fear…She was not expecting him…He slowly assesses all the stock she has displayed…moves on to the chair and sits down emotionless…)*

MLITSHE I am very thirsty and very hungry.
TSOARELO I…I…Oh, please, my God…This…Eh!…
MLITSHE Would you be kind enough to give me something to drink, please?
TSOARELO *(Shaking as she brings it)* Please…ke kopa tsoarelo hle! Forgive me…
MLITSHE *(After two or three sips)* Ah!!…That's it, feels better now…don't you have bread today? Even if it's two slices, that will do…*(Given four and tea)*
TSOARELO I am terribly sorry for what I have done…but…the money…the children…
MLITSHE Tsoarelo my beloved wife…I am very sorry for what I have been doing to you, the way I have been treating you…If you were another woman you would have long left me by now…You have given me two beautiful children, stood by me when I was doing the worst to you without any reason…Shit me! Shit friends! Shit beer! Shit! Shit! Shit!…*(Crying hysterically)*…I am a useless somebody! I am worse than a pig!…Tsoarelo, I am not fit to belong to you…Please leave me!…
TSOARELO Through pain and happiness you are mine…Didn't we make vows in church, witnessed by all?
MLITSHE *(Moving away from her)* Tsoarelo…I have something to tell you…
TSOARELO Just say anything…I'll understand…
MLITSHE Oh! How should I start?
TSOARELO Mlitshe, are you leaving me?…Have you impregnated someone?
MLITSHE Tsoarelo, why do you think I did not give you any money this month?
TSOARELO Well I thought…the usual…
MLITSHE It is now three weeks that I have lost my job…*(Crying)*…
TSOARELO Three weeks! But you wake up every morning going to work?
MLITSHE I woke up to look for a job all this time…
TSOARELO Why didn't you tell me?
MLITSHE I thought I will get another job before you knew I was fired…But I have not had any luck, nothing…I even went to iSangoma and she told me all about us, how useless I am and how lucky I am to have you as my wife. She also gave me umuthi [herbs] to help me get a job, but nothing…and I can't hide this anymore! I can't pretend to be working when I know I don't! Pretending to be full when I know I am hungry! Pretending to be happy when I know I am not! And I can't!…I can't!…I can't!…*(Breaking down)*
TSOARELO You know what? You will find another job, don't worry…All you need to do is just pray and God will answer…Okay!
MLITSHE Okay!!…*(They hug, clinging to each other)*

And all this…you did for the children?
TSOARELO When you stopped me from working, and we started having financial problems, I could not write to my mother to say we do not have money for the children…So behind your back I started to

secretly sell this to subsidize towards that end.

MLITSHE Ja! Wena ngakukhethelwa amadlozi...Thank you my ancestors for giving me such a beautiful and sensible wife...*(He cries hysterically clinging to her.)*

TSOARELO Thula Baba thula! [Don't cry baba]...Sh!!!

(Maybe some song – "Niboyigcina lentandane")
(Fadeout)

Scene 7

*(Late afternoon...*TSOARELO *is busy dancing to the business song. Time and again looking at the watch, worriedly, but a bit hopefully...Suddenly enter* MLITSHE *singing a Christian song and dancing with enthusiasm...He encourages her to join...)*

TSOARELO I don't have to ask...You got the job?...

MLITSHE No!...

TSOARELO *(A bit disappointed)* No...but then...?

MLITSHE Remember when I used to suffer...I was like...

(Playback – He goes to the door. TSOARELO *sings a usual song of business in a free spirit, and the business flourishes. A knock at the door.)*

TSOARELO Come in!...*(Enter* MLITSHE *dejected)* Nothing I suppose...

MLITSHE I feel useless...

(Another knock at the door)

TSOARELO Come in! *(Enter the* CHILD*)*

CHILD I want sweets and...*(She sees him.)*...Jo! *(Running back to the door afraid)*

TSOARELO No come back...There is bread there...Hey! It's okay, come and buy...The water is boiling.

MLITSHE Just prepare the food and I will serve your customer...*(The* CHILD *runs away as* TSOARELO *goes to get food.)*

Why?...Come my child, I won't harm you...*(The* CHILD *comes back agitatedly and buys.)*

You want two rands kipkip and sweets for 50c...Okay!...Here is your change...

(He tries to play with the CHILD *and she cries fearfully...End of playback and re-enter* TSOARELO*.)*

TSOARELO I will never forget those days...

MLITSHE But now I am...Guess what?...I am...*(Hand in pocket and out comes the Bible)* BORN AGAIN!...Glory Jesus!

TSOARELO You born again...Come on!

MLITSHE He needs all of us, the rich, the poor, the happy, the sad, the sinners, the do good, the ugly, the beautiful, the educated, the illiterates...All of us...Hallelujah!!

TSOARELO Am I not dreaming?...

MLITSHE Brothers and sisters – let us forget the earthly things and talk about the spirit and faith and the Gospel...Forget the money, your sufferings, go street by street, corner to corner, without fear and shame all shall be well...Give all you have to the Lord, a tenth of all you earn must go to the church of the Lord, so says the Bible, the Holy book...My wife I am saved, I feel brand new!

TSOARELO Are you sure of what you are saying?

MLITSHE I invite you too to join me...

TSOARELO Are you sure to attend home cells? And pray as many times as possible?

MLITSHE Praise the Lord!

TSOARELO I am not sure I can cope with all the demands...And anyway you know I belong to the Dutch Reformed Church...

MLITSHE May the Lord show you light, and I know He will...Come let us pray...Jesus, Lord of Lords! King of Kings! You are the Master in Heaven and earth, we pray and praise your name...

(Fadeout in prayer)

Scene 8

(In the train/on foot in the street. MLITSHE *with plastic bags full of groceries at his feet, preaching...)*

MLITSHE Bazalwane abathandekayo enkosini, Beloved people in the name of the Lord, even those who don't want to listen! The Lord is alive! Alleluia!...I was a sinner and unemployed...and I gave myself up to the Lord Jesus, this word came to me and I heard it...Everyday I woke up to look for the job and to find more soldiers for the Lord...I preached even to those I asked for the job from...Amen! He died and rose after three days!...And after three months I got a job...Praise Him!...Yes, of course I earn peanuts, but I dare say half a loaf is better than nothing!...Now look!...Look! I can buy groceries and do all my services for my church in the name of the Lord!...Even though I arrive very late everyday my wife is happy...I am happy and the Lord is happy...Now I invite all those who now feel they are prepared to hand their lives to the Lord to lift up their hands and I pray for them...*(Lifts his hands and a song is started and he starts to pray emotionally.)*

(Fadeout)

Scene 9

(MLITSHE *arrives and* TSOARELO *already is counting a lot of money on the table.)*

TSOARELO Awu!...You are back?...
MLITSHE Yes!...
TSOARELO Wait a minute...

(She leaves excitedly to the other room...He looks on the money...Stealingly he counts it...takes out his wallet, counts his money and his face changes...He is not happy with this...For a moment he stares at one point, thinking deeply...)

TSOARELO Baba!...*(Silence)*...Mlitshe!...
MLITSHE Yes!...*(Tone changing)*
TSOARELO How was it at work today?...
MLITSHE Getting used to it now...*(She comes carrying a new dress.)*
TSOARELO Tarara!...*(Showing off)* How does your wife look like?
MLITSHE How much?
TSOARELO You don't look happy about it...
MLITSHE How do you spend without consultation?...My agreement!...
TSOARELO Mlitshe, this money I worked for...I don't need any permit for it...
MLITSHE Oh!...*(Sarcastically)*
TSOARELO What's the jealousy for?...
MLITSHE Where are you going to wear that?...Didn't you refuse indirectly to commit yourself in my church?...And now this...Mh!...You don't need a permit!...Mh!...You worked for it...*(Looks up)* Lord forgive me!...Now that you have a lot of money you forget I am still your husband here...
TSOARELO *(Trying to answer)*...
MLITSHE In my house now you have your own things and decisions?...where do you get all these filthy ideas?...You indirectly mean I am useless?...Don't answer me back!...
TSOARELO I thought you will appreciate the fact that I bought myself something that you can't afford to...
MLITSHE Shut up!...You are insulting me, shut your mouth now...Or I will shut it for you!...Lord forgive me, this woman is tempting me...*(There and then he leaves banging the door.)*

(Slow fadeout)

Scene 10

(Next evening, TSOARELO *keeps checking the time...Looking afar...Paces up and down...Sits down and tries and falls asleep. The light gradually fades to indicate passing time...Blackout. The light comes up slowly, the clock rings and wakes her up...She looks at it and gets mad...She goes back to sit on the chair, then moves to the bed and lies at the bottom...and falls fast asleep. The lights go very bright...then gradually fade out but not to blackout...It is night. She wakes up, puts on her nightdress and goes back to sleep...*MLITSHE *is heard singing a church song, "God is so Good to me, now I am free"...A loud knock is heard and she's rudely awoken...Lights gradually come up.)*

MLITSHE *(Drunkenly)* Vula man!...
TSOARELO *(Goes to the door and flings it open)* Where do you come from?
MLITSHE *(He enters dead drunk.)* Don't ask me rubbish! This is my house...
TSOARELO My God! what is this?...Am I dreaming or what?...I don't believe what I see before me...
MLITSHE You better believe it, you are not dreaming...
TSOARELO So, it's back to square one again?...But why?...
MLITSHE I don't need your permit for anything I do...I don't need a permit from a woman for anything I decide to do!...Give me my plate!... (TSOARELO *contains her anger and gives him his plate.* MLITSHE *eats and spits)* Hey, wena! this pap is stale! Do you think I am stale!...Look...this is not my plate!...*(Throwing the plate down)*...
TSOARELO Please Baba, stop it!...
MLITSHE Nywa nywanywa!...Nywanywa a!...Votsek!...You think you are clever? My money buys food and yours you save it and buy clothes...From today all the money is controlled by me...You get that?...By me...

TSOARELO You better come to sleep, you are drunk...

MLITSHE Me drunk?...

TSOARELO Tomorrow you must wake up and go to work...

MLITSHE Forget it...I am not going to work anymore!...And for your information...I have drunk all the money I have earned so far!...

TSOARELO Basadi! [Women!]...Are you mad!...

MLITSHE Me, mad!...Ha ha ha!!!...You make a lot of money to maintain this family. All I would do is to control what comes in and out...You don't pay rent here!...

TSOARELO My money, never...This money is for my children...For that you better kill me!...

MLITSHE Woman!...Mfazi!...Where do you get that attitude? *(To himself)* Yes, guys are right, if you don't beat up a woman she takes you for granted, she takes you cheap...It's worse once she starts having more money and you earn nothing...She thinks she is a king...And yet you bought this thing...It's worse once you start attending church...She starts jollying around, suddenly you see she is having new this, new that...Yeyi!...A man is a man, is a man, is a man, is a man! *(To her)* And wena!...I will kill you...I tell you...One day is one day...

TSOARELO Just try me, just dare try...I respect you as my husband, but mind you I am not afraid of you and your threats, a lousy drunkard like you...If I had wanted I would have long killed you, I could have just poisoned your food, and you would die just like a dog, or I could have just hacked you with your axe in your sleep, and you would wake up in hell!

MLITSHE *(Eyes wide open)* Hey, wena!...Yeyi!

TSOARELO *(Rising from bed)* Stop barking and come to action...

MLITSHE *(Getting mad)* Hey! I will kill this...So you would know me!!...*(And he makes fists)*...

TSOARELO *(Goes to bed)* If you want to challenge me, just dare touch me...Jesus! I am tired of you...I have had enough of you.*(Going back to bed)*

MLITSHE *(To the audience)* Hey broer! the world is going mad!...This one I will kill her with my bare hands...I mean, I am not wrong, man! You see once women starts having control of money, they want to control we men as well...Never, over my dead body!...Not me, not Mlitshe!...The stone that never breaks!...Where is that meat? *(Goes and takes meat from the plate on the floor, tries to clean by blowing and wiping it. Sits on the chair...chewing)*

(Fadeout)

Scene 11

(Morning. MLITSHE *is asleep on the table and snoring.* TSOARELO *is loading her goods on to the trolley to go and sell. As he lifts his head she doesn't even look at him. He tries to pretends to be asleep, but realizes this is in vain...and he wakes up.)*

MLITSHE Awu! I slept on the chair!...Sweetheart, how could you leave me like this?...Where are you going? Why?...

(TSOARELO *does not look at him.)*

Eish, My head!...Heyi! You know, the other night I met Bra Willie, you remember Bra Willie?...*(No answer)*...The one who drinks too much, the one from exile – remember him?...I was so depressed you see, at work they said they will call us when there is a lot of work to be done...But you are not even listening to what I am saying... (TSOARELO *still doesn't speak; she leaves him like that pushing her trolley.)*

MLITSHE Nxa!...Damn shit...*(He is silent for some time, and he begins to search firstly himself, finds nothing, then everywhere: her clothes, under the mattresses, under pots, under carpet, almost everywhere. Suddenly he thinks about it...The pillowcase. He walks on the bed to hers, rips it open and there it is, two rows of ten- and twenty-rand notes, R450, he gives a sly smile, goes to the wardrobe and takes the dress, and rushes to the doorway, victory written on his face, leaving the room upside down.)*

R30...Okay R20, come on take it for your wife...Ah! you, idiots...

(Fadeout)

Scene 12

(TSOARELO *arrives to find the house upside down, she goes mad. And, realizing the money is missing, tears go down her cheeks and she starts to cry like a child...After a few moments she starts to assess the damage step by step. She realizes her dress too is missing...She stands still deep in thought, and then she decides what to do. She counts the money she has brought and goes to sleep.* MLITSHE *and* BRA WILLIE *are heard singing from far. The song is "Let the Good Times Roll," both are dead drunk. A loud knock...)*

MLITSHE Hey, Vula! open up!..."The boss is back! Ha ha ha! He is a hero!...He is a heeeroo!!"...Bra Willie ngena...Come in!...This is my house Bra Willie...You will sleep here. No in fact you must come and stay with me here if you don't have a place to stay.

WILLIE What about...*(And he points)*

(BRA WILLIE *sees a plastic bag of popcorn on top of the clothes on the floor. He takes it excitedly and starts to eat wildly.)*

MLITSHE This is my house...and you are my friend. If you don't have a place to stay, you will stay with me whether she likes it or not!...I am a man, man...Hey Bra Willie what are you eating? *(Tasting from the plastic bag, and spitting)*

Ayi man, Bra Willie you are eating these things. *(To* TSOARELO*)*...Hey wena! Vuka! Wake up and make us food!

WILLIE Leave her Stoney...It's half past two in the morning.

MLITSHE So, what? You shut up...You don't have a wife. *(He goes to* TSOARELO *and pulls her blankets.)*

TSOARELO What do you think you are doing?

MLITSHE Wake up and make food, woman!

(She tries to go back to sleep, but he pulls the blankets off her trying to beat her, but she pulls the blankets and he falls and she jumps on him, beating him with fists.)

MLITSHE Wenzani? Uyazimbambela? *(He tries to advance but he is overpowered.)*

TSOARELO Do you get me?...I am tired...of you *(She beats him harder and sits on him.)*

MLITSHE Yo! Mama! Yo! Leave me wena...I will kill you, uyangizwa!...Yo!!...Yo!...Yo!...

WILLIE Ayi man...woman!...You can't do...Tsoarelo! Tsoarelo!...

TSOARELO Votsek wena!! *(*WILLIE *tries to pull her away but she takes an axe and turns to him.)*

WILLIE Mina ngenzeni? What have I done?...Yo!!!!

TSOARELO Usabuza? You are still asking? *(She hits him and he runs out, followed by* MLITSHE, *who is pulled back and loses his T-shirt and runs out bare-chested and crying.)*

MLITSHE I'll kill this woman! You beat me because I'm powerless, I am drunk! You will pay for this! *(*TSOARELO *advances and he runs away, then she locks the door.)*

WILLIE Broer, mina I'm leaving you. I'm going back to the shebeen.

MLITSHE Just leave me wena! *(He turns to* TSOARELO.*)* Heyi wena Tsoarelo, I will report you to your elders for this... Ngiyotshela abakini! Open up! *(He bangs on the door, then after some time...)* Awu Sweetheart...it's cold here...Let me in...please or give me something to wear...Please...

TSOARELO Heyi wena...Stop making all that noise!...uyangirasela man! Go to the toilet!

MLITSHE Please Tsoarelo...I am sorry...I will never do anything wrong again...I will die here...

TSOARELO Why don't you die? You are a man, man. *(She goes to sleep.)*

MLITSHE Tsoarelo, what will people say if they see me like this? Open up! Please...please...please...My God...My God, why have you forsaken me?

(Fadeout)

(The lights come up. It is morning and MLITSHE *knocks gently on the door.)*

TSOARELO Wait, I am coming...*(She opens the door.)*...Oh...it's you...*(Taking the axe)*...What do you want...Some more...

MLITSHE *(Falls to his knees)* Please Tsoarelo, let me in.

TSOARELO Why? To mess up my life again!

MLITSHE What can I be without you? Nothing!

TSOARELO That is what you are.

MLITSHE From today I will change, it will be like before *(He starts crying.)* Please...

TSOARELO I know that song, just get out...now!

MLITSHE If I ever do it again, kill me.

TSOARELO I won't dirty my hands. You are finished! You are dead already! I have stomached so much pain from you...hoping you will change...thinking of our marriage, our children...

MLITSHE Tsoarelo, out there in the cold, I have had time to think more about it...

TSOARELO I have fed you and your children

and let you think just because you paid lobola for me I am your furniture...

MLITSHE Tsoarelo, the Gospel truth is that I felt like all other men...So powerless with less money than you made...But from today, if you forgive me for the last time, I will prove to you that I have changed...I want to work for you.

TSOARELO What?

MLITSHE We will be husband and wife only in bed...But I will go and buy stock for you, clean, sell...I will work under you...Give me one last chance. Please!

TSOARELO Last chance it is...

MLITSHE Thank you, my wife...Thank you! *(He moves to hug her.)*

TSOARELO Don't get carried away! You must pack everything properly and set up the stock for my customers. *(MLITSHE jumps to do his duties.)* Hey! Come here!...I don't want to seem like I'm treating you bad, but don't think I'm giving you powers to mess things around...Take it easy, don't jump...

MLITSHE Awu Tsoarelo! *(He kneels down clinging on to her dress crying tears of happiness.)*

TSOARELO Mlitshe...

BOTH *(They embrace.)*WEEMEN.

(Blackout)

Muthal Naidoo

> I decided to take their lives and do something with them, and chose to do it from a feminist point of view. Just take all the women out and let them explore who they are and what they want to be, rather than just producing heroes for the Mahabarath because that was their function in the epic – simply to be the mothers of this great hero and that great hero.

Educator, director, and playwright Muthal Naidoo was born in Pietermaritzburg, but lived in Ladysmith, Pretoria, and Durban. She has been involved in theatre for over forty years, starting with her first play at the age of 14. According to Muthal, "I would have liked for it to have been my vocation, but it's been more of an avocation because mainly I had to earn a living. I couldn't earn a living here in the theatre." After high school, Muthal earned a two-year teaching certificate, and later a B.A. from the University of Natal-Durban. She taught high school, where she also worked with children's theatre.

During the early 1960s, she became active with the Durban Academy of Theatre Arts (DATA), which developed out of a series of workshops spearheaded by Krishna Shah, an East Indian who had studied and worked in the United States. In 1963 Muthal was one of the founders of an offshoot of DATA called Shah Theatre Academy in honor of Krishna Shah, which focused on indigenous plays.

In 1965, Muthal was awarded a Fulbright Fellowship at the University of Indiana to study for a Ph.D., which she completed in 1972. Immediately after receiving her doctorate, Muthal worked for several years in the St. Louis area. Her first position was with the renowned choreographer/dancer Katherine Dunham in her drama program in East St. Louis. Her next position was with the Head Start Program, teaching English at Southern Illinois University, in the East St. Louis area. At the same time she was working with the Black Artists Group – college-age students who were creating plays and skits based on local issues – in St. Louis.

From 1972 to 1976, Muthal worked as a lecturer in the departments of Black Studies and Performing Arts at Washington University, teaching black drama and history. She developed a black theatre program where she directed such productions as Soyinka's *Trial of Brother Jero* and *Strong Breed*, *Our Land*, and *No Place to Be Somebody*. One of her students was Ron Himes, who later became one of the founders and artistic directors of the St. Louis Black Repertory Company.

In 1976, Muthal returned to Durban and resumed activities with Shah Theatre. Despite having a Ph.D., she could only find work as a teacher at the high-school level since her American degree was considered "inferior" for a post at a university: "And being a woman, they didn't consider what I did important." At the high school, she developed her writing skills by adapting novels for the stage. Muthal's active involvement in politics and the protest movement often found her at odds with the school administrators, resulting in her being "chased out of schools". The 1980s witnessed a surge in school boycotts. Muthal identified with the students' opposition to apartheid and the inferior educational system. After a series of battles with officials, Muthal left teaching and pursued professional theatre on a full-time basis. "I did it for two years and became broke." During those two lean years, she wrote all of her plays, starting with *Of No Account*, which was produced at the Market Theatre in 1982. *Of No Account* explores racism and sexism through the relationships among an Indian man, an African man, a white woman, and a white man, who all work in the same office. Muthal's other works include *We Three Kings* (1992), about the South African Indian Council Elections, and *Oh God!*, a title that was considered blasphemous. She changed the title to *Lucy's Dilemma* (short for "Lucifer"), and still she couldn't get it produced. She also wrote *Ikhayalethu* (meaning "our home"), *Nobody's Hero*, and *Masks*, one of Muthal's most interesting plays. In an article published in *Theatre Journal* (March, 1997) Muthal states:

> Of all the plays I have written, the play that most overtly represents the search for identity is *Masks*. The play takes place in the mind of a woman who is of Indian and Coloured parentage and all the characters that appear on the stage are various manifestations of her split personality. Her psychosis is born out of racism, and it is only when she can acknowledge all elements of her heritage and accept them as valid within herself that she becomes a whole human being again.[1]

Muthal's plays are usually social, political, and humorous. Her plays were sometimes banned:

> All of my plays were flops because people saw the name "Naidoo" and thought, "this must be an Indian play" and were not interested. There's no big following of Indians.

Muthal is an officer in the Regional Department of Education in Giyani.

ARTISTIC STATEMENT

I had been watching on the M-Net station the *Mahabarath*, and I thought everyone is going back to their roots, so let me see what I can find. At the same time I was reading all of Mary Daly's books, the feminist author. I like the way she turns everything on its head, the way she turns language on its head. I think she's probably learned from the black movement. So I put all of these things together. The *Mahabarath* was full of women characters with wonderful potential. I decided to take their lives and do something with them from a feminist point of view. Just take all the women out and let them explore who they are and what they want to be, rather than just producing heroes for the *Mahabarath*, because that was their function in the epic – simply to be the mothers of this great hero and that great hero. I spent a year or two thinking about it. Reading all of Mary Daly's books and experiencing the *Mahabarath*, the *Ramayana*, and all these Indian epics that are now on television. In a sense it's good they're showing them so everyone can view, but they're totally ghettoized on television. They're on a station called East-Net, which is subscribed to by Indians, so it's another form of apartheid. They feel only Indians would be interested. In these epics, women get so stuck in stereotypical roles and we need to see liberated women. So I wrote the play based on all of these experiences. I'm now looking at the *Taming of the Shrew* to see how I can reclaim the shrew.

THE ROLE OF THEATRE IN SOUTH AFRICA

I don't see the role of theatre changing that much over time. I think the role of theatre is – as Shakespeare put it – "to hold a mirror up to nature" so that we can examine ourselves and see what we are, and move on from that if it's not good and preserve what there is that is good. That's what I feel that theatre should be about. It's about challenging existing norms and standards. We still have to challenge the existence of apartheid at other levels.

HAVE SITUATIONS IMPROVED FOR BLACK WOMEN IN THEATRE IN THE NEW SOUTH AFRICA?

I'm not sure. To some extent yes, but not really.

1 Naidoo, Muthal, "The Search for a Cultural Identity: A Personal View of South African 'Indian Theatre'," *Theatre Journal* 49(1), March 1997: 29–39.

I think a lot of lip service is being paid to gender issues. We have a long way to go.

HAVE THINGS IMPROVED IN GENERAL IN THE NEW SOUTH AFRICA?

We've got a new government, and now we have a whole lot of new rich people – but we still have the same lot of very poor people who are not reaping the benefits of the changeover. On the surface it looks good, because we've got lots of blacks and women in government. A lot of new people are getting advantages in this society and are being recognized. But it's always those people who've managed to achieve wealth, education, or something like that. The ordinary poor people are still ordinary poor people and nothing has really changed for them.

Interviews conducted July 1996 and July 1997, in Johannesburg.

Photo by Kathy A. Perkins.

8 Flight from the Mahabarath

Muthal Naidoo

This play attempts to look at the *Mahabarath* from a woman's point of view.

In casting the play, the characters should represent the rainbow nation of South Africa and any tendency towards ethnic stereotyping should be scrupulously avoided. Performers should be chosen for their ability to interpret the roles.

Traditions, customs, rituals should also come from the diversity of the South African cultural context. African, Western, Indian music, dances and traditions should inform the life of the play. For this reason, I have called the performers of religious rituals shamans, rather than priests, sangomas, inyangas, etc.

Characters

Women

DRAUPADI
RADHA
GANGA
SUBADHRA
KUNTHI
HIDIMBA
URVASI
UTTARAI
GANDHARAI
OTHER WOMEN

Men

BRIHANNALA
SIKANDI

(The WOMEN *come running in, helter-skelter, through the audience. They are dressed in classical Indian style with loads of jewelry, hair bound up, tightly draped saries. When they arrive on stage, they stand together, listening, alert, watching out for pursuers. Once they are certain that they have not been followed, they break the silence.)*

DRAUPADI We did it.

(There is a joyful outburst. The women laugh and hug one another.)

GANGA This is our space.

RADHA Here I can speak. I have a voice. In the epic, the *Mahabarath*, I was just a footnote. *(The women laugh and some embrace her.)*

DRAUPADI We can be ourselves. *(She pulls down her tresses and then pulls off the wig that she is wearing to reveal a short, boyish hairstyle.)*

KUNTHI But Draupadi, your beautiful hair.

DRAUPADI You mean this wig. This is not me. I wore it in the *Mahabarath*. It was bound and decorated when I was a respectable woman, loose and flowing after I had been defiled. Now my hair is short because that is the way I want it.

(All the women clap and begin throwing off the shackles of their previous existences in the Mahabarath.*)*

GANGA I am so glad to get rid of this ridiculous crown and with it the crazy notion that I have to be divine in order to be the mother of a hero of the *Mahabarath*. Women, I want you to bear witness: I give up this crown and with it the enslaving tradition of motherhood. *(She flings the crown away.)*

KUNTHI Have you never wanted to be a mother?

GANGA Never.

SUBADHRA Is that why you drowned seven of your babies right after they were born?

GANGA I didn't drown them. Vyasa did. He wrote the epic. Give him his due, he is a very skillful writer. What an intriguing introduction; a woman, actually a goddess, throwing her newborn babies into the river year after year for seven years. Sensational! But I was his instrument. I had to kill off babies that I would never have had in the first place.

SUBADHRA But they weren't killed. By drowning the babies, you released their souls into the hereafter and spared them the sinful life on earth.

GANGA You can believe that if you want. I am like a river, free flowing, creating my path on the *earth.*

(She pulls off her sari; underneath is a free-flowing garment. She dances around. The other women pull off various items of clothing and are revealed in shorts and jeans and other non-restrictive forms of dress. Some women play musical instruments and others join in the dance with GANGA*. While they are prancing about,* GANDHARI*, blindfolded, struggles toward the stage, falling and feeling her way forward.)*

GANDHARI *(Calling out.)* Kunthi, my sister-in-law, where are you? Kunthi, can you hear me?

DRAUPADI Gandhari? What is *she* doing here?

SUBADHRA Poor woman, look at her crawling. I will help her.

DRAUPADI *(Stopping her.)* No, she must help herself.

SUBADHRA But she is helpless.

DRAUPADI No, she is not. She chooses to wear that blindfold.

GANDHARI Kunthi, where are you?

KUNTHI *(Coming forward.)* Here I am. *(She touches* GANDHARI*.)*

GANDHARI *(Grabbing hold of her.)* Why did you leave me?

KUNTHI But I explained it all to you. I asked you to come with us.

GANDHARI You know I cannot.

DRAUPADI How did she get here? How did she find us? Kunthi, did you tell her? I think she is a spy. She will lead the others here.

KUNTHI I had to tell her. After all, she is a woman.

DRAUPADI If she wants to join us, she will have to remove that blindfold. *(She comes forward and pulls on* GANDHARI*'s blindfold.* GANDHARI *screams.)*

GANGA *(Pulling* DRAUPADI *away from* GANDHARI*)* Stop this. Do you want to go back to the epic? There you can force people to do what you want.

DRAUPADI I'm sorry, but I get so angry when I look at her and see how she is wasting her life.

GANDHARI Wasting my life! What does she mean? How can she speak of me like that?

KUNTHI Draupadi is very impatient; you must forgive her.

GANDHARI But why does she say I am wasting my life? I have dedicated my whole existence to my husband and my children. I put on this blindfold to join Dhritarashtra in his blindness so that he would understand he had a true, faithful and obedient wife. I bore him a hundred sons.

DRAUPADI And what about you? What do you want for yourself?

GANDHARI But I've just told you. I want to be a good wife and mother.

DRAUPADI Then what do you want here? Go back to the epic; your husband and sons are there.

GANDHARI Why is she speaking to me so harshly? What have I done?

KUNTHI Stop persecuting Gandhari.

SUBADHRA Aunt Gandhari, have you come to stay with us? Have you decided to leave the epic too?

GANDHARI *(Shocked.)* Leave the epic! Have you left the epic? Oh no. You can't do that. Kunthi, you must come back; tell the others to come back too. Kunthi, I beg of you, come back with me. *(She clings to* KUNTHI*.)* Kunthi, you must come back.

DRAUPADI You see. I told you she was here as an agent. Who sent you, Gandhari?

GANDHARI Sent me! No one sent me. I came on my own. I missed my dear Kunthi. I didn't know you had left the epic. How can you do that? Don't you see the harm you are doing? You are destroying a great masterpiece.

RADHA If it cannot accommodate my speaking, it needs to be destroyed.

DRAUPADI If it demeans my sexuality, it needs to be destroyed.

GANGA, SABADHRA, KUNTHI If we are simply vessels for producing warriors, then it needs to be destroyed.

HIDIMBA If I am to be a scapegoat to be sacrificed so that clans can keep their unity without resolving their real internal conflicts, then it needs to be destroyed.

GANDHARI *(Drawing in her breath sharply.)* The witch! Is that the witch? Keep her away from me. I see it now. She has influenced you. How can you believe her? She is evil. She wants to destroy the proud heritage of a whole nation.

HIDIMBA We have no power to destroy the epic. It exists in another time and space.

DRAUPADI So does she. She doesn't belong here. Send her away.

GANDHARI I won't go without Kunthi. *(She clings desperately to* KUNTHI.*)*

KUNTHI I am so sorry, Gandhari. I cannot go back with you.

GANDHARI But why do you want this? It cannot replace the epic.

HIDIMBA We are not trying to replace the epic; we are building our new home.

KUNTHI I'm sorry, Gandhari, we have chosen what we want to do. You must do the same. Go back if that's what you want; but try to make some changes. This blindfold, for instance.

GANDHARI Are you mad? Do you expect me to interfere with tradition?

GANGA Yes, we do. *We* have, by leaving the epic. You must do what you can.

GANDHARI You are mad. You are all mad. What has happened to you? It's that witch or some god must have cursed you.

(All the women burst out laughing.)

KUNTHI Stop this. She lives by the old values. She does not understand. Gandhari, my dear sister-in-law, I am sorry but we cannot go back with you.

GANDHARI Oh, Kunthi, this is terrible. Perhaps I can find a god or a rishi to come and break the spell. I will go back. I understand my mission now. You are quite right. I have to do something new. I have to find help for all of you. I am leaving but will be back. *(She stumbles out the way she entered.)*

SUBADHRA What's going to happen to us? If she comes back with her hundred sons...

GANGA What if she does?

SUBADHRA They could take us back.

GANGA Do you want to go back?

SUBADHRA No. I couldn't be myself there. I was either Krishna's sister or Arjun's second wife or Abhimanyu's mother; but in myself I was nobody. I don't ever want to go back.

GANGA Then you are quite safe.

URVASI But Subadhra's right; how can we withstand a hundred men?

KUNTHI We have already. We're here, aren't we?

SUBADHRA But how are we going to protect ourselves?

DRAUPADI We don't have to. This is our space. We decide what happens. Didn't you see that Gandhari couldn't enter here?

RADHA Come on, Subadhra. Your fears belong in the epic. This is our play. We have exciting times ahead of us. Let's get on with it.

(They begin to pick up all the clothes and accessories that they discarded.)

URVASI What are we going to do with all these things? We do not need them any more.

UTTARAI Let's burn them. Make a huge bonfire.

RADHA No. We need to preserve them as reminders of the way in which we lived. They must go into a museum so that future generations of women can see them and never repeat the mistakes that we made.

(The women start to pack the items in a box.)

GANGA *(Laughing)*. Yes, that is a wonderful idea. As long as we are alive, we can visit the museum and remind ourselves of the ghosts we used to be.

(At this moment, two men come running in. One is BRIHANNALA, *the persona adopted by Arjun when in hiding in Virata during the thirteenth year of the Pandava's banishment. The other is* SIKANDI, *the male form of Amba. The women gather together at the edge of the stage somewhat apprehensive.)*

URVASI Subadhra was right. They've come for us.

DRAUPADI It's my husband, Arjun, but disguised as Brihannala.

SUBADHRA Why is he disguised as a woman? Has he come to take us back?

(The two men come to the edge of the stage and greet in the Hindu way.)

BRIHANNALA AND SIKANDI Namasthe.

GANGA Namasthe.

DRAUPADI Arjun, I know it is you. Why have you adopted that awful disguise again?

RADHA Are you trying to pass yourself off as a woman so you can deceive us?

SUBADHRA If you have come to take us back, we won't go. You will have to kill us first.

GANGA Stop this. No one can take us back without our consent. *(Turning to the men.)* Now tell us, why have you come here?

BRIHANNALA If you will allow us, we would like to join you.

WOMEN Join us!

GANGA We are a group of women. Why do you want to join us?

SIKANDI We cannot continue to live at odds with ourselves.

DRAUPADI What do you mean?

SUBADHRA I know. Sikandi was a woman too. He was Amba. Ganga, he was trapped in this form because Vyasa needed an instrument to destroy your son, Bhishma, Ganga.

HIDIMBA But if you have left the epic why have you retained your masculine form? You have the freedom to change.

SIKANDI Are you going to exclude us because we are men?

GANGA Why do you want to join us?

BRIHANNALA We want to be free.

RADHA You, Arjun, of all people, you had freedom. You had opportunities to become the most renowned warrior. In addition, you became an accomplished dancer and musician. You were the darling of the gods. What more did you want?

BRIHANNALA But I wasn't myself.

SIKANDI We are both victims, just as you are. Your roles made you uncomfortable; ours did too.

HIDIMBA Our society might prove equally restrictive to you.

BRIHANNALA Not if we can be ourselves.

RADHA Why didn't you fight for freedom in the epic?

SIKANDI Traditions! We could not get past traditions.

DRAUPADI They want what we want. Let them join us.

RADHA No. How do we know that they are not here to sabotage us?

BRIHANNALA We want to be free, just like you.

DRAUPADI Let them join us. They can't do us any harm. We are in our own space.

SUBADHRA Yes, let them join us.

GANGA Arjun, as you can see your two wives are eager to have you with us. But what will you do here? We have banned war. We do not have a place for warriors.

BRIHANNALA That is why I have come to you. I am sick of war. I am a dancer, musician and story teller. I want to devote myself to these arts.

RADHA Now this is unbelievable. You, the greatest living warrior? You are prepared to give up glory, fame and reputation to be a dancer?

BRIHANNALA Yes, I am.

RADHA *(To* SIKANDI*)* And what about you? Why do you continue to retain your male form?

SIKANDI I was born this way. But that's beside the point. I have apprenticed myself to Brihannala and I too wish to devote myself to the performing arts.

BRIHANNALA If you do not feel comfortable about having us here, we will understand and move on.

SUBADHRA Back to the epic?

BRIHANNALA No, we cannot go back.

GANGA *(Turning to the other women.)* Well, what do you say?

DRAUPADI I say we accept them.

GANGA What do the rest of you say?

RADHA I don't really understand but I suppose there's no harm in it. They won't be able to divert us from our course whatever they do.

URVASI With their artistic skills they'll be useful in helping us with our play.

GANGA Does everyone agree? *(Chorus of yeses.* GANGA *turns to the two men.)* Arjun and Sikandi, you are welcome to join us.

(As the two men step onto the stage, DRAUPADI *rushes forward and throws her arms around* BRIHANNALA.*)*

DRAUPADI Oh, Arjun, I am so glad you are here. I have missed you dreadfully. Now this place will be paradise for me.

BRIHANNALA *(Extricating himself from her embrace.)* Please, I am Brihannala.

DRAUPADI *(Laughing.)* Yes, I can see that. Well, go and change so that we can see my handsome warrior husband, Arjun, again.

*(*BRIHANNALA *gives her a searching look, then exits with* SIKANDI.*)*

RADHA Draupadi, don't get carried away.

Arjun was your husband in the epic. This is not the epic.

DRAUPADI *(Dancing about.)* Yes, this is not the epic. I am so glad. Arjun will be my husband and my only husband. I won't be saddled with four others just to satisfy Vyasa's prurient imagination. I love Arjun. I love him. I love him. I love him.

RADHA What about you Subadhra? He was your husband too.

SUBADHRA Who? Brihannala?

DRAUPADI No, not Brihannala; that's only a disguise. Arjun, Arjun.

SUBADHRA I don't know. I don't know whether I loved Arjun in the epic either. My marriage was arranged by my brother, Krishna. I never knew whether he was doing it for me or for himself.

GANGA Well, let's forget all that now and begin our work.

RADHA It's not going to be easy. Where do we begin?

GANGA Certainly not with me, drowning babies.

RADHA But why are we trying to compete with Vyasa? Why do we want to rewrite the *Mahabarath*. We are creating a new world for ourselves. In the epic, we are not real people; we are mythological characters created to fulfill other people's needs.

KUNTHI Yes. I want a real existence; one that I am author of.

SUBADHRA How do we go about this?

KUNTHI We will tell our own stories.

SUBADHRA What good will that do?

KUNTHI We will reveal how we see the world.

RADHA Not full of violence, war and victims. Our play will be life affirming.

HIDIMBA *(Dryly)* We hope.

GANGA I agree with Radha. We will celebrate life; we will be creative, exciting and full of joy.

SUBADHRA But the epic is exciting because of violence and conflict. I don't see how we can make our play exciting if we exclude violence and conflict.

RADHA That is our great challenge.

SUBADHRA What if we fail?

GANGA Screw your courage to the sticking place and we'll not fail.

SUBADHRA Lady Macbeth said that to incite her husband to violence. The killing of the king provided the excitement of the play.

RADHA We'll change that. We can learn from Vyasa in that. Look how he took Ganga's drowning of the babies and turned it into a good deed; how he justified the killing of the Kauravas in the *Bhagavad Gita*...

DRAUPADI No, no, no. We can't copy him. Through his crooked logic he justified violence. Besides, in his epic, I had to have five husbands all at the same time. In our play, I don't want five husbands. I want only one.

KUNTHI Draupadi is right. Vyasa made us accept death and violence.

RADHA So then, where do we begin?

KUNTHI I still say, we must tell our stories.

RADHA And present ourselves as victims? I don't like it.

GANGA What do you suggest then?

RADHA We've got to show our new world and we can't do that until we have created it.

KUNTHI Can't we do both? Tell our stories and at the same time create a new world?

DRAUPADI Let's try. We can look at our lives and where we colluded in our own oppression, change the circumstances to meet our new needs.

GANGA Well, I have already begun something like that. In my story, I will not marry and have any babies.

RADHA You will have to go much further. It's not what you don't do; it's what you do that has meaning.

DRAUPADI Let's begin with my story. It is also, in part, Kunthi's story, since she was my mother-in-law. Now that Arjun has joined us, there are three of us to make contributions. We can always come back to the other stories and decide how to fit them all together.

GANGA Well, women, shall we begin with Draupadi's story?

(The women agree.)

DRAUPADI *(Running off)*. I'll call Arjun.

HIDIMBA She's chasing an illusion.

SUBADHRA Why do you say that?

HIDIMBA She's looking for Arjun.

KUNTHI Well, he was her husband.

*(*DRAUPADI *comes back dragging* BRIHANNALA *behind her.* BRIHANNALA *is dressed in a karate outfit. They are followed by* SIKANDI *who is also wearing a karate outfit.)*

DRAUPADI Come on, Arjun. We need you here.

BRIHANNALA But I told you, I am Brihannala.

DRAUPADI Don't make me laugh. You've taken off all that foolish fancy dress.

RADHA Why are you wearing karate gear?

SIKANDI We've taken up karate. It is a martial art but used only in self-defence and it's good exercise. Do you want to see us perform a kata? It's like a dance but it's a fight with an imaginary opponent.

RADHA Let's see it. Perhaps we can use it in the play.

(SIKANDI and BRIHANNALA perform a kata. At its completion, the women clap.)

GANGA This is something that we will have to learn. We have always depended on others to defend us; now we're on our own.

RADHA Brihannala and Sikandi, will you organize classes for us?

SIKANDI With the greatest pleasure. You see, Bri, we aren't out of place here.

(BRIHANNALA looks unconvinced.)

DRAUPADI Come on, let's begin with my story. Arjun…

BRIHANNALA Please, I am Brihannala.

DRAUPADI *(Impatiently.)* Yes. Yes. Brihannala, Partha, Dhananjaya and Arjun. *(BRIHANNALA looks decidedly unhappy.)* Those of us who need to change, let's get into costume.

SUBADHRA What part am I to play?

GANGA Who would you like to be?

SUBADHRA Could I be a musician? I don't feel ready for a major role.

GANGA Fine. *(She puts on a mask.)* I am Drupada, Draupadi's father. Radha, where is your mask?

RADHA I've got it. *(She puts it on and jumps into the midst of the others and begins whirling around with her mace like a demon. She laughs a loud, raucous laugh.)* Where's Draupadi? I'm going to eat you alive. *(She chases DRAUPADI around the stage.)*

(Everyone laughs.)

KUNTHI You really love playing Duryodhana, don't you?

RADHA It's all that pent-up energy I couldn't use in the epic. *(She wields her mace and faces up to BRIHANNALA. She speaks in a loud growl.)* Come on, cousin. You think you are the greatest warrior on earth. I'll show you. *(She whirls her mace. Brihannala dodges it by jumping over it, sliding under it and then with a few karate movements catches her from behind and disarms her.)*

BRIHANNALA Are we going to portray violence in the play?

GANGA We can't deny that violence is out there.

RADHA But we're not going to glorify it. We are not going to have heroes and villains, force the audience to take sides, encourage them to adopt a punitive attitude and so stimulate a blood lust.

HIDIMBA But that's what excites them. *(Pointing to audience.)* You can't change that.

SIKANDI It will take time but it can be done.

DRAUPADI Oh, come on. Let's get on with it. Who is going to be the story teller?

SIKANDI I will. Bri has been teaching me. *(He smiles at BRI, who smiles back.)*

DRAUPADI *(Annoyed.)* Well, I don't know.

GANGA Sikandi, doesn't have any part right now. Let him do it. Now put on your sari and your wig.

DRAUPADI *(Begrudgingly.)* Oh, all right.

GANGA Let's begin.

RADHA (DURYODHANA) *(Speaking to audience.)* I am Duryodhana, Prince of Hastinapura. You met my mother, Gandhari, earlier. You know the one with the blindfold. I am the sworn enemy of my cousins the Pandavas, Arjun and his brothers. *(Sighing.)* So that makes me the arch villain of the *Mahabarath*.

SIKANDI (NARRATOR) We begin our story of Draupadi on the day she chooses her husband. She has organised a huge music festival. All the musicians, dancers and singers of the land are here to perform. People from all over the country have come to attend the festival.

(A group of musicians, singers and dancers occupy centre stage. These are all the other women who were not assigned specific parts. They wear masks. They begin to perform. They can mime to background music because we already know that they are not the real musicians.)

RADHA (DURYODHANA) What kind of foolishness is this? I came here thinking this would be Draupadi's swayamwara. *(Pauses. Looks at SIKANDI. SIKANDI shrugs. RADHA takes off mask.)* Tell them *(Pointing to audience.)* what a swayamwara is.

SIKANDI Oh, right. A swayamwara is an occasion when a girl chooses her husband from an assembly of suitors. *(Thumbs up sign to* RADHA.*)*

RADHA (DURYODHANA) *(Resuming her mask.)* My brothers and I came thinking this was Draupadi's swayamwara. That's what it was supposed to be. This Woodstock thing is not in the epic. Be that as it may, swayamwara or not, I will get Draupadi. With the help of my brothers, I am going to carry her off before she can make her choice. You think that's boorish. No it isn't. It's part of our tradition. Tradition allows an exceptional man simply to abduct a woman at her swayamwara and make her his bride. And as you can see, I am an exceptional man.

(The music and dancing become very lively and exhilarating. BRIHANNALA, *who has been watching, spontaneously joins in, plays and dances with the group.* DRAUPADI *becomes very excited and applauds enthusiastically. When they have finished,* GANGA, *as King Drupada, awards a prize to the best performers. Then* DRAUPADI *moves forward, takes the garland from her neck and puts it around* BRIHANNALA. *He takes off the garland and puts it back on her neck. She then puts the end of the garland around his neck and they are yoked together.)*

GANGA (DRUPADA) My daughter, what does this mean?

DRAUPADI Father, this is the man I want to marry.

RADHA (DURYODHANA) *(Whirls in between them with his mace.)* You cannot allow this. This is not a swayamwara. Besides, this man, my cousin, Arjun, is poor and lives a nomadic life in the forest. I am a prince in full standing; I claim your daughter as my prize.

GANGA (DRUPADA) My daughter, you cannot marry a poor man. You are used to a life of luxury.

DRAUPADI If I cannot marry him, I will not marry at all.

RADHA (DURYODHANA) *(Grabbing hold of her arm.)* You are mine. You will come with me.

GANGA (DRUPADA) Let go of her. As you have already pointed out, this is not a swayamwara; if you try to abduct her you will be committing a crime.

RADHA (DURYODHANA) If this is not a swayamwara, she cannot choose a husband.

GANGA (DRUPADA) Nevertheless, my daughter has made a choice.

RADHA (DURYODHANA) You cannot ignore our customs. She will come with me.

(The women who have been musicians doff their masks, assume their roles as women and surround DURYODHANA.*)*

WOMEN Duryodhana, if you cannot accept Draupadi's decision, leave this place. We will not allow you to commit any violence here.

RADHA (DURYODHANA) *(Laughs.)* Are you *women* going to stop me?

(He wields his mace. The women take up karate stances. He comes to attack them. They trip him and remove his mace.)

WOMEN Please leave.

*(*DURYODHANA *glowers at them and then begins to walk off. One of the women runs after him and gives him his mace. He takes it from her roughly.)*

WOMEN *(Shaking hands with* BRIHANNALA *and* SIKANDI.*)* The karate lessons really paid off. Thanks.

GANGA (DRUPADA) *(Clearing her throat loudly to remind them that the scene is not yet over.)* Draupadi, are you certain that you want to marry this man?

DRAUPADI Oh yes, father. I have never been more certain of anything in my life.

GANGA (DRUPADA) Very well, I consent. Shall I make arrangements for the marriage or will you?

BRIHANNALA Wait a minute, why am I not being consulted?

GANGA (DRUPADA) Sorry, did you want to arrange the wedding? Draupadi is such a good organiser…

BRIHANNALA No, no. I don't want to get married.

(Everyone is surprised.)

GANGA (DRUPADA) You object?

BRIHANNALA Yes, I do.

(There is a bit of a stir among the women.)

SIKANDI Oh, come on, Bri. This is only a play

you know. You're acting a part. You're supposed to accept.

BRIHANNALA But this is the same thing all over again. I may as well be in the epic.

SUBADHRA It's not the same. This was not a swayamwara.

DRAUPADI Most important of all, you are my only husband. I have not been saddled with all your brothers as well. We two will be together all the time.

GANGA *(Doffing her mask.)* Yes, we have changed the story. Women are not ignored here.

*(*BRIHANNALA *is about to protest but* SIKANDI *whispers in* BRIHANNALA*'s ear and the two of them move off,* BRIHANNALA *still obviously agitated.* DRAUPADI *starts to go after them but is called back by* GANGA.*)*

GANGA Draupadi, where are you going? We have to prepare for the next scene.

DRAUPADI All right. I don't know what's the trouble with Arjun.

SUBADHRA He played his part all right.

DRAUPADI He doesn't seem to be himself.

RADHA Well, this is a come-down for him; he was the hero of the epic. Anyway, let's get on with the next scene. *(She gives* SUBADHRA *a blindfold.)* Here put this on. You'll play my mother. *(She puts her own mask on.)*

SUBADHRA Gandhari! We should have let her join us. Then she could have played this part.

HIDIMBA No, she loves her blindfold too much.

GANGA *(Calling.)* Sikandi! We need you to introduce the next scene. Radha, where's my mask. I am playing Dussasana now.

RADHA You're playing my brother, my extremely evil brother, who wants to but can't quite match up to my excesses.

GANGA Is that a challenge? Just watch me in the next scene. I'll outdo you. *(Gets her mask and puts it on and roars.)* Sikandi, where are you?

SIKANDI *(Running in.)* Bri is going to narrate. He doesn't want a part in this play.

GANGA Tell him to hurry.

SIKANDI He's coming. He's just getting his guitar. He thought he might sing parts of the narration.

*(*BRIHANNALA *comes running in with his guitar.)*

DRAUPADI Why don't you want to be in the play?

BRIHANNALA For the same reason that you don't want to be in the epic.

DRAUPADI But this is different. There is freedom here.

BRIHANNALA Is there?

GANGA Shall we begin?

HIDIMBA Sikandi get dressed. Hurry up.

*(*SIKANDI *takes off karate jacket, puts on* DRAUPADI*'s sari and wig.* BRIHANNALA *speaks the introduction to the next scene strumming his guitar in accompaniment.)*

BRIHANNALA Despite Draupadi's rejection of him, Duryodhana is determined to capture her and he and his brother, Dussasana *(A roar from* GANGA.*)*, seize her while she is walking in the garden.

*(*SIKANDI, *dressed in the sari* DRAUPADI *wore earlier, walks about, humming. S/he is happy and does little pirouettes.* DURYODHANA *and* DUSSASANA *stalk her/him and suddenly spring on her/him. S/he struggles and tries to scream but* DURYODHANA *knocks her/him out. Then he and his brother carry her/him off.)*

BRIHANNALA Duryodhana and Dussasana bring Draupadi to their mother, Gandhari.

RADHA (DURYODHANA) Mother, look at the bhiksha we have brought.

GANGA *(Laughing.)* That's a good one; the Pandavas couldn't have put it better.

SUBADHRA (GANDHARI) Bhiksha? Alms? Why have you been begging for alms? At any rate, you know I can't see, so share it among yourselves.

RADHA (DURYODHANA) *(Guffawing.)* Amongst all my brothers?

SUBADHRA(GANDHARI) Yes, of course.

RADHA (DURYODHANA) Well, well, well Draupadi. This time you'll have a hundred husbands, not just five. And I am the first.

KUNTHI *(Entering.)* What is going on here? What are you doing with my daughter-in-law?

RADHA (DURYODHANA) She is not your daughter-in-law. She is my wife, our wife. Isn't that so mother? You told us to share her, didn't you?

KUNTHI For goodness sake, can't you be original? Quoting straight out of the *Mahabarath* and not even your lines.

GANGA (DUSSASANA) They should have been ours in the first place. We know how to satisfy a woman. Your sons can't appreciate this tasty morsel. We'll show her a good time *(To* SIKANDI*)*, won't we darling?
RADHA (DURYODHANA) Don't hide behind that sari; it won't protect you. *(*DURYODHANA *catches hold of one end of the sari and starts to pull it off her.)*
KUNTHI *(Comes forward to intervene but* DUSSASANA *wards her off.)* Gandhari, are you going to allow this disgrace to your family. Look at what is happening.
RADHA (DURYODHANA) *(Laughing.)* My mother will never remove her blindfold.
KUNTHI Gandhari! Your son is attempting to violate my daughter-in-law.
SUBADHRA(GANDHARI) Where is Krishna? He helped before.
KUNTHI Gods and magic tricks! For goodness sake, this is not the epic. Come on Gandhari stop your son.
SUBADHRA (GANDHARI) How can I? I am blind.

(As DURYODHANA *comes to the end of the sari, he and* DUSSASANA *are full of glee.* SIKANDI *hides his identity with the long hair of the wig.)*

RADHA (DURYODHANA) *(Laughing uproariously.)* In the epic, the sari never came to an end. *(He pulls the end off* SIKANDI*. Then walks around, showing off the sari.)* Behold ladies and gentlemen, one ordinary sari, with an end. *(He laughs.)*

*(*SIKANDI *stands with head bowed.* DURYODHANA *throws the sari to one side and rubs his hands in anticipation.)*

RADHA (DURYODHANA) And now for the prize.

*(*SIKANDI *begins to whimper.)*

RADHA (DURYODHANA) *(To* BRIHANNALA*)* Hey, Arjun. This is my feast. You can have the scraps when I'm through.
GANGA (DUSSASANA) *(Also to* BRIHANNALA.*)* No, when all of us are through. All hundred brothers. You know five was never enough for her. *(Laughs.)*

*(*BRIHANNALA *suddenly comes at them both in a rage. They grab hold of him and push him to one side.)*

RADHA (DURYODHANA) *(Advancing on* SIKANDI.*)* You're much better off with me. That is no man. *(He kneels before* SIKANDI.*)* Now, come and sit on my knee.

*(*DUSSASANA *grabs hold of* SIKANDI *by the hair, removing the wig as he plops* SIKANDI *onto* DURYODHANA*'s thigh.* DURYODHANA *stares for a moment at* SIKANDI*, then jumps up in horror.)*

RADHA (DURYODHANA) This is a man.

*(*SIKANDI *sidles up to* DURYODHANA*, who pushes him away. Everyone watching begins to laugh.)*

SIKANDI *(Pursing his lips, pursues* DURYODHANA *and* DUSSASANA.*)* Oh baby, baby, baby. Come to me. I'm dying for you.

*(*DURYODHANA *and* DUSSASANA *flee from* SIKANDI *in homophobic terror. The women capture* DURYODHANA *and* DUSSASANA *and hold them down.)*

WOMEN *(To* SIKANDI*)* Come on, Draupadi. Time for revenge. Don't you want these tasty morsels.

*(*SUBADHRA/GANDHARI*, who removed her blindfold when the excitement began mounting, comes forward laughing heartily. She embraces* SIKANDI*, then finds* BRIHANNALA *and embraces him too.)*

SUBADHRA (GANDHARI) *(Holding the hands of both* SIKANDI *and* BRIHANNALA.*)* My wonderful sons. What a sight for sore eyes you two are. What a trick to play on those dreadful boors. I am proud of you, Duryodhana and Dussasana.
RADHA (DURYODHANA) Mother, you have removed your blindfold.
SUBADHRA (GANDHARI) I had to take if off; I couldn't miss all the fun. *(She hugs* SIKANDI *and* BRIHANNALA.*)* My wonderful sons.
GANGA (DUSSASANA) But mother, they are not your sons. We are.
SUBADHRA (GANDHARI) What? *(To* SIKANDI *and* BRIHANNALA.*)* Is this true? *(They nod.)*

*(*GANDHARI *walks slowly over to* DUSSASANA *and then to* DURYODHANA.*)*

SUBADHRA (GANDHARI) *(Recoiling sharply.)*

Where's my blindfold? *(Someone gives it to her. She puts it on hastily.)* I'm happy the way I am.

(Everyone bursts out laughing. RADHA *and* GANGA *take off masks.)*

RADHA We showed them, didn't we?
GANGA Thought we couldn't defend ourselves because we were a bunch of women. But we fooled them.
RADHA Sikandi, you were great.
GANGA I'm glad you joined us.
SIKANDI What did you think, Bri?
BRIHANNALA Over-the-top. You call that acting?
SIKANDI What! You jealous old cow.

(The two of them engage in a mock fight.)

DRAUPADI That's enough now. Let's get on with the play.
URVASI Oh come on, Draupadi. We're just having a little fun.
DRAUPADI You may be, but I am not.
GANGA All right. What's our next scene?
DRAUPADI We should tackle your story.
GANGA My story! But I have no story now that I am just an ordinary woman who does not marry and have children.
RADHA Just listen to yourself. Are you saying that unless you become a wife and mother, you have no identity?
KUNTHI Are women nothing in themselves?
SUBADHRA Do women have to marry and have children?
GANGA No, it was that way in the epic.
RADHA Now if you tell us you have no story, you are confirming the epic.
HIDIMBA I told you we wouldn't change anything.
GANGA No. No. No. I have a life of my own and a reality that I create.
RADHA Well come on then. Let's have it.
GANGA All right.
SUBADHRA *(Taking mask.)* I am going to play Santanu, Ganga's husband.
GANGA Only in the epic.
BRIHANNALA This is the story of Ganga, a very beautiful woman, who meets King Santanu on the banks of the Ganges. They fall madly, passionately in love.
SUBADHRA (SANTANU) You are the most beautiful woman I have ever met. I cannot live without you. Please be my wife.
GANGA I love you too, but I cannot marry you.
SUBADHRA (SANTANU) Why? Are you married already?
GANGA No, I just don't want the responsibilities of marriage.
SUBADHRA (SANTANU) How can you say such a thing? If you love me, you'll marry me.
GANGA Can't we just be lovers?
SUBADHRA (SANTANU) That would never be accepted by my people.
GANGA Then we must forget each other.
SUBADHRA (SANTANU) I can't give you up.
GANGA I love you and I am willing to live with you but I will never marry you.
SUBADHRA (SANTANU) But our children will be outcasts.
GANGA Children? I am not going to have any children.
SUBADHRA (SANTANU) Don't you want children?
GANGA No.
SUBADHRA (SANTANU) But that is unnatural.
GANGA Why?
SUBADHRA (SANTANU) You are a woman. It is your function.
GANGA No, not unless I choose it. Tell me, why are you so desperate for children?
SUBADHRA (SANTANU) Well, every man wants a son and heir.
GANGA To carry on the line?
SUBADHRA (SANTANU) That's only natural.
GANGA I'm not so clear about what is natural.
SUBADHRA (SANTANU) You're not thinking clearly. You love me and I love you. What could be more…
GANGA Natural?
SUBADHRA (SANTANU) Yes. It's natural to get married and raise a family.
GANGA That's not my dream.
SUBADHRA (SANTANU) *(Kneeling before her.)* I swear that if we marry, nothing will interfere with your dreams. I will not tie you down in any way.
GANGA You are happy not to have any children?
SUBADHRA (SANTANU) Must it be like that?
GANGA You should put children out of your mind. You are not destined to beget a long line.
SUBADHRA (SANTANU) What are you talking about?
GANGA I'm sorry to disappoint you but if you

knew the truth, perhaps you wouldn't be so bound by tradition. *(She signals for the family tree. The family tree could be a slide projection or a chart held by two women.)*

SUBADHRA (SANTANU) What are you doing?

GANGA I have taken this family tree from the epic. There are some things we can't change.

SUBADHRA (SANTANU) My family tree?

GANGA Yes. Do you see how abruptly your line ends? There are no grandchildren here.

SUBADHRA (SANTANU) But the epic began with me. That means that I am father to all that followed.

GANGA You were meant to think that. But it didn't work out that way.

SUBADHRA (SANTANU) *(Examining the family tree.)* But I have three sons.

GANGA One, my son Bhishma, took a vow of celibacy and never married. The other two, your sons by your second wife, Satyavati, died before they produced any heirs. Your line disappeared completely.

SUBADHRA (SANTANU) That is a lie. The main conflict in the *Mahabarath* is between the Pandavas and Kauravas and both clans are descended from me.

GANGA Look at the tree. The real fathers of the *Mahabarath* are Parasar and his son Vyasa, the father of Dhritarashtra, Pandu and Vidur.

SUBADHRA (SANTANU) But Ganga, the epic begins with me, with us, you and me.

GANGA But Vyasa wrote the story and fathered the Kurus. It seems that he wanted authorship in every sense of the word. I guess he was just as obsessed with paternity as you are.

SUBADHRA (SANTANU) But why did he begin the epic with me?

GANGA You have to admit, it is a gripping opening. A mother drowning her newborn babies, a father paralysed, unable to stop her. Vyasa knows how to capture attention.

SUBADHRA (SANTANU) *(Getting rid of the family tree.)* I don't believe this. All I know is that I want you. *(SANTANU grabs holds of her.)* You will marry me.

BRIHANNALA (NARRATOR) Santanu married Ganga. He was happy. Because they were passionately in love, he was confident that they would have children. But a year went by, then another and another. Ganga did not conceive.

(KUNTHI puts on mask of SANTANU'S MOTHER.)

KUNTHI (SANTANU'S MOTHER) Santanu, this woman you brought home from the banks of the Ganges; this woman whom you could not live without; this woman is barren.

(SIKANDI puts on mask of BHISHMA, son of GANGA.)

SIKANDI (BHISHMA) No, she can't be. She has to give birth to me. I have a major role in the epic.

KUNTHI (SANTANU'S MOTHER) Who are you?

SIKANDI (BHISHMA) I am Bhishma, the famous son of Ganga.

GANGA Go away, Bhishma. We don't have a place for you here.

SIKANDI (BHISHMA) But mother, I am a major character; the soul of integrity in the epic.

GANGA You, the soul of integrity. Don't be ridiculous.

SIKANDI (BHISHMA) *(To SANTANU.)* Listen, Santanu, don't let her play games with you. I am your pledge of immortality.

GANGA How can you be? The line ends with you. You remain celibate all your life.

SIKANDI (BHISHMA) *(To SANTANU.)* Don't listen to her. Stand up for your rights as a man. She owes it to us to become a mother.

KUNTHI (SANTANU'S MOTHER) I told you not to bring that woman into my house. She's just a whore. Tell her to get out.

SUBADHRA (SANTANU) I can't mother. I love her.

KUNTHI (SANTANU'S MOTHER) Love, love. What's all this rubbish about love. She's not a woman. Attending meetings all day long. Meeting, meetings. Bringing all kinds of funny people here. And all they do is plant trees. Plant trees. I ask you. Tell her to go.

SIKANDI (BHISHMA) No, grandmother. Don't chase her away.

SUBADHRA (SANTANU) Mother, you don't understand her.

KUNTHI (SANTANU'S MOTHER) Understand? What's to understand? She's a witch. She can't have babies. Get rid of her.

SIKANDI (BHISHMA) You can't get rid of her. If she goes, I won't be born. Your memory will die without me.

GANGA It never lived anyway.

KUNTHI (SANTANU'S MOTHER) This

woman can't give you children. Send her away. I will find you a proper wife.

SIKANDI (BHISHMA) Make her stay. My life depends upon it.

GANGA There's no need to trouble yourselves. It does not depend on you, whether I stay or go. It depends on me and I have decided to go.

KUNTHI (SANTANU'S MOTHER) Good. Go away. We don't need you. We have gardeners to plant our trees.

SIKANDI (BHISHMA) *(Grabbing hold of* GANGA.*)* Santanu, stop her. Don't let her go.

SUBADHRA (SANTANU) Ganga, please don't go. I don't care about having children. I just need you by my side.

SIKANDI (BHISHMA) Can't we compromise? You don't have to have eight babies; one is enough.

GANGA I am sorry, Santanu. But I think it is better if we part. We want different things from life and I can't give you what you really want. Your mother is right. You should let her find you a woman who wants to be a wife and mother.

SIKANDI (BHISHMA) No, it's your duty to have children. *(Pushes her forward to* SANTANU.*)* There take her....by force. She is your wife. You have every right.

SUBADHRA (SANTANU) There's no point. She wants to go.

SIKANDI (BHISHMA) *(To* GANGA.*)* What about me? If you go, I will be aborted.

GANGA If I stay, I will be. I'm sorry, I want my own life.

SIKANDI (BHISHMA) But mother, you're killing me. *(He drops to his knees.)*

GANGA Goodbye. I have a mission: to keep the earth green. It's bigger than you or me. *(She leaves.)*

SIKANDI (BHISHMA) *(Screaming with pain.)* There should be laws against abortion. Help me. Help me. I am being torn from the womb. *(He dies.)*

SUBADHRA (SANTANU) *(Takes off* SIKANDI's *mask and examines it fondly.)* I could have had a son but he was aborted.

SIKANDI *(Sitting up.)* Rubbish. He wasn't even conceived in our play. Quite frankly, I am glad I could help get rid of Bhishma.

BRIHANNALA But you gave such a performance; I mean introducing the whole abortion angle.

SIKANDI Really Bri, I am a method actor, you know. I gave myself to the part completely.

SUBADHRA *(Taking off her mask.)* I really believed you. I thought you were going to persuade Ganga with your abortion argument.

SIKANDI *(Laughing.)* Ganga wasn't going to fall for that.

SUBADHRA What do you mean?

GANGA It was a matter of abort or be aborted. *(Pointing to the audience.)* They don't really know us, the women. If you ask them out there, they can only identify us as mother of, or wife of, or sister of, but not as individuals in our own right.

SIKANDI That's how they know me too, as an instrument; if they know me at all.

BRIHANNALA It's not just the women who are trapped. We are too. Just because we get the action does not make us any the less puppets.

DRAUPADI I don't know why you're complaining. Men control everything; what we do, think and believe. You're a man; you can make choices.

BRIHANNALA That's not true. From the time you are little, people keep stuffing toy weapons in your hands and pushing you towards violence.

DRAUPADI No, no. It's different for men. You are not trapped by your gender.

BRIHANNALA Yes, I was.

DRAUPADI *(Laughing sarcastically.)* The only time you were trapped was when you were forced to disguise yourself as Brihannala.

BRIHANNALA It was the only time I was not forced.

DRAUPADI But you were in drag. You had to play the part of a gay musician.

BRIHANNALA It wasn't a part.

DRAUPADI *(Very upset.)* I don't want to hear this.

BRIHANNALA No, you want to keep me locked in an image that is not of my making. This is not what I expected here. *(He walks out.)*

SIKANDI Bri is right, you know. With our customs and traditions, we keep building cages for ourselves, for both men and women.

HIDIMBA Have you built a cage, Draupadi?

DRAUPADI I don't want to hear your rubbish about cages.

SIKANDI But I was born in one. Let's examine my story.

DRAUPADI I am not interested in your story.

SIKANDI Why? Because I am a man?

DRAUPADI You eradicated Bhishma. Without Bhishma, you don't exist.

SIKANDI That was Ganga's story. I remained within her framework. We have to expand that framework to include my story.

DRAUPADI But your story is irrelevant.

HIDIMBA *(To* SIKANDI*)* I warned you about cages right from the beginning.

SUBADHRA Sikandi, you are a man; we came here to find freedom as women. You are confusing us.

SIKANDI No, no, not confusing; I am trying to fuse our stories. We have to break through barriers, all barriers.

GANGA Look Sikandi, we have suffered long enough. Now we have taken charge of our own lives, we cannot have a man come here and tell us what to do.

SIKANDI All right, go ahead and build your narrow world. It won't be any better than the one you left.

RADHA Wait a minute. I don't understand what's going on here. Why can't we examine Sikandi's story?

GANGA We don't want to be dominated by men.

SIKANDI Only by women?

GANGA No, we don't want domination of any kind. But we have to help ourselves first.

RADHA Then we will change nothing. That is exactly how people have always thought; we'll free ourselves first and then help others. Unless we build together, we will only build cages.

HIDIMBA Are we capable of building anything else?

DRAUPADI Don't get Hidimba started on her one and only theme.

SUBADHRA I don't really understand what's going on here but I would like to hear Sikandi's story.

KUNTHI I don't know what's wrong with all of you. You know that Sikandi didn't begin life as a man.

SIKANDI No, wait a minute.

KUNTHI You wait. Sikandi was forced to take on a man's role in order to be able to defeat Bhishma in the great Kurukshetra war.

UTTARAI I don't understand.

RADHA Sikandi was born as a woman, Amba.

SIKANDI But that's not my story.

RADHA Just be quiet and let me finish. Amba loved Bhishma and when he rejected her, she was reborn as a man so s/he could take revenge.

URVASI Well, why didn't someone say so in the first place? Come on, we're doing Sikandi's story.

RADHA What's the matter, Draupadi? Do you have something personal against Sikandi?

DRAUPADI I don't know what you mean.

RADHA Is it because of Sikandi and Bri....

DRAUPADI *(Interrupting)* Oh, for goodness sake. Let's get on with it. I don't care whose story we tell next.

GANGA Then let's get ready for the next scene. Someone call Brihannala.

SIKANDI I'll fetch him.

DRAUPADI No, I will. You get ready for the scene. It is your tale, isn't it? *(She exits.)*

SIKANDI No, it isn't.

GANGA Don't take any notice of Draupadi.

SIKANDI I know.

RADHA I am going to play Ambika.

KUNTHI And I will be Ambalika.

SIKANDI Who's going to play Amba?

URVASI Why you, of course.

SIKANDI But I can't.

RADHA (AMBIKA) AND GANGA (AMBALIKA) *(Arms outstretched to* SIKANDI*)* Dear sister. Isn't it wonderful. We are all soon to be married. *(They hold hands and romp in a circle,* SIKANDI *most unwillingly.)*

SIKANDI *(Protesting)* No, wait a minute. I can't play this role.

GANGA Don't be so modest. You're a wonderful actor.

KUNTHI How are we going to play this scene? We need someone to abduct the girls.

RADHA That's Bhishma. We need a Bhishma.

SIKANDI I'll play Bhishma. I played him before.

GANGA That's right and he was aborted. We can't have a Bhishma.

DRAUPADI *(Entering in time to hear this)* I told you we'd have problems with this story.

RADHA Let's have Bhishma in the scene. We can find some way of justifying his existence later.

HIDIMBA Aha, now we resort to magic tricks. *(Calling)* Bring the dead back to life.

RADHA Shut up, Hidimba! Haven't you heard of poetic licence? We'll work it all out later.

SUBADHRA Don't worry, Ganga. Bhishma won't be connected with you in any way.

HIDIMBA You can change his name.

RADHA We can't *(Pointing at audience)*, for their convenience. They know Bhishma.

HIDIMBA If they've read the *Mahabarath*.

DRAUPADI Hidimba, stop putting obstacles in the way.

HIDIMBA I beg your pardon. Don't take any notice of me. I'm not even here.

DRAUPADI Are we ready?

SIKANDI I can't play Amba. Don't force me to play this role.

URVASI Stop arguing. You are the obvious choice for the part.

GANGA Yes. Who's playing Bhishma? Here's his mask.

BRIHANNALA I'll play Bhishma. *(Puts on mask.)*

SIKANDI Bri, you traitor.

BRIHANNALA Have you forgotten? This is a play. You're only acting a part.

GANGA Draupadi, you'll have to narrate.

DRAUPADI *(Narrating unwillingly.)* This is the story of the woman, Amba, whose life was ruined by Bhishma and against whom she swore revenge...

SIKANDI I'm sorry to interrupt, but that is how it happened in the epic.

DRAUPADI *(Viciously)* Do you want to narrate and play the main role as well?

GANGA Draupadi, you play King Salwa. I'll narrate. *(She hands* DRAUPADI *her mask.)*

GANGA This is the story of Amba.

SIKANDI But that's not my story.

GANGA Be patient. I'm getting to it. Now stop interrupting. This is the story of Amba, the woman who became a man in order to control her own destiny. We begin with the scene of the swayamwara of Amba, Ambika and Ambalika the three daughters of the King of Kasi; who were to choose husbands.

*(*SIKANDI *shakes his head in frustration but resigns himself to the role of* AMBA. *The others as a group of suitors pretend to enter a great hall and seat themselves. The three young princesses enter and are seated near to the throne of their father. The king makes a grand entrance and is seated. The king is about to explain the proceedings when* BHISHMA *jumps into the midst of the assembly.)*

BRIHANNALA (BHISHMA) *(Loud, authoritarian and challenging.)* "Of all the ways of choosing a bride, the sages have mentioned, the noblest is that in which a maiden is acquired by force from amidst a valiant gathering such as this." *(Changing to an explanatory tone and addressing the audience.)* This is a direct quote from R.K. Narayan's book, *The Mahabharat*, London, 1978, page four.

SUBADHRA (KING OF KASI) What do you mean by this uncalled-for behaviour?

BRIHANNALA (BHISHMA) This is what I mean. *(He dashes forward, grabs the three young women and rushes off with them. All the princes go after him and he demolishes the lot of them with his sword, karate kicks, etc. Bodies fall all over the place. He grabs hold of the girls again.)*

SIKANDI (AMBA) You've killed them all. *(Struggling with him.)* Let me go. I want to be with my beloved, King Salwa. Have you killed him, you monster?

KUNTHI (AMBALIKA) *(Swooning over* BHISHMA.*)* Monster, oh no. You're my hero. So handsome, so brave.

RADHA (AMBIKA) *(Also swooning.)* So strong and forthright.

SIKANDI (AMBA) You brute, let go of us at once.

RADHA (AMBIK) and KUNTHI (AMBALIKA.) *(Clinging to* BHISHMA.*)* Our hero. We are the luckiest women alive.

SIKANDI (AMBA) Are you mad? This is a savage. Salwa, Salwa, my beloved. I will come back to you.

(BRIHANNALA/BHISHMA *carries off the girls.* AMBIKA *and* AMBALIKA *go willingly and help him to control* AMBA, *who is kicking and screaming.)*

HIDIMBA *(One of those killed by* BHISHMA, *sitting up and taking off mask.)* I don't believe this.

GANGA You understand now, why I didn't want to be his mother, don't you.

UTTARAI *(Another one of those killed by* BHISHMA, *sitting up and taking off mask.)* Did you hear what he said? Taking the women by force was the noblest way to do it!

URVASI *(Another one of those killed by* BHISHMA, *sitting up and taking off mask.)* Glorifying rape. That's what he was doing!

UTTARAI We are going to have to think seriously about including Bhishma in the play.

URVASI I'm afraid we have to have him. Rape is a very common problem. We may have banished it from our world but they *(Pointing to the audience.)* have not.

DRAUPADI Can we get on with the next scene? I'd like to get this part of the play over with.

GANGA (NARRATOR) Bhishma brings the princesses to Hastinapura as brides for his stepbrother, the King Vichitravirya.

SIKANDI (AMBA) Why did you bring me here? I want nothing to do with you. I want to go back. I will never marry you.

RADHA (AMBIKA) and KUNTHI (AMBALIKA) But we will. You don't need her. We'll make you forget all about her.

RADHA (AMBIKA) You are so strong and brave; the way you vanquished all those other princes.

KUNTHI (AMBALIKA) And you did that, just for us. Such a great prince. You wanted us! We are so grateful.

RADHA (AMBIKA) and KUNTHI (AMBALIKA) It will be an honour to be your wife. *(They touch his feet.)*

SIKANDI (AMBA) I will never marry you. I will kill myself first.

(Enter UTTARAI *as* SATYAVATI, BHISHMA*'s stepmother.)*

UTTARAI (SATYAVATI) *(Melodramatically.)* Oh, my dear Bhishma, you have brought three brides. You are so noble and pure of heart.

BRIHANNALA (BHISHMA) *(Equally melodramatic.)* Mother, I gave you my word that the Kuru clan would never die out.

SIKANDI Talk about over-the-top.

UTTARAI (SATYAVATI) My dear child, *(Coming forward to embrace* AMBA.*)* I know how grateful you are. This is such a wonderful opportunity for you.

SIKANDI (AMBA) I will never marry this barbarian.

RADHA (AMBIKA) and KUNTHI (AMBALIKA) But we will. He is our knight in shining armour. *(They stand on either side of him.)*

UTTARAI (SATYAVATI) Oh, my dears. This is not your husband-to-be. He has taken a vow of celibacy. He brought you here as brides for my son, the King of Hastinapura.

RADHA (AMBIKA) and KUNTHI (AMBALIKA) Oh, Amba, isn't it wonderful. We are going to be queens. Surely you must consent now.

SIKANDI (AMBA) Never. Let me go. I want nothing to do with any of you. I made my own choice long ago. I will marry King Salwa and no one else.

UTTARAI (SATYAVATI) Oh, dear Bhishma. What an unpleasant creature. Are you sure this is a princess? Sister of these two?

BRIHANNALA (BHISHMA) She's the real prize mother. The kind of woman who will produce brave, strong, noble sons. Ah, if only I hadn't been so rash in my vows...

UTTARAI (SATYAVATI) Well, I don't think she will do at all. Besides, I don't know if I can trust you.

BRIHANNALA (BHISHMA) Oh mother, I am pained. I gave my word. I am called Bhishma. "One of firm vow" *(Changing to matter of fact tone and addressing audience.)* Ibid., page four.

UTTARAI (SATYAVATI) I do trust you, my son. But I fear she will not make my boy a good wife. *(Sotto voce.)* She'll scare him to death. I expected you to bring only one girl. One is hard enough for my son to cope with; two will make him very nervous; three will kill him. And especially one like her. *(Indicates* AMBA*)* I think we should send her back.

BRIHANNALA (BHISHMA) Mother, your wish is my command. *(Turning to* AMBA.*)* Well, Princess, it would not be right to keep you here against your will...

*(*AMBA *laughs cynically.)*

BRIHANNALA (BHISHMA) You will be sent to King Salwa as you request. Are you sure you want to go?

SIKANDI (AMBA) Yes.

(Masks are changed and new attitudes adopted. DRAUPADI *plays the* KING OF SALWA. SUBADHRA *plays his* COUNSELLOR; UTTARAI *is the* MESSENGER.*)*

GANGA The scene now moves to the court of King Salwa.

UTTARAI (MESSENGER) *(Entering the King's presence.)* Your majesty, we have an entourage from the court of Hastinapura.

DRAUPADI (SALWA) Who leads the group?

UTTARAI (MESSENGER) Bhishma, sire.

DRAUPADI (SALWA) Bhishma himself. Well, well, well. Is this diplomacy or audacity? What do you think Counsellor?

SUBADHRA (COUNSELLOR) One could hardly call him diplomatic after he snatched Amba and her sisters from their swayamwara.

DRAUPADI (SALWA) He was perfectly within the law. A master stroke of diplomacy; to take the most difficult and manly route. I must say, I was lost in admiration.

SUBADHRA (COUNSELLOR) Then his attendance here today must be more evidence of diplomacy. You should receive him and his retinue, your majesty.

DRAUPADI (SALWA) Very well. *(To* MESSENGER.*)* Show them in.

(BRIHANNALA/BHISHMA, SIKANDI/AMBA, *who have been standing with their backs to the scene, turn around and are in the presence of* KING SALWA.)

DRAUPADI (SALWA) *(Startled at the sight of* AMBA.*)* Why, it is Princess Amba.

SIKANDI (AMBA) *(Trying to push past* BHISHMA, *who holds her back.)* Salwa, Salwa, I am so glad to see you.

BRIHANNALA (BHISHMA) *(Greeting* SALWA *and his* COUNSELLOR.*)* I am most grateful to you for receiving us. I have come on a very delicate mission.

DRAUPADI (SALWA) I see you have brought your wife with you. I must say Bhishma, you swept those girls off, with style. I envied you. So you have finally given up that foolish vow of celibacy. Eh?

SIKANDI (AMBA) I am not his wife. How could you think such a thing?

DRAUPADI (SALWA) Excuse me, I need to confer with my Counsellor for a moment. *(The group turn their backs on* KING *and* COUNSELLOR.*)* Counsellor, what do you make of this? Why does he allow his wife to speak out of turn?

SUBADHRA (COUNSELLOR) He does not seem to have any control over her, sire.

DRAUPADI (SALWA) No control over his wife! Doesn't he beat her?

SUBADHRA (COUNSELLOR) Your majesty, this Amba has a reputation. She is quite a little fury. You had a lucky escape there.

DRAUPADI (SALWA) Escape? What do you mean?

SUBADHRA (COUNSELLOR) Well, sire, it is no secret that she meant to choose you at her swayamwara.

DRAUPADI (SALWA) *(Embarrassed.)* Oh, was that common knowledge?

SUBADHRA (COUNSELLOR) I am sure the little minx spread the rumour herself. You would not have been party to such a thing; not with a woman like that, would you sire?

DRAUPADI (SALWA) *(Embarrassed.)* No, no. Of course not. Well, let's find out what they want.

SUBADHRA (COUNSELLOR) Honoured guests, the king is ready to hear you now.

DRAUPADI (SALWA) My dear Bhishma, I am a little confused. Your delegation seems to be in some disarray. You and your wife do not seem in agreement.

SIKANDI (AMBA) I am not his wife. Why do you keep assuming that?

BRIHANNALA (BHISHMA) Your majesty, Princess Amba is not my wife.

DRAUPADI (SALWA) You sly old dog, you. Well, my estimation of you goes up even more. Panache, that's what it is. I'm afraid I lead a less colourful life.

SIKANDI (AMBA) *(Breaking free and confronting* SALWA.*)* You admire this man for abducting me?

DRAUPADI (SALWA) What he did was courageous beyond words.

SIKANDI (AMBA) Other princes challenged him. Why couldn't you? You should have been in the forefront; if you loved me you wouldn't have let him get away.

DRAUPADI (SALWA) But this is Bhishma.

SIKANDI (AMBA) Were you afraid of him? Or did you fall in love with him at the swayamwara?

DRAUPADI (SALWA) How dare you speak to me like this? *(To* BHISHMA*)* Get your woman away from me.

BRIHANNALA (BHISHMA) I'm sorry, your majesty. I thought you two had an understanding.

DRAUPADI (SALWA) What if we did? You have won her and your claim supersedes mine.

SIKANDI (AMBA) He assaulted my rights as a human being. How can you respect that?

DRAUPADI (SALWA) What he did was perfectly legal. In fact it was sublime. A tradition for the bravest of the brave. If we don't respect our traditions, we cannot have a civilized society.

SIKANDI (AMBA) Is that a law? A law that allows me to be violated? You call that civilized?

DRAUPADI (SALWA) He has not dishonoured you. He has paid you the highest compliment a man can offer. He demonstrated his supreme manhood, his incomparable courage for you.

SIKANDI (AMBA) I don't believe this! You are in love with him!

DRAUPADI (SALWA) There is no doubt that I have the greatest admiration for him.

SIKANDI (AMBA) Your admiration for him is much stronger than your love for me.

DRAUPADI (SALWA) Bhishma, what has brought you here today? It is a very auspicious occasion and I am honoured to have you as my guest.

BRIHANNALA (BHISHMA) Your majesty, I am at a loss. I came here to return Amba to you, her rightful husband. She had fixed her choice on you at her swayamwara.

DRAUPADI (SALWA) Well, she obviously does not understand our traditions. I have no claim on her whatsoever. You won her fair and square.

BRIHANNALA (BHISHMA) But your majesty, I have taken a vow of celibacy. I cannot marry her.

DRAUPADI (SALWA) That is not my problem. She belongs to you.

BRIHANNALA (BHISHMA) She has chosen you for her husband; I think that is a stronger claim.

SIKANDI (AMBA) Gentlemen, don't trouble yourselves further. What happens to me is no longer any concern of yours. I don't need either one of you. *(She turns on her heel and walks out.)*

DRAUPADI (SALWA) Poor confused woman. If only she knew her place, she would save herself so much trouble.

BRIHANNALA (BHISHMA) This is quite embarrassing.

DRAUPADI (SALWA) Oh, let's put it behind us. As it happens, you have arrived on my wedding day. I would be honoured if you would attend the ceremony.

BRIHANNALA (BHISHMA) Thank you, you are very gracious. I had no idea it was your wedding day. Please forgive me for my unceremonious arrival.

DRAUPADI (SALWA) No, no. You must forgive me. I am the one who has been discourteous; I should have informed you of the wedding and invited you to attend.

(They move off together, each trying to outdo the other in his apologies.)

SUBADHRA You see Draupadi, there was no harm in exploring Sikandi's story. It's perfectly relevant.

SIKANDI But that wasn't my story.

GANGA Not your story? Of course, it's your story.

SIKANDI That was Amba's story.

GANGA But you are Amba. You became a man only to destroy Bhishma.

SIKANDI All that is in the epic. I am not Amba. I look exactly like her, but I am not Amba. I am her grandson.

RADHA Her grandson?

SUBADHRA No, that can't be. Vyasa turns you into a man, puts you in front of Arjun in his chariot during the war so that Bhishma won't attack because he knows you are really a woman.

GANGA Another stroke of Vyasa's genius. A very clever twist in the story.

SIKANDI No, no. It's not. It is demeaning. Amba is simply an instrument, a shield to protect Arjun.

RADHA *(Shaking her head.)* It's becoming clearer and clearer; women in the epic are simply there to be exploited.

SUBADHRA Well, we've left all that behind now.

RADHA Have we? Look how we just jumped to the conclusion that Sikandi and Amba were the same person. Shows you our thinking is still determined by the epic.

GANGA We are going to have to watch ourselves very carefully to see that we are not still perpetuating the old ways.

UTTARAI Hidimba, don't say "I told you so."

KUNTHI So what do we do now?

SIKANDI Tell my story. You owe it to me.

GANGA All right. Shall I continue to narrate.

SUBADHRA I think you should play one of the roles. I'll take over the narration.

GANGA Shall I be the shaman? No, I'll be Sikandi's aunt.

RADHA I'll be his mother and Brihannala can be his friend.

SUBADHRA (NARRATOR) This is the story of Sikandi, the grandson of Amba. When Amba realized that she couldn't live with either Bhishma or Salwa, she went to live in the forest. She eventually married a man who, like her, wanted more freedom than customs and traditions would allow. Their son was the father of Sikandi.

(SIKANDI is playing a musical instrument and singing.)

RADHA (SIKANDI'S MOTHER) Sikandi, what are you doing? You have to get ready for the tournament. You are the best stick-fighter in the village.

SIKANDI *(Protesting.)* Mother.

RADHA (SIKANDI'S MOTHER) Well, you will

be after the competition today. Now get ready. *(She leaves.)*

*(*SIKANDI *picks up the skin he is supposed to wear, the shield and stick. He looks around and sees other clothes. He drops what he has picked up and goes to examine the other clothes – women's clothes. He begins to fondle and play with these and then begins to put them on. He puts on make-up, looks at himself in a mirror and laughs. He begins to prance around. His friend enters.)*

BRIHANNALA (SIKANDI'S FRIEND) *(Dressed in traditional stick-fighting gear.)* Hey, Sikandi, are you ready? I am going to beat the daylights out of you today. *(Stops and stares for a long moment.)*

SIKANDI *(Whirling around* FRIEND.*)* Well, what do you think?

*(*FRIEND *is tongue-tied.)*

SIKANDI *(Stops dancing around.)* Oh, all right. I'll change. I'll get ready for the stick fight.

BRIHANNALA (SIKANDI'S FRIEND) No, don't. *(*SIKANDI *looks at him a little puzzled.)* You look beautiful.

SIKANDI *(Laughing.)* Are you smitten?

BRIHANNALA (SIKANDI'S FRIEND) *(Confused.)* You are so beautiful.

SIKANDI Come, dance with me.

(They begin to dance, and the dance clearly develops into an expression of love. SIKANDI'S MOTHER *and* AUNT *enter.)*

RADHA (SIKANDI'S MOTHER) What's going on here? Stop this at once.

GANGA (SIKANDI'S AUNT) *(Staring at* SIKANDI *in shock.)* It is your mother-in-law, Amba, returned from the dead.

RADHA (SIKANDI'S MOTHER) Don't be ridiculous. This foolish boy is always getting up to this kind of nonsense. *(She rubs the make-up off* SIKANDI*'s face.)* Why do you keep on doing this? Haven't I told you, I don't want you dressing up in women's clothes? *(Turning on* SIKANDI'S FRIEND.*)* And what were you doing? Encouraging him in this sick fantasy?

GANGA (SIKANDI'S AUNT) *(Still awe-struck.)* The boy is possessed. His grandmother, Amba, has taken over his body.

RADHA (SIKANDI'S MOTHER) Rubbish. He just looks like her, that's all. Why he couldn't have taken after my side of the family, I don't know. His father was like this too.

GANGA (SIKANDI'S AUNT) He's haunted.

RADHA (SIKANDI'S MOTHER) *(Quite apprehensive.)* Don't talk such nonsense.

SIKANDI Mother, I'm sorry. I'll get dressed for the stick fight. *(Starts to pull off clothes and put on gear for a stick fight.)*

BRIHANNALA (SIKANDI'S FRIEND) I'll go on ahead of you. See you at the ground. *(He leaves hastily.)*

GANGA (SIKANDI'S AUNT) *(Shaking her head.)* He needs help.

RADHA (SIKANDI'S MOTHER) I don't know.

GANGA (SIKANDI'S AUNT) Oh sister, I have seen this before. There was a girl in the village. She rode on a motorbike, then she began to dress like a boy. She was haunted too; they had to beat it out of her. Only after she was exorcised did she come right.

RADHA (SIKANDI'S MOTHER) *(Clearly disturbed.)* Exorcised? But these are just naughty pranks. He'll get over it.

GANGA (SIKANDI'S AUNT) But he's been doing this for a long time. He must be exorcised. I'll call the shaman.

SIKANDI Mother, I'm sorry. I was just fooling around. I'm going to the grounds. I'll be late for the competition.

RADHA (SIKANDI'S MOTHER) No, you stay right here.

SIKANDI But mother, I can be champion. I know it. Don't you want that?

(Enter the SHAMAN/URVASI *with* SIKANDI'S AUNT. SIKANDI'S MOTHER *goes through the payment routine and then they proceed with the ceremony throughout which* SIKANDI *protests and thus brings down upon himself harsher and harsher treatment. At the end,* SIKANDI *is left lying exhausted and unhappy.)*

RADHA (SIKANDI'S MOTHER) *(Showing the muti she has obtained from the* SHAMAN.*)* I have to mix this with Sikandi's food every day and he should be all right after a few weeks.

GANGA (SIKANDI'S AUNT) You've done the right thing. I will go and see the other boy's mother. I think he is possessed too. *(She leaves eagerly.)*

RADHA (SIKANDI'S MOTHER) *(Kneeling next to her son.)* My poor boy. *(She strokes him.)* You have the same delusions as your father. But you will be better now. There, there.

Sleep. I'll be back in a little while. *(She leaves.)*

*(*SIKANDI *gets up slowly; looks for the women's clothes he had on before. He puts them on, puts on the make-up. He spreads out the clothes he has taken off in the place where he lay and then runs away.* SIKANDI'S MOTHER *enters with some food.)*

RADHA (SIKANDI'S MOTHER) Sikandi, sit up and eat a little; it will give you strength. Sikandi, where are you? *(She looks about and then notices his clothes spread to assume his shape.)* What's this? Oh my god, what's happened here? *(She stares at the clothes.)* He's been transported. Utterly transported. The spirits have claimed him as one of theirs. *(She stands up stoically.)* Perhaps it is for the best. In his confused state, his life would have been nothing but misery.

SUBADHRA (NARRATOR) Sikandi never returned to his family. He joined various groups of actors and performed all over the country. Then he met Brihannala and teamed up with him.

DRAUPADI That's ridiculous. Brihannala is not a real person. That was just an identity that Arjun assumed when he was in hiding in the thirteenth year of our banishment.

BRIHANNALA Look, are we reliving the *Mahabarath* or is this something new?

SIKANDI Arjun and banishment belong in the *Mahabarath.*

DRAUPADI I have my roots in the epic.

GANGA All right. We cannot entirely forget our origins but here we make our own lives.

DRAUPADI *(Confronting* BRIHANNALA.*)* Are you denying that you are Arjun?

BRIHANNALA Yes I am. I choose to be Brihannala.

DRAUPADI But why? Arjun is noble, kind, sensitive, courageous and an intrepid warrior.

BRIHANNALA I don't want to be a warrior. Look at how Arjun was brought up. He was trained in the martial arts. He was taught to kill and he became very good at it.

DRAUPADI Yes, you are the bravest and most devastating fighter. Noble, handsome and the soul of propriety; forerunner of the knights of the round table.

BRIHANNALA Draupadi, look at me. Do I look like a knight?

DRAUPADI This is your disguise. And it's a wonderful disguise. Nobody could suspect that the great and noble Arjun could take on such a form. Even I found it distasteful.

SIKANDI I think he's beautiful. He wasn't turned into a complete woman; it was an imaginative, dramatic and titillating ploy of the author to make his story exciting and to resolve a difficult situation.

GANGA There's no doubt. Vyasa had a wonderful imagination.

SUBADHRA Admit it Draupadi, you too were used to appeal to people's fascination with sex. You, with five husbands all at the same time.

DRAUPADI But I wanted only one. *(She looks at* BRIHANNALA.*)*

KUNTHI Well, it was my word that made you take five. Even when I retracted, Vyasa wouldn't allow it. He was the author, so he entered the story to make you accept the situation.

DRAUPADI But I loved only one.

SUBADHRA And where is that story? It was silenced because it did not fit in with the author's plans. Only at the end do we hear that you could not enter heaven because you loved Arjun too much.

DRAUPADI Why are you telling me all this? I know we were treated as instruments. But are we free now. We can be ourselves That is why I don't understand why Arjun insists on this masquerade.

BRIHANNALA It is not a masquerade and you do not love me. You admitted just now that you are repelled by Brihannala. You love Arjun and I am not Arjun the great warrior.

SIKANDI Your protector, your guardian, your lover.

SUBADHRA Brihannala is a man made in his own image.

DRAUPADI No, no, no. Give up this perversion and be your real self. My Arjun. My husband. I want to be your wife. Don't you care about me any more?

BRIHANNALA I am not Arjun.

DRAUPADI You are. You are my husband. You should be ashamed to call yourself Brihannala. Brihannala is not a man.

BRIHANNALA What is a man? Someone who proves himself by killing? Someone who beats women? Someone superior to women? Someone whose authority depends on a woman's servitude? If a man is all that, then you are quite right; I am not a man.

DRAUPADI *(Kneeling before him and clasping*

him.) Don't do this. Don't torture me. I love you.

BRIHANNALA *(Gently raising her.)* I'm sorry. I cannot be your husband.

DRAUPADI *(Furious.)* Oh, damn you. Stop pretending. It's because you are involved with that, that...*(Pointing to* SIKANDI.*)* pervert.

RADHA *(Shocked.)* Draupadi!

DRAUPADI You've all seen it. *(To* SIKANDI.*)* You have made him into this.

RADHA Draupadi, you'd better go away and calm yourself.

DRAUPADI It was better in the epic. This is no life.

KUNTHI Draupadi, come with me. Let's go for a walk.

DRAUPADI Let's do more than that. Let's walk right out of here. This is no place for any of us. This life is unnatural. Look at what it has done to him *(Pointing at* BRIHANNALA.*)*. We must go back to the epic.

RADHA Draupadi, calm down.

GANGA *(To* BRIHANNALA *and* SIKANDI.*)* Why don't you two just go and prepare for the next scene.

DRAUPADI *(Seeing them walk off.)* Where are they going? *(Shouting after them.)* You know you're doing wrong. That's why you're skulking off like that.

GANGA Stop it, Draupadi. I asked them to leave.

DRAUPADI I don't care what you say. You know that this is wrong. We've tried the experiment but it doesn't work. Now let us admit that there is no other way for us. We are women; we were born to be mothers and wives. That is what we were in the epic. That is our birthright and we should be proud of it.

RADHA Draupadi, just calm down. You don't know what you're saying.

DRAUPADI Are you coming back with me or not?

SUBADHRA Draupadi, you can't be going back just because of Arjun.

DRAUPADI At least in the epic, he is my husband and he loves me.

KUNTHI Are you prepared to endure all the abuse again?

DRAUPADI It's clear that none of you know what it is to love a man. I am prepared to go through hell for him.

SUBADHRA Are you sure?

GANGA But he doesn't love you.

DRAUPADI He will be mine again in the epic.

RADHA But he will not be a free agent. He will simply be fulfilling the destiny mapped out for him. Can you call that love? At least here, there is truth. He doesn't love you and you know it.

DRAUPADI I don't want to hear this. I am going back. Are any of you coming with me? *(Nobody responds.)* Very well, I shall go back alone.

KUNTHI *(Coming forward with her sari and wig.)* Here, you had better put these on. You won't be accepted there looking like this.

(The women help her to dress and then she leaves. They watch her sadly as she makes her way through the audience.)

HIDIMBA *(Holding out blindfold.)* We should have given her this blindfold. She's going to need it.

(BRIHANNALA *and* SIKANDI *come back.)*

BRIHANNALA Has she really gone? I don't believe it.

RADHA She's very confused.

SUBADHRA I followed her here. She inspired me.

KUNTHI *(Sighing.)* But she can't give up Arjun.

HIDIMBA Arjun was your son. Have you given him up?

KUNTHI *(Putting her arm around* BRIHANNALA.*)* This is my son.

BRIHANNALA Thank you, mother.

GANGA Now that Draupadi's gone, I suppose I shall have to take over the task of calling us to order. What is next?

RADHA It's time for a different kind of story. We have only dealt with your stories, stories of the privileged classes. Let us tell the story of peasant women like me.

SUBADHRA I didn't know you had a story.

HIDIMBA *(Laughing.)* Radha, the ever optimistic. Think you can change the world. You haven't even changed attitudes here.

GANGA Everyone has a story. Depends on the author, whose story gets told. You've been reading too many his-story books.

HIDIMBA Poor little Subadhra. Doesn't want to go slumming, eh?

SUBADHRA Hidimba, you don't have to gloat. Anyone can make a mistake. I apologize, Radha. I should have known better. I was automatically referring to the epic again. I wish I could stop doing that.

RADHA I understand. We are all still tied to the epic in many ways; but we will overcome.

(HIDIMBA *hums mockingly, "We shall overcome.")*

RADHA You can laugh all you want, Hidimba, but we will overcome.

GANGA Come on, let's begin Radha's story.

RADHA It's Hidimba's story as well as mine.

HIDIMBA I'm being conscripted here. My participation is under protest.

KUNTHI So what's new? Come on Radha, let's hear your story.

UTTARAI (NARRATOR) This scene begins in Radha's village, a day after a hut of one of the families was destroyed by lightning. Two children were trapped in the hut and burned to death. The incensed villagers believe that Hidimba is a witch and is responsible.

(The VILLAGERS *are chasing* HIDIMBA.*)*

HIDIMBA Leave me alone. Get away from me. *(She picks up a twig and shakes it at her pursuers.)*

SUBADHRA (VILLAGER) Careful, she must have some magic in that stick. *(She picks up a stone and aims it at* HIDIMBA. *A flurry of stones comes flying at* HIDIMBA. *She screams and falls to her knees.)*

(The group surrounds her. They accuse her, pick up stones and begin to stone her. RADHA *jumps into their midst and shields* HIDIMBA *from them.)*

VILLAGERS Get out of there, Radha. Don't interfere. This woman is evil. We must kill her. How can you touch the vile creature? Radha what's wrong with you?

RADHA You have no right to persecute this woman.

VILLAGERS Woman! Hidimba is not a woman. She is a witch, an evil demon.

KUNTHI She killed two children last night; burned them to death while they were sleeping.

RADHA How do you know she did it?

GANGA Who else would do such a horrible thing?

RADHA Everything is so dry around here. The hut could easily have caught alight.

SIKANDI Yes, that's another thing; this drought. It's her wickedness that has caused it.

RADHA You don't believe that.

KUNTHI She's a witch; she can do anything.

BRIHANNALA Look in her bag. You'll see the proof there.

SUBADHRA It's full of body parts.

GANGA Ask her what she is doing with the body parts.

SUBADHRA She's been stealing children and cutting them up to make magic. She deserves to die. *(Throws a stone and the others pick up stones too.)*

*(*RADHA *picks up bag. The others move away in horror.* RADHA *empties bag in front of them. All kinds of herbs and roots fall out. The* VILLAGERS *stare in amazement.)*

RADHA *(Picking up some herbs and holding them in front of* SUBADHRA*'s face.)* Whose child is this?

SUBADHRA How did she do it?

RADHA Do what?

SUBADHRA Change the body parts into plants?

RADHA Did you look into this bag before you accused her?

SIKANDI We didn't have to; we all know Hidimba is a witch.

BRIHANNALA Yes, she's a witch. Kill her. Kill her.

(They pick up stones again and are about to pelt her. RADHA *picks up the herbs and roots and throws them at the crowd.)*

RADHA There, take your children's body parts and leave this woman alone.

(The VILLAGERS *scatter to avoid contact with the plants.)*

VILLAGERS *(As they retreat.)* Radha, Hidimba has bewitched you. You will die. *(They leave.)*

RADHA *(Helping* HIDIMBA *up.)* Are you all right? Did they hurt you?

HIDIMBA I'm all right, thanks to you. I think I should move away from this village.

RADHA It won't help; they'll just find someone else. We've got to stop this kind of thing. *(She begins to gather up the herbs and roots and puts them in the bag.)*

HIDIMBA How do you do that? If I were a

witch, I could make some magic to put an end to it. It needs a miracle; you can't reason with these people.

RADHA We have to find a way. We can't go on like this. It's destroying us all.

HIDIMBA You'll never change them. They are tied to their superstitions.

RADHA If they understood about lightning and other natural elements, they wouldn't feel so helpless.

HIDIMBA They turn everything they don't understand into symbols. And symbols are difficult to demystify. I am a symbol of evil because I live alone, don't have children and make medicines.

RADHA That's it. It's the symbols. We have to explode the symbols. These symbols blind them to reason and rationalize their fears and insecurity.

HIDIMBA Are you going to explode me? That will save them the trouble of trying to murder me.

RADHA Oh don't joke about it. We have to make them understand.

HIDIMBA Be careful they don't come after you with their stones and curses.

RADHA But we can't go on like this; looking for scapegoats instead of dealing with the problems.

HIDIMBA You'll never change them. They want easy answers.

RADHA I won't give up. I'll find a way.

HIDIMBA *(Saluting.)* Hail, Saint Joan of Arc.

(HIDIMBA *marches out with* RADHA. *The* VILLAGERS *come back cautiously.)*

KUNTHI There she goes. She has taken Radha with her. The poor woman is bewitched. She's walking like a zombie.

GANGA We must get rid of Hidimba. She has brought a curse upon our land.

BRIHANNALA It hasn't rained for years. All our cattle are dying and our crops have failed.

SIKANDI The river is dry and the water holes empty.

KUNTHI The shaman must tell us what to do.

(The SHAMAN, URVASI, *enters dancing.)*

KUNTHI *(Greets the* SHAMAN *in the proper way.)* O great seer, we have come to you because we are in trouble and need your wisdom and advice.

URVASI (SHAMAN) What do you seek from me?

KUNTHI It is the terrible drought; we are dying. Please help us.

(The SHAMAN *throws the bones. All the* VILLAGERS *participate in the ceremony.)*

URVASI The ancestors are angry. You are harbouring an evil witch in your midst. She has created the drought. Bring her to the place of sacrifice just before sundown. I will cleanse her and then her blood will cleanse the land. And it will rain.

(The VILLAGERS *pay their respects to the* SHAMAN. URVASI *takes off her mask and puts on the villager mask again. The* VILLAGERS *begin a hypnotic song and dance, which prepares them for the acts that they are about to commit. They exit dancing.)*

(Enter HIDIMBA. *She is looking for herbs and roots.* RADHA *comes rushing in.)*

HIDIMBA Radha, what's the matter?

RADHA They're coming for you. You have to hide. I think they mean to kill you.

HIDIMBA Here's your chance to explode a myth.

RADHA This is not the time for jokes. Come on, let's get away from here. They want to take you to the sacrificial place; they are to kill you at sundown.

HIDIMBA Is this from the shaman?

RADHA Yes. Come on, now. We must hurry.

HIDIMBA Did he say it would rain after the sacrifice?

RADHA We haven't got time for all this now. Come on.

HIDIMBA *(Insisting.)* Did he say it would rain?

RADHA Yes, he did. Now come on.

HIDIMBA That's a wily old bird. Look at the sky.

RADHA Hidimba, are you mad? The villagers are coming to kill you. Can't you hear them? You're in danger.

HIDIMBA My dear Radha, you have lived in this village all your life, surely you have learned to read the sky. Look and tell me what you see.

RADHA We don't have time for weather forecasts. Let's go.

HIDIMBA Look and tell me what you see.

RADHA *(Quite frustrated.)* Yes, yes. I see the clouds, but they mean nothing. They don't produce rain.

HIDIMBA Do you see where these clouds are coming from?

RADHA Over the mountain. Over the mountain! That means it's going to rain. That's wonderful; I'll go and tell the villagers.

HIDIMBA They won't believe you. Besides the shaman won't let you near them. Women are not allowed at these ceremonies. Except as sacrifices of course.

RADHA I'll find a way.

HIDIMBA The shaman will not allow you to interfere. He knows it is going to rain. He is no fool; he has read the skies.

(The singing of the VILLAGERS *becomes louder.)*

RADHA We've got to get out of here. Come on.

HIDIMBA No, we won't run. We'll join them.

RADHA Are you mad?

HIDIMBA I sincerely hope so. *(Hands* RADHA *a mask and puts one on herself.)* Here, they won't find us. We'll become invisible in the crowd.

(They put on masks. The VILLAGERS, *singing and dancing, enter and begin to look for* HIDIMBA. *Unnoticed,* RADHA *and* HIDIMBA, *join the search.)*

KUNTHI She is not here.

GANGA Radha must have warned her.

BRIHANNALA What will we do now?

URVASI (SHAMAN) She must be found. We must perform the ritual as the sun goes down or the ancestors will be very angry and we will all be destroyed. *(He closes his eyes and performs ritualized movements.)* She is close by. I can feel her presence. Search for her.

(The VILLAGERS *spread out. Their search takes the form of a dance that becomes quite frenzied. They eventually fall into positions of supplication before the witch doctor. The witch doctor goes into a trance and then speaks in tongues.)*

URVASI (SHAMAN) I have consulted with the ancestors. They say that if we cannot find the witch, there is another amongst us who is evil. *(He looks around the group. Everyone trembles with fear. Then he points to* SIKANDI.*)* That is the one. Take him to the sacrificial place and prepare him.

(The VILLAGERS *grab hold of* SIKANDI.*)*

SIKANDI No, no, stop.

BRIHANNALA Why are you taking him? He is not the evil one.

GANGA The ancestors have chosen him. He will be our sacrifice.

(They carry him and parade around the stage. BRIHANNALA *fights to free* SIKANDI. *The* VILLAGERS *overpower* BRIHANNALA *and* RADHA *and* HIDIMBA *hold him prisoner as the procession moves toward the sacrificial place.)*

URVASI (SHAMAN) Get him ready. *(He looks at the sky.)* Hurry, or it will be too late.

(Some VILLAGERS *pull off some of* SIKANDI's *clothing. The* SHAMAN *chants and performs some rituals and then asks the* VILLAGERS *to hold* SIKANDI *in the right position to be stabbed through the heart. During this whole procedure,* BRIHANNALA *has been struggling and shouting. As the* SHAMAN *gets his knife ready and is about to plunge it into* SIKANDI, RADHA *and* HIDIMBA *let go of* BRIHANNALA, *who runs forward and stops the* SHAMAN. *Some of the* VILLAGERS *grab hold of* BRIHANNALA *and threaten to kill him.* RADHA *and* HIDIMBA *run forward and help* SIKANDI. *Then* HIDIMBA *and* RADHA *unmask and reveal themselves.)*

HIDIMBA Stop! You wanted me for the sacrifice. Well, here I am.

VILLAGERS Hidimba!

URVASI (SHAMAN) Seize the woman. We will not have time to prepare her. The hour of the sacrifice has almost passed. *(He raises his knife.)*

BRIHANNALA *(Grabs knife and throws it aside.)* You don't know what you're doing. First you wanted to sacrifice Hidimba, then Sikandi, now it's Hidimba again. Does it matter who you kill?

RADHA No, it doesn't. He just needs to kill someone to make you believe in his power. But look the time has come and gone. The hour of the sacrifice is over.

VILLAGERS *(Wailing.)* We have lost our chance for rain. We are all going to perish.

RADHA The rain will come. Look at the sky. See, the clouds are coming over the mountain. We don't need to sacrifice for rain.

HIDIMBA *(Coming to the* SHAMAN.*)* You have deceived these people.

URVASI (SHAMAN.) Seize them. They must be punished for entering the sacred place. These women have defiled the grounds.

(The VILLAGERS *grab hold of* RADHA *and* HIDIMBA. *Just then it begins to rain.)*

HIDIMBA Stop. Can't you feel the rain?

RADHA It's raining. It' raining. You don't have to kill for rain.

VILLAGERS *(Feeling the rain with their bodies.)* I feel raindrops. It is raining. *(They revel in the rain for a few moments.)*

RADHA *(Turning to* SHAMAN.*)* You knew it was going to rain and you wanted us to believe that you had the power to make it rain. You blamed Hidimba for the drought.

HIDIMBA I do not have the power to control such things; neither do you. But we both know how to read the sky and we can make predictions.

RADHA *(To* VILLAGERS.*)* That is something that we can all learn. Instead of being victims of our fears, we can learn to understand and take control of our lives. Then we will be free.

KUNTHI I am glad it is raining. I don't know why the ancestors took pity on us...

GANGA It was because our shaman was threatened. They did it to save his life.

RADHA No, that's not true. It had nothing to do with ancestors and shamans and magic.

*(*KUNTHI *begins a chant in praise of the ancestors and the* SHAMAN. *The* VILLAGERS *carry him off in triumph.)*

HIDIMBA *(Laughing.)* There you are. You have exploded the myth.

RADHA It's not funny. How can they still believe the shaman?

HIDIMBA He's easier to believe than you are. They can't make head or tail of what you are talking about.

RADHA All I want is for them to take charge of their own lives and not be victims.

HIDIMBA All the shamans asks is that they believe in him. That's much easier. They don't want to take any responsibility.

RADHA You're just cynical. I believe that they will change. They have to. Look at the devastation of this land. We are just destroying ourselves. What will we leave our children? Lives of endless suffering in a wasteland?

HIDIMBA Oh give up, Radha. You can't change anything.

RADHA We can make this world into an Eden again. I believe that. I am going to work for it.

SIKANDI *(Coming forward.)* Radha, I believe what you say. I think you are right.

BRIHANNALA So do I.

RADHA Are you willing to help me?

HIDIMBA She's not asking for much. She just wants to change the world.

BRIHANNALA Hidimba, I'm beginning to understand why you are cynical. We talk about freedom and yet we are full of prejudices. I was actually willing to believe you were a witch. Please forgive me.

SIKANDI I was too. I should have understood, after all I have been through. Please forgive me too.

HIDIMBA Nothing to forgive. Actually, I am a witch.

*(*SIKANDI *and* BRIHANNALA *laugh.)*

HIDIMBA I am you know. I don't live in cages the way you do. That's why people pick on me. They envy my freedom.

RADHA But then you're all alone.

HIDIMBA And free. *(Exits laughing and singing "I have overcome".)*

RADHA *(Shouting after her.)* Not if you're alone.

SIKANDI *(Looking out over the audience.)* Someone's coming. Is it another escapee from the epic?

BRIHANNALA It's Draupadi.

RADHA She's come back. I'm delighted. I'll round up the others. This calls for a celebration.

BRIHANNALA *(Coming forward to greet* DRAUPADI.*)* Have you come back to stay?

DRAUPADI *(Wearily.)* Yes.

SIKANDI I'm glad.

DRAUPADI You're glad. I thought you wanted me out of the way.

SIKANDI No, we need you here.

BRIHANNALA I felt very guilty when you left. I thought it was my fault.

DRAUPADI No, it was my fault. I didn't really understand. I was no better than Vyasa and the characters from the epic.

BRIHANNALA Why do you say that?

DRAUPADI Because of how I feel about you.

SIKANDI I think I'll go and help Radha.

DRAUPADI No, please stay. This concerns you too. I was jealous of you.

BRIHANNALA We didn't blame you.

DRAUPADI But I blamed you. I felt you had

betrayed me. What I didn't realize was that I had blamed you even in the epic. I never admitted it, even to myself. I was deeply wounded when you insisted on sharing me with your brothers. Even after your mother admitted she had spoken impulsively and in ignorance, you made us all adhere to her words.

BRIHANNALA But I didn't have a choice.

DRAUPADI I understand that now. You were bound by the structure of the epic and so was I. That is why I kept silent.

SIKANDI Did you speak up when you went back now?

DRAUPADI I still couldn't. I was back in that structure, locked into the pattern again. But this time I was aware of it. I found I was standing outside of myself, watching what was going on. I couldn't get involved. I could see that we were all in our cages of customs and traditions.

BRIHANNALA But we need customs and traditions.

DRAUPADI Not dead ones. When they lose their meaning and become magical rites that we perform out of superstitious fear, they distort and deform us.

SIKANDI What about the others in the epic? Don't they question?

DRAUPADI I don't know. Perhaps they feel alienated but they don't question. I looked at Gandhari and I thought she was right to wear a blindfold. That way she could close her eyes to her oppression. *(After a thoughtful pause.)* But perhaps she was wearing the blindfold because she was grateful to have her life structured for her.

SIKANDI Whatever her reason, she cannot be herself.

BRIHANNALA She has made that choice for herself.

DRAUPADI But she doesn't understand that she has other choices.

BRIHANNALA Then she can't be unhappy.

DRAUPADI Does suffering have to be conscious? All the Pandava brothers, Yudhistira, Bhima, Nakula and Sahadev, are happy to remain in the epic because they are heroes.

BRIHANNALA Even Yudhistira? He believes in non-violence; I didn't think he would want to remain.

DRAUPADI He does everything by the book. He would never challenge conventions.

BRIHANNALA But you challenged. Why did Vyasa allow you to challenge?

DRAUPADI He likes feisty women. It was my function to titillate and excite.

SIKANDI I was created as a man/woman for the same purpose.

DRAUPADI At any rate, I am glad I was not a subservient woman in the epic. I wouldn't be here now, if I had been.

BRIHANNALA I wouldn't be here either if I had been straight throughout the epic.

DRAUPADI That is the way I wanted you. Still want you.

BRIHANNALA I thought you understood.

DRAUPADI I do. I know you cannot love me but I have always loved you. When I went back to the epic, I realized that my love for you would be a cage; you could never be yourself in a relationship with me. How can I put you in a cage, when I don't want to live in one myself.

BRIHANNALA But you still have feelings for me?

DRAUPADI You accused me earlier of loving a romantic ideal, Arjun, hero, protector, lover, destroyer in one. Master of my destiny. But is that what I really want? Or is that what I am expected to want? As long as I am in this confusion, I do not feel I have genuine love to offer. So, you see, I still have a long way to go.

BRIHANNALA *(Taking her hand.)* Draupadi, I do love you...you are my beloved sister, my friend, my mentor.

DRAUPADI *(Taking* SIKANDI*'s hand and placing it over* BRIHANNALA*'s.)* And I will learn to love you both as friends and brothers. I am happy that you found each other.

(All the other players enter.)

KUNTHI *(Rushing forward and embracing* DRAUPADI*.)* Draupadi, I am so glad you have come back.

GANGA My dear sister, we missed you dreadfully.

HIDIMBA So you flew the coop.

SUBADHRA If you hadn't come back, I think I would have weakened and gone back too.

RADHA Rubbish, you've been having too much fun here.

SUBADHRA *(Embracing* DRAUPADI*.)* I am so happy to see you.

RADHA Yes, the old sergeant-major's returned.

DRAUPADI *(Laughs.)* You know when I went

back, I kept looking for you. I missed your wisdom and advice. It was hard to know that I couldn't ever speak to you. That you were only a footnote.

RADHA So you came back for me. And here I thought you were pining for Brihannala.

DRAUPADI I missed you all and most of all I missed myself. *(She flings off the sari and wig.)* Burn these. I never want to see them again.

KUNTHI No, no. They go back into the museum.

DRAUPADI And this time they'll stay there.

HIDIMBA I thought this was a celebration? Where's the music?

RADHA Hidimba! You, going for this stereotyped ending? What's happening here?

(They sing and dance, songs and dances of the rainbow nation of South Africa.)

Duma Ndlovu

> *Sheila's Day* is a tribute to the woman who brought me into this world, Sara Manala maNkosi Ndlovu, who single-handedly raised me and my four siblings after my father had died. It is also a tribute to all those women who raise their children and tell them to become somebody against all odds.

Duma Ndlovu is a poet, journalist, director, producer, and playwright. Born in Soweto, he attended the once prestigious Sekano Ntoane High School in Senaoane. After graduating, he began writing for the *World Newspaper* during the turbulent 1970s.

In 1975 he founded the Medupe Writers Association, a national group that encouraged young black writers. He served as the organization's president until October 1977, when the government banned the group and seventeen others that had been active in the Black Consciousness and anti-apartheid movements.

Shortly afterwards, Duma left South Africa for the United States. After completing a Master's degree at Hunter College in New York, he embarked on a career as a theatrical producer. Duma was responsible for the upsurge of interest in South African township theatre in the United States. Among his producing credits are *Asinamali*, *Woza Albert*, *Sarafina* (all by Mbongeni Ngema), The Woza Afrika Festival at New York's Lincoln Center, and a score of other productions. His highly acclaimed *Sheila's Day* has been performed throughout the United States by university and regional theatres, and it enjoyed a New York run in 1996.

In 1985, Duma founded the Woza Afrika Foundation, to raise money to support the arts in South Africa. Through the foundation he also produced theatre and music festivals that featured South African artists. During his last two years in the U.S., Duma taught African American literature and music at the State University of New York, Stony Brook.

Duma returned to South Africa in 1992, where he founded Word Of Mouth Productions, to mount music, theatre, and television productions. In South Africa he wrote *Bergville Stories* (1994), which had successful runs in Durban at the Playhouse, the Grahamstown National Arts Festival, and the Market Theatre. *Bergville Stories* includes song and dance, and examines the conflict among rival ethnic groups. The play focuses on a group of itinerant Zulu labourers barricaded in a township that does not want them. Duma was inspired by an actual event from 1956, when twenty-three men were sentenced and hanged on the same day for the murder of five policemen during a drug raid. In 1995, *Bergville Stories* received thirteen regional Vita Award nominations (the equivalent of the prestigious American Tony Award) and one national citation. *Bergville Stories* received the 1997 award for best original score from the First National Bank–South African Music Association, and was nominated for the Kora Music Awards. The play was also chosen for the second Woza Afrika Festival at the Lincoln Center in July, 1997. South African Broadcast Company TV (SABC-TV) has commissioned a screenplay adaptation.

In 1996, the Windybrow Centre for the Performing Arts commissioned Duma to do a play on women in prison. *The Game* went on to win a Vita Award and was featured on the main stage of the 1997 Grahamstown Festival. Duma wrote and produced a thirteen-part drama series for SABC-2, *Muvhango*, which was the first drama in the minority Venda language in the history of South African television. Duma is the editor of *Woza Afrika!: An Anthology of South African Plays*.

In all he does, he always give tribute to the major force of inspiration in his life – Steven

Bantu Biko, the visionary young Black Consciousness leader who was tortured to death in 1967 by the security police in Port Elizabeth.

ARTISTIC STATEMENT

I spent fifteen years in the United States, and lived fourteen of those years in black communities. One of the reasons was the recognition of the commonalities and the fact that I felt mostly at home in those communities. I felt like I was back home in South Africa.

But most of the time we take the commonalities for granted. It is true that we have a shared experience of apartheid, oppression in the south and various other common experiences. But it is not until we go deeper into some of the more intense, latent experiences that we discover just how deep the commonalities run.

I had always been concerned about the plight of domestic workers, since my mother had been a domestic worker in South Africa all her life. So when Mbongeni Ngema and I decided we wanted to do a project with both South African and African American women, the subject was a natural for me. It was when I started doing research into the lives of common folks [and their] contribution to the struggles of both societies that I felt even stronger about the story line. The more I read, the more I discovered similarities in various aspects of our lives. Some of the discoveries were scary. Domestic workers both in South Africa and the U.S. got their day off on Thursday, The day, Thursday, is called "Sheila's Day" in South Africa because of that reason; the name Sheila having been used because in most cases white madams were too lazy to learn to pronounce the domestic workers' African names and therefore settled for the easier "Sheila". Interestingly, "Sheila" seems to have its origins in Australia, where madams commonly referred to their domestic workers by this name.

But even more interesting and astounding for me were the similarities between the death of Jimmy Lee Jackson, who died trying to protect his mother in Marion, Alabama, in 1965, and Mthuli Shezi, in Germiston, South Africa, who, in 1972, came to the rescue of domestic workers at a train station and got pushed in front of a moving train. Both men were refused treatment at white hospitals, both died seven days after sustaining their injuries at the hands of insensitive white policemen, and both their tombstones were desecrated, at different times in different parts of the world.

THE ROLE OF THEATRE IN SOUTH AFRICA

Theatre, since time immemorial, has played a significant role in the lives of Africans – since the days when grandmother storytellers used to sit in front of fires and tell their grandchildren tales of animals who used to rule the world and transform themselves into the animals as they animatedly captivated the young ones, to the early 1900s when black people moved to the cities and underwent urbanization and hence had to find newer ways of entertainment. Blacks, as storytellers, have always created exciting theatre. Thus, the theatre that was created in the 1950s did not move too far from the original role that theatre always played in black society, theatre as a form of entertainment and as a way of helping people pass time. So it was that in the early 1960s right through to the seventies, when white rule was more and more entrenched and people had to react to their oppression, the theatre started assuming a new role of conscientizing and sensitizing people to their plight. But this theatre always had to retain the element of entertainment. That is why when Gibson Kente penned his classic musical, *How Long*, people left the theatres in tears because of the reminder of harsh pass laws, but they also left the theatres entertained by the music, dance, and humour that was Kente's ultimate signature.

Woza Albert, the collaborative play by Mbongeni Ngema, Percy Mtwa, and Barney Simon, was perhaps the best example of a highly political play that was also largely entertaining. Theatre in South Africa has had to meet several challenges – challenges that most changing societies have to deal with. The transformation from apartheid to democracy has meant that the theatre has had to find a new voice, a new language, has had to move from protest theatre back to its original role of entertaining. But because every experience is a learning curve, our theatre will be more vibrant and more informed. Our theatre will triumph and move onto the next millennium. Our theatre will find new voices and new meaning. Theatre always finds a way to examine a society and comment on that society. So theatre in South Africa will comment on the transformation, will set trends and lead a way to a future.

HAVE THINGS IMPROVED IN GENERAL IN THE NEW SOUTH AFRICA?

The political dispensation that South Africa has undergone in the last few years has been the most exciting. While some of us have been skeptical of the process of change and its aftermath or after-effects, we can, however, not question the fact that society has undergone transformation. There is all the evidence that in the years to come the quality of life for the majority of the people will change for the better.

South Africa under white rule was in a state of a mess. Blacks in general were worse off. Anything, we argued then, would leave them better off. We have witnessed a new government and new players with a game plan that, although slow, is seeking to transform and change society for the better. To that extent, yes, there have been changes in South Africa.

But when one sits down and analyzes society piecemeal, then one is confronted with situations that are difficult. For instance, in the area of the arts or any specific area, it will be easy to pinpoint things that need to change or that will have to be addressed seriously for there to be changes. There is still the major problem of some of the Old Guard politicians, remnants of the old system, who still operate within the current structures. No doubt these individuals, with their Eurocentric mind-set, still find themselves with other vested interests and are usually quick to try and sabotage any effort that seeks to empower black people.

PRODUCTION HISTORY

Sheila's Day was first performed at Crossroads Theater, September 1989, in New Brunswick, New Jersey, with the original cast featuring Stephanie Alston, Gina Breedlove, Carla Brothers, Irene Datcher, Thuli Dumakude, Ebony JoAnn, Annelen Malebo, Letta Mbulu, Tu Nokwe, Valerie Rochon, and Gina Torres. Khaliq Al Rouf was featured playing a variety of horns.

Interview conducted via phone and e-mail during 1996 and 1997.

Photo by Thomas Khosa.

9 Sheila's Day

Duma Ndlovu
Conceived and created by Duma Ndlovu and Mbongeni Ngema

Time
The present

Characters
QEDUSIZI MAPHALALA
RUBY LEE THOMAS JOHNSON
AND AN ASSORTMENT OF OTHER CHARACTERS PLAYED BY TEN OTHER WOMEN

The set
The empty space that is transformed by the actors into various locations in the American South and in South Africa. A configuration of two or three black cubes (boxes) is upstage centre. These are used as chairs, and various other objects throughout the play. Along the upstage wall is a prop table.

Prologue
KHALIQ AL ROUF *walks in, playing a clarinet solo. He goes towards the audience to the right of the stage and sits on a chair in the last row.*

TU NOKWE *walks in playing a guitar and singing. She goes and sits on the boxes at centre stage and continues to play.*

LETTA MBULU *walks in and goes towards the boxes centre stage.)*

LETTA (*as* QEDUSIZI) He Tu, waze wayidlala kamnandi leyongoma. [Hey Tu, the song you are playing is beautiful.]

TU Hey Qedusizi, kunjani! Ngiya rehearsa sisi, ngi rihesela tonight. I want us to do this song tonight. [Hey Qedusizi, I am rehearsing for tonight.]

(EBONY JOANN *walks in and joins them.)*

EBONY JOANN (*as* RUBY LEE) *(In Zulu)* He Qedusizi, kunjani? [Hey Qedusizi, how are you?]

QEDUSIZI Ngikhona, Ruby Lee, how are you? [I am fine.]

(STEPHANIE ALSTON *and* ANNELEN MALEBO *both walk in together from another door, directly behind where* KHALIQ *is sitting.)*

STEPHANIE Ruby Lee, Ruby Lee, Skwiza got lost again today on her way here.

SKWIZA (ANNELEN) He Tu, He Qe, I got lost again today. *(And general laughter)*

RUBY LEE *(She walks over to* TU.*)* Hey Tu, remember the song that we rehearsed last night?

TU What's wrong, you don't like this one?

RUBY LEE No, no, I love this one, but remember that one from yesterday?

ANNELEN She means *Bayajabula.*

TU You mean the Mbaqanga song? You are speaking my language. How do you want it, fast?

(She starts the song on the guitar and the whole group joins in singing.)

Siyajabula, thina x4
Sihlanganis'izizwe
Sihlanganis'iAfrika

Bayajabula x4
Bayajabula bonk'abantu
Yo-Iyoyoyoyoyo mama

Bayajabula x6
Bayajabula bonk'abantu.

(On the end of the first verse of the song, THULI *walks in followed by* CARLA*, then* GINA BREEDLOVE, VALERIE ROCHON, IRENE DATCHER *and* GINA TORRES*. They all each have a pan of cans that they use as part of the "can dance" that they break into as soon as they walk in.)*

(At the end of song, lights out)
(Lights)

VALERIE ROCHON *(Is standing on top of the boxes.)* This is a gathering of spirits. We gather in this room every Thursday to rehearse, and part of our ritual has been to talk about our lives, what moves us, what drives us.

IRENE DATCHER And this gathering is by no coincidence. I truly believe, deep in my heart, that nothing is by coincidence.

GINA TORRES Para mi, esto es una reunion de espiritos y una celebracion de nuestra fuerzas como mujeres. [For me this is a reunion of spirits and a celebration of all our spirituality as women.]

ANNELEN MALEBO We meet on Thursdays, Sheila's Day, so as to honour our mothers, the domestic workers, the Sheilas of this world on their day off.

CARLA BROTHERS It is in these meetings that we realize the truths about our lives.

THULI DUMAKUDE In my hometown of Thembisa, in South Africa, a tombstone on the grave of Mthuli kaShezi was shattered to pieces, because it had stood in the form of a clenched fist, as a symbol of Black Pride.

STEPHANIE ALSTON In my hometown of Marion, Alabama, a tombstone at the grave of Jimmy Lee Jackson was desecrated. When they could not destroy it, they blasted it with shotgun bullets. The question as to why these things keep happening is what drives us.

TU NOKWE I am so excited.

GINA BREEDLOVE Because women, collectively, have a power to change this world.

QEDUSIZI My journey has been propelled by the impact that the death of my cousin, Mthuli kaShezi, I will never rest until his dream, of a free South Africa, is realized.

RUBY LEE The death, in 1965, of Jimmy Lee Jackson, my dear friend, changed my life. And that, for me, was the beginning of my journey.

(Lights out as the women move to sit on the boxes and take their respective positions.)

One

RUBY LEE My name is Mary Ruby Lee Thomas Johnson. I was born in Marion, Alabama, and I was raised mostly by my grandmother because my mother always did sleep-in work. She always made sure that she got Sundays off, because we come from a tradition of churchgoers. Both of my parents have always been holiness. I was raised in a small Pentecostal Church in Perry County and for me my mother was important in that church. She brought the church to life. Mama was blessed with a singing ministry and when she sang the whole church shouted. I can remember as a little girl, walking into the church holding hands with both of my parents. The first thing I would do would be to look for my school friends. I would find my cousin Albert Turner, then I would have to search for Jimmy Lee Jackson because they had to be separated or they would cut up during church service. Jimmy Lee's folks would be sitting behind him like guards, there would be Mr Cager Lee, his grandfather, his little sister and his mother, Miss Viola. I would be sitting in between my parents and at a certain point during the service my mother would walk to the front of the congregation and lead the congregation in a song. I remember her favourite song *(She starts the song.)*

(Now) Let us all
All go back
Go back to the old
Old Landmark
(Now) Let us all
All go back
Go back to the old
Old landmark
(Now) let us all
All go back
Go back to the old
Old landmark
And (kneel and) stay in the service of the Lord
Stay in the service of the Lord

Now let us kneel and pray
Kneel and pray
Like we did in the old time way
Old time way
Now let us kneel and pray
Kneel and pray
Like we did in the old time way
Old time way
Now let us kneel
Kneel and pray
Like we did in the
Old time way

He'll be near us
He will hear us
We'll be given
Bread from heaven
Then he will feed us till we want no more
Feed us till we want no more

(Now) Let us all
All go back
Go back to the old
Old Landmark
(Now) Let us all
All go back
Go back to the old
Old Landmark
(Now) let us all
all go back
Go back to the old
Old Landmark
And (kneel and) stay in the service of the Lord
Stay in the service of the Lord

That was my mother, she would sing till the spirit came down.

(She goes back to sit down and QEDUSIZI *comes up.)*

Two

QEDUSIZI MAPHALALA My name is Qedusizi Maphalala. I was born in a small village in Bergville, Zululand, in 1936. I was named after my paternal great-grandmother, Qedusizi, who I was told I resembled very much.

My father's brother was a traditional doctor, and was greatly respected for his knowledge of the earth, the trees, the roots and their relationship to man and his existence. My aunt was a sangoma, a spiritual medium. Throughout my youth I was surrounded by people who communicated with the spirits all the time.

My father was a very special person. He was a major influence in my life. I have vivid images of him taking me with him to feasts and ceremonies. It is the exuberance and the pulsating rhythms of those ceremonies that gave me an inspiration about my people's music. My father was a dancer, the best dancer in the village. He was known as the "earthshaker." My people were known for their powerful indlamu dances and their intricate harmonies that rang all over the world when they sang. I still remember my father's favorite song. The song of hope, he called it.

THULI *(Starts a song while* QEDUSIZI *continues her monologue.)*

We Madala bo!
Wazungelez' umuzi weny' indoda
Owakho!
Owakho wawushiya nobani.

QEDUSIZI That's the song! That's the song! Whenever the men started that song, we all knew what they wanted. Oh yes! It was a challenge to Nqolobane, my father, to show them what he could do. And at that stage he could not resist. He would start circling the men, leading them first in the clapping of hands.

THULI *(Out loud)*

Uyeyeni!
Wazungelez, umuzi weny' indoda
Kanti unjani lomuntu
Owakho wawushiya nobani.

And his body would be transformed, then his legs would fly to the sky and come down to earth with thunderous thuds;

Uyeyeni!
Wazungelez', umuzi weny' indoda
Kanti unjani lomuntu
Owakho wawushiya nobani.

QEDUSIZI There was a sense of unity in the music, a sense of community and a sense of hope in the music. Not only did he take me with him to all these functions, he also let me stay in school until I finished. From a very early age I had a strong desire to teach. So upon finishing high school I went to train as a teacher, but when I came back to Bergville I could not find a job. The only places where there was a shortage of teachers were in the big cities, Johannesburg and Durban. And you could not work in the cities unless you had the right papers. That presented a big problem for those of us who were born in the rural areas, because our passes did not permit us to work anywhere else, but in the rural areas.

I decided to take the risk and go to Johannesburg to try my luck, even without papers. But before leaving for Johannesburg,

I went to my uncle who slaughtered a goat for me, asking the ancestors to guide and protect me throughout my travels.

(At the end of her monologue QEDUSIZI *walks back to the boxes and* RUBY LEE *comes back down.)*

Three

RUBY LEE As soon as I was old enough to work I had to leave Marion because there certainly weren't any jobs there. I hated to leave my friends but my mother found me a sleep-in job in Montgomery. I will never forget my first day at work. *(Chuckle)*...I was in the living room cleaning when that scrawny-looking white woman came in:

MRS DOBSON (AS GINA TORRES) Girl, make sure that you use plenty of elbow grease.

RUBY LEE Well, I spent half the morning looking for that elbow grease. *(Laughs)* I couldn't find it so I just put more effort into my work. Well, she didn't complain, I finally figured out that "elbow grease" simply meant that she wanted me to clean like my arm was on fire. Now, the next morning she came back again and sent me into the bathroom to clean the toilet bowl without a brush.

MRS DOBSON Ruby Lee, just get on your knees and swish that rag around in the bowl. Make sure that you get it nice and clean now.

RUBY LEE With that stupid grin on her face. It wasn't that the work was so hard, it was just that she wanted you to do everything the hard way. That woman wasn't happy unless you were down on your knees. Then, when Thursday rolled around she told me that I couldn't have my day off because they were going away the following weekend and that she didn't want to leave me in the house by myself. So I would take next weekend off, without pay, and report to work the following Monday.

Well, my first day off in Montgomery finally arrived. I will never forget that day if I lived to be 150, December 1, 1955. I went to catch the Cleveland Ave bus to my aunt May Ella's house. Well, I was lucky enough to get a seat in the first row after the white section next to another coloured woman. There was a coloured lady and a coloured man sitting across the aisle. Well, two stops later the bus took on some white riders near the Empire Theater. The driver yelled out for the four of us to "get up and move to the back of the bus".

At first didn't none of us move. Then the driver, a big hairy cracker, got up and came towards us. "You all better make it light on yourselves and let me have them seats."

So, I eased my shoes back on and stood up. In fact we all moved except for the woman across the aisle from me. She said she didn't think she should move because she was not in the white section. Then the driver said: "Gal, the white section is wheresonever I decide it is."

Then he stormed out of the bus and came back with two white policemen. Now you know, them Alabama policemen ain't got no time for no belligerent coloured womens. Well, they came inside the bus and called the woman a black so and so and told her to give up her seat or go straight to jail because she was breaking the Alabama Bus Segregation laws. They then hauled her off to jail and that was that. We continued to Cleveland Avenue and after I put that mess out of my mind, I enjoyed my weekend at my aunt May Ella's house. That following Monday, December 5, I was fixing to go back to work when I found out that them Negroes in Montgomery had lost their minds. There were millions of coloured people out in the streets that morning talking about they wasn't gonna ride the buses on account of some coloured lady had been arrested because she had refused to give up her seat for a white man. It turned out to be the same woman I was on the bus with Thursday last.

I had to walk more than three miles to work that day. I was mad and scared. I didn't want no trouble, I just wanted to get to work. I got there late and that woman fired me on the spot. Threw my pay at me and slammed the door. I tried to find another job but with that bus boycott going on it proved impossible.

That bus boycott lasted over a year, 381 days from December 5, 1955 to December 21, 1956. I hung in there as long as I could but when I couldn't get another job it got hard on my aunt May Ella and I had to return home to Marion.

I never forgave that woman for making me lose my job, whatsaname...uh...uh...

THE CAST *(Agitated that she does not remember the name.)* Rosa Parks!

(RUBY LEE *shrugs and goes back to her seat as* QEDUSIZI *comes up.)*

Four

QEDUSIZI Yes, that's when I left for Johannesburg where I stayed with one of my cousins. She and her husband introduced me to various people who were known to have connections with petty officials who could fix my papers, for a fee, of course. But for a strange reason all those people would meet me with enthusiasm and would inexplicably disappear whenever they were supposed to take me to their contacts, to fix my papers.

Before I knew it I had been in Johannesburg for a whole year, without the right papers and without being able to work. I started looking for odd jobs just to keep myself busy, doing washer work for white women. This is not what I wanted to do but I had to make ends meet.

Then one day, the house I lived in was raided for permits. This was not the first time. We had been raided two times before.

The first time they had arrested me and I spent fifteen days in jail. They released me and told me to leave Johannesburg.

The second time they arrested me and sent me to jail for a month. When I was released, my cousins bribed a policeman and I was not sent back to Bergville.

This was the third time and I knew that I had struck out. The judge just looked me over once and said: "Have you ever dug potatoes with your bare hands? Guilty! Six months hard labour. Bethal prison farm."

When we got to Bethal, this one policeman huddled us together and just threw us into the office. Then another policeman said:

GINA BREEDLOVE (*as* POLICEMAN) (*Gets up)* Right. Tables!

(STEPHANIE *and* VALERIE *go to one side, stage left and form a table,* GINA TORRES *and* CARLA BROTHERS *go to stage right and form another table.)*

Where is my chair!

(TU *rushes and crawls under* CARLA *and* GINA TORRES, *and becomes a chair.* POLICEMAN *comes and sits on chair.)*

POLICEMAN Name.

QEDUSIZI Qedusizi Maphalala.

PRISONERS Louder!

QEDUSIZI Qedusizi MAPHALALA.

POLICEMAN Place of birth.

QEDUSIZI Bergville, Zululand.

PRISONERS You've got to talk loud in here sister.

POLICEMAN Date of birth.

QEDUSIZI September 24, 1936.

POLICEMAN Marital status.

QEDUSIZI Single.

POLICEMAN You don't get enough, hey! Offence!

QEDUSIZI No house permit.

POLICEMAN Illegal alien hey! Let's go you cheeky Kaffir. *(They go to get fingerprints on a table close by.)*

QEDUSIZI Qedusizi Maphalala prisoner number 48!

SKWIZA Wom A hom iyelele Wom A hom
Wom A hom iyelele Wom A hom
Wom A hom iyelele Wom A hom

(GINA, *as* GUARD, *leads the women to their cells and locks them in.)*

(QEDUSIZI *and* SKWIZA *are at the offices cleaning.)*

SKWIZA Qedusizi.

QEDUSIZI Skwiza.

SKWIZA Khawundiphe icuba Skwiza man, ndinqanqathekile tu, Chom'am. [Please give me a cigarette, I am craving, my friend.]

QEDUSIZI Hay man Skwiza, you always want to get me in trouble. This is dangerous.

SKWIZA Hay Skwiza man! Nginqanqatheke very bad man. Help me, Skwiza, just one cigarette. [I have a bad craving Skwiza.]

QEDUSIZI I can't be always stealing cigarettes for you, I don't even smoke.

SKWIZA I'll see you in the kitchen, Qedusizi.

QEDUSIZI You are a pain, Skwiza man. Hold on. *(She goes to the box with a telephone and is about to take out a cigarette from a box on the table when suddenly the phone rings and startles her. She runs back to where she was cleaning, and continues to clean as the phone rings. When she is sure that the "coast is clear" she comes back again and takes one cigarette from box and hands it to* SKWIZA *through a hole between the two offices/cells.)* Skwiza, there's a hole at the corner, down there.

SKWIZA Where Qedusizi? *(She fumbles all over the office looking for the hole and finally finds it and she snatches the cigarette in excitement.)*

(Lights a cigarette, jumps about in excitement, then moves upstage and calls out)

SKWIZA Next!

(The PRISONERS *jump up and in a mad rush go to line up for food.)*

SKWIZA *(Is dishing out the food)* Right!

*(*PRISONERS *come one by one to get the food until* QEDUSIZI *gets to the top of the line.)*

QEDUSIZI Skwiza man.
SKWIZA Hi! Skwiza, it's you.
QEDUSIZI Ja skwiza, more meat, Skwiza *(*SKWIZA *gives* QEDUSIZI *extra food.)*
OTHER PRISONERS Hey, what's happening up there, she's giving her more food.

(When they finish they go and lay in a clump, GINA BREEDLOVE *comes in as guard.)*

GINA Right! Qedusizi, come with me. *(Takes her by hand and disappears with her. All the* PRISONERS *look towards* IRENE/BUSI, *who is closest to the window, and ask her what happened.)*
IRENE He is taking her...
STEPHANIE Where is he taking her to?
IRENE I don't know, you should know, he took you last night.

(They all rush towards a window to peep except for RUBY LEE.*)*

Five

RUBY LEE Of course...

Of course, there was still no steady work in Marion. So I took in laundry for white folks, some sewing on the side, and took care of children. But I still could not make ends meet. Ends meet? I couldn't even get them to wave at each other. I watched the children play their games as I dreamed about getting out of Marion and getting a real job.

But on weekends Marion came to life. Saturday night, I'd get myself together, and go on by my girlfriend Nomareen's juke joint, The Flat Top.

The WHOLE CAST *transforms and they become patrons at* NOMAREEN*'s juke joint.)*

NOMAREEN How you all doing this evening. Ruby Lee, it's sure good to see ya. Welcome. Y'all here to have a good time? Look here now, if you ain't here to have you a good time tonight, you need to get the hell out of here!!! Yeah!!!
GINA BREEDLOVE I was always sneaking into Miss Nomareen's Flat Top every Saturday night. I wasn't supposed to be there because I was too young. Oh, but I didn't care, I had to be there, because there was always so much going on. Like this particular Saturday night I wasn't there but five minutes when I looked over and who did I see all up in the corner with Ms Elmira Henderson's husband...but Donna Lynn. Now I don't have to tell you what Ms Elmira said when she showed up.
ELMIRA HENDERSON She said, "Gal, what you doing over there in the corner with my husband, he's ol' enough to be your daddy."
DONNA LYNN 'Cause Daddy don't need his mama no mo!
LETTA Oh, I need me a cigarette.
ANNELEN I need a drink.
ELMIRA Well, that's all right, I don't want him no more anyway, cause his feet stink and he ain't going to heaven when he dies.
DONNA LYNN *(Coming over to fight)* His feet don't st...
NOMAREEN *(Breaks up the fight, pushes* DONNA LYNN *away)* And he don't love his Jesus! Now, there'll be none of that in here. No!!!
RUBY LEE Now, Nomareen would keep the peace until she got into her liquors, then she would jump up on top of the tables and sing the Black Blues.
NOMAREEN *(On top of table starts to sing)* "Down and out Blues". Are you my daddy baby, then why do you do me the way you do?

Chorus
Ohhhh,
Are you my baby, then why do you do me the way you do?

RUBY LEE I don't know why Nomareen sing them kinda songs.
NOMAREEN

Why turn your back on me, baby,
Walk away and leave me so blue?

RUBY LEE Nomareen got a good husband.
NOMAREEN *(Responding to* RUBY LEE*)* Hey you watch it!

Who's gonna love me sweet papa, and who's gonna warm my bed at night? (Repeat)

Cause when that winter wind gets to blowing
who's gonna hold me so tight.

RUBY LEE *(Joins* NOMAREEN *for the last few lines of the song.)* Well, Nomareen would sing the blues way past the midnight hour into the wee hours of Sunday morning. Without fail Vera would come to collect her husband, who by this time was with that husband-snatcher, Donna Lynn. I'd have to go there and save Donna Lynn because that woman was gonna kill her. *(Grabs* DONNA LYNN *by the hand.)* Gal, why don't you leave them women's husbands alone. *(*DONNA LYNN *tries to say something but* RUBY LEE *goes.)*

And then I'd change the music

(Changes the song that was going on under her monologue.)

Well see, see rider
Lord see, what you done done
See see rider, see what you done done
You know you made me love you
now your gal done come.

I'm gonna buy me buy me a pistol
Just as long as I am tall
Lord lord lord shoot that man
Catch that cannonball
Cause if he won't have me
Won't have no gal at all.

(At the end of the song they transform immediately to "Highway to Heaven".)

It's a highway to heaven
None can walk up there
but the pure in heart.
It's a highway to heaven
I am walking up the king's highway

(Repeat verse)

RUBY LEE It always tickled me that the same folks partying all night long in the juke joint were the first ones to arrive at church on Sunday morning.

(They all assume their positions in church.)

Yes, yes Lord yes Lord
Yes Lord, yes, yes Lord yes

VALERIE Amen, at this time we would like to ask for testimonies. And we shall receive them by saying Amen.

GINA BREEDLOVE

Many things about tomorrow
I don't seem to understand
But I know who holds tomorrow
And I know who holds my hand

I sing because I'm happy
I sing because I'm free
His eye is on the sparrow
And I know he watches me

First giving honour to God and to this assembly. I want to praise God for being here and I want you to pray much for me.

DONNA LYNN

Real he's real
Jesus is real to me
So many people dying
I can't live without him
That is why I love him so
Jesus Is Real to me

Giving honour to God and all the saint, I'm asking you to pray much for me, for I am only one of his lost sheep. I need your prayers. Amen.

RUBY LEE Giving honour to God, the pastor, deacons and missionaries, saints and friends. I thank the Lord that I have been able to return to His house once again. I thank the Lord that I was able to come back, finding my dear mother yet a soldier in God's army. *(Goes to audience and finds elderly woman and talks to her.)*

For mother dear, when I was a child, all I got out of church was the music. Under your leadership, the ministry of music was very strong. The spirit was always there. Now that I have been out in the world I understand that it was your guidance…God working through you, that helped me grow in a deeper understanding of faith and fellowship with the Holy Spirit. Mother, continue me in your prayers as I continue my search for spiritual fulfillment.

My mother is a soldier
She has her hand on the gospel plow
But one day she got old
Couldn't fight anymore
She said I'll stand here and fight anyhow.

Chorus
We are soldiers in the army

We've got to fight although we have to cry
We have to hold up the blood-stained banner
We have to hold it up until we die.

I'm glad, we are soldiers
Got our hands on God's gospel plow
But one day we'll get old
Can't fight anymore
Well just stand up and fight anyhow
Ohhh

Chorus
We are soldiers in the army
We've got to fight although we have to cry
We have to hold up the blood-stained banner
We have to hold it up until we die.

(At the end of the song, IRENE *goes over to the box with the phone and starts dialing.)*

Six

IRENE (*as* ALBERT TURNER) *(Talking on the phone.)* Hey Cousin, how you doing.

RUBY LEE Albert is that you. What's happening?

IRENE You. Listen, Are you interested in a job?

RUBY LEE You bet your beebee.

IRENE I spoke to the manager of the Woolworth Store and he might have a job for a dishwasher. When can you come up to Greensboro?

RUBY LEE As soon as I get off this phone. I took a Greyhound bus northbound. I got a room with a real nice coloured family and worked steady for the first time in my life.

Then one day I got a bad feeling at work, it was the same feeling I had gotten on that bus back in 1955. You see, four coloured college students came into the store and strolled over to the lunch counter just as calm as you please. With books in their hands. *(*VALERIE, LETTA, TU *and* ANNELEN *walk in as the four college students.)*

VALERIE Excuse me ma'am, could you kindly get us a waitress as we would like to be served.

RUBY LEE I just wanted to throw my hands up in the air and cry out: Please Lord, why me? Now why were they trying to put my job on the line like that. Then the manager showed up.

GINA TORRES (*as* MANAGER) Girl, why don't you try and talk some sense into your people. If they want to be served I'd be happy to serve them in the basement. You know I don't want no trouble now. I don't bother niggers. Tell them to leave the store.

STUDENTS We won't move! We won't move! We won't move!

RUBY LEE Well they didn't move. In the days to follow they brought the whole school with them, and spectators, and reporters.

IRENE *(Jumps up and becomes reporter and goes over to* STEPHANIE.*)* Excuse me ma'am, what do you think of the disturbances in the store? *(*THULI *is on the floor miming the old television cameras, winding as she follows the action.)*

STEPHANIE (*as* SOUTHERN WHITE WOMAN) First I'd like to say God bless. Well, as you know, we Southern folks are God-fearing people. Now I believe that if a person has the means to open their own store, they should be able to do and serve whom ever they want. These niggers are outside agitators, and communists. God bless you!

(The STUDENTS *start a song, "We Shall Not Be Moved", as* GINA BREEDLOVE, THULI, CARLA, STEPHANIE, IRENE *walk into the audience and start interviewing the audience about the sit-ins. When they finish the interviews they come back and join the rest of the cast as they sing "We Shall Not Be Moved".)*

(GINA TORRES *as* MANAGER *walks over to the wall downstage and posts a sign on the wall: STORE CLOSED IN THE INTEREST OF PUBLIC SAFETY.)*

RUBY LEE *(As song continues underneath)* The manager called us employees over to him to tell us we must go home and wait until he called us back to work. In the meantime I took a sleep-in job to keep myself busy. I guess you know I was never called back to work, even after they integrated the lunch counters.

Seven

QEDUSIZI I was released from prison after six months. My father had died while I was in prison and I had to go home to pay tribute to my father.

(VALERIE *gets up and becomes* QEDUSIZI*'s shadow; they both do the lines together.)*

BOTH I got home at sunset, even the cows were already in the kraal.
QEDUSIZI Kwakunomehluko, uma ngifika ekhaya.
VALERIE Something strange/different about home this time.
QEDUSIZI Isigqiki sakhe sasingekho endaweni yaso.
VALERIE I noticed that his stool was not where it usually is.
QEDUSIZI Wayethanda ukuhlala ebaleni, abheke ngasesibayeni.
VALERIE He used to sit in front of his hut facing the direction of the kraal.
QEDUSIZI Acule ingoma yakhe, eculela izinkomo zakhe.
VALERIE And would sing his favorite song to his cows.
THULI
We Madala bo!
Wazungelez'umuzi walendoda.
QEDUSIZI Amasimu ayegcwele ukhula.
VALERIE The fields were unkempt.
QEDUSIZI Kubonakala ukuthi ubaba akasekho.
VALERIE I could tell my father was gone.
QEDUSIZI Ngangena endlini, ubabomncane nomamncane bangibingelela, bangitshela amazwi kababa okugcina.
VALERIE I got inside the house, my uncle and my aunt greeted me and told me of my father's last words.
QEDUSIZI Ukuthi kwakuyisifiso sakhe ukuthi angahambi emhlabeni, angakaboni abazukulu bakhe.
VALERIE That he wished he could have lived to see his grandchildren.
QEDUSIZI Lokho kwangenza ukuthi ngihambe ngiye ethuneni likababa.
VALERIE At that moment I knew it was time to pay my respects to my father.
QEDUSIZI Ngahamba nobaba omncane saqonda khona oThukela.
VALERIE My uncle took me down the path towards Uthukela River.
QEDUSIZI Kwakukhanya unyezi nge! Ngalolosuku siya ethuneni likababa.
VALERIE The light of the moon shone through the trees and lit the way to my father's resting place.
QEDUSIZI Ngagaqa ngamadolo ngaze ngafika ethuneni likababa.
VALERIE As I neared my father's grave I fell to my knees and crawled until I found myself at my father's feet.
QEDUSIZI Baba, ngihlupheke kakhulu emadolobheni.
VALERIE Baba, I've gone through a lot in the city.
QEDUSIZI Ngicela uhambe nami ukubuyela e Johannesburg.
VALERIE Please go back with me to Johannesburg.
QEDUSIZI Ngifuna ukuba uthisha.
VALERIE I want to be a teacher.
QEDUSIZI Ngifundise izingane.
VALERIE To teach the children.
BOTH Maphalala.
QEDUSIZI Mqedankani, giligili, Mahlasela onkone, nkomibomvu ihlabana ngebala. Yanyomfa abakwa Khoza yabaqeda inkani.
THULI
Uyeyeni!
Wazungelez'umuzi weny'indoda
Owakho
Owakho waw'ushiya nobani.

Eight

MRS POOL What did you say your name was?
QEDUSIZI Qedusizi Maphalala.
MRS POOL Khedu, khedu, khedusiz Qa, Qa. Oh well, why don't I just call you Sheila. Ha ha ha! Anyway. I like girls from Zululand. They don't lie and steal like the girls from the city. Listen. Here are the rules. You will sleep in that room outside, next to the swimming pool. Under no circumstances can you bring boyfriends here. That is a no no no. You should never touch the bread in the white bread bin. That is a no no no. Always wash dishes immediately after mealtime. In the morning when you come into my bedroom to bring our tea you must knock. Qo qo qo and say, "Good morning madam, good morning master, may I please come in." Now you try it.
QEDUSIZI Good morning master, good morning madam, may I please come in.
MRS POOL No, you did not knock.
QEDUSIZI I'm sorry. Ko ko ko, may I please come in.
MRS POOL Now say, "Madam here's your tea."
QEDUSIZI Madam here's your tea.
MRS POOL Yes, but smile.

(They both smile.)

QEDUSIZI I worked for her for seven years,

then it was time for her to take me to the pass office, at Polly Street, the Women's Native Affairs Department, to have my papers fixed so I could qualify to work in Johannesburg legally. One Sunday madam was sunbathing in the pool, and I decided to take advantage of her good mood.

MRS POOL *(Sitting by swimming pool,* QEDUSIZI *appears apparently with a tray,* MRS POOL *kicks water to* QEDUSIZI*'s face, and* QEDUSIZI *is embarrassed.)* Khedu, qu, khequsizi, khequ. Khequ-sizi!

QEDUSIZI Yes madam.

MRS POOL Oh good, I've been practising. *(To say her name.)* Did you wash the breakfast dishes, press the master's pants, shine his shoes, walk the cat and prepare my lunch?

QEDUSIZI Yes madam. Madam, I've been working for you for seven years...

MRS POOL Yes, yes, yes, and you have been a good girl. Truly one of the family.

QEDUSIZI Well madam, I was wondering if you could take me to Polly Street to fix my papers.

MRS POOL Oh, yes, yes, yes. Come sit down with me and enjoy the sun. It's so hard to get a tan. *(Splashes water to* QEDUSIZI*'s face.)*

QEDUSIZI Hayi madam I'm busy. I have a lot of work to do. Madam, about my papers.

MRS POOL Oh you know, I would absolutely love an ice-cold glass of orange juice.

QEDUSIZI Yes madam.

MRS POOL And don't forget my medicine. My medicine on the rocks, that is.

QEDUSIZI Yes, madam. *(She goes to the props table and comes back with a glass.)*

MRS POOL *(Singing and monitoring her tan.)*We are marching to Pretoria, Pretoria, Pretoria. We are marching to Pretoria, ha ha ha ha ha.

QEDUSIZI Well madam, here's your ice-cold drink. It is so nice and warm madam. And your tan is nice and brown madam. As I was saying madam...about my papers.

MRS POOL Oh I am. I am brown. Oh thank you, thank you. I have been trying so hard. I said yes. Of course for you anything.

TU NOKWE *(Sitting on top of the boxes, centre stage, while the other women stand on a line behind her.* ANNELEN *is sitting on a box front stage right, as a pass office official.)* I was there at Polly Street the day that Qedusizi walked in with that white woman.

I remember that day very well. There were many women at the pass office. As usual. Others were there to apply for passes, others were there to get special permits to work in Johannesbug. Some had been told to leave Johannesburg in seventy-two hours. I was there with a group of church women to apply for passports. We were preparing for an Easter revival in Swaziland. Qedusizi walked in behind a white woman, just look at her.

MRS POOL *(Walks in, followed by* QEDUSIZI.*)* Come, come, come Khedusizi, Qa, qa.

(They proceed to where a white pass official – ANNELEN *– is sitting.)*

MRS POOL Good afternoon sir.

ANNELEN *(Nonchalantly)* Good afternoon.

*(*MRS POOL *turns around and motions to* QEDUSIZI *to bring the passbook.)*

TU They walked in and did not even stand in line.

MRS POOL My girl has been working for me for seven years and now she needs a stamp to...to...to... *(Turns around and looks at* QEDUSIZI.*)*

QEDUSIZI ...to qualify to work in Johannesburg.

MRS POOL Ah, ja, qualify to work in Johannesburg. *(Hands* ANNELEN *the passbook.)*

ANNELEN *(as* THE WHITE OFFICIAL*)* *(Pages through the passbook.)* Here tog, she's got to be out of Johannesburg in seventy-two hours. Or go to jail.

MRS POOL What? Why?

ANNELEN She's got a prison record.

MRS POOL What? Why didn't you tell me about the prison record? You stupid Kaffir.

QEDUSIZI Madam, you did not ask me.

MRS POOL What do you mean I did not ask you? Don't you know that you went to jail? *(She then turns to the white official/*ANNELEN.*)* Excuse me Sir. Do you have any girls here with papers?

ANNELEN Plenty!

(The group of women who have been standing in line start coming towards the madam with their passes, and a maddening rush starts as the other women recite their qualifications to the madam, showing her their passbooks.)

MRS POOL *(Points to* THULI *and* THULI *rushes forward to the madam and hands over her papers.)* You, you, the short Zulu girl.

THE OTHER WOMEN What short Zulu girl?

Oh that one, she's deaf and dumb madam, she can't cook, she can't speak English.

MRS POOL What is your name?

THULI Nomathemba Shange.

MRS POOL Any Nqo Nqo Nqo in your name?

THULI No, I don't have a Nqo Nqo.

MRS POOL Good! Come with me. *(Then they leave.)*

QEDUSIZI *(Looking totally dejected, goes to the center and sings.)*

Eloi Eloi elamasabakatani
Eloi Eloi elamasabakatani

Thixo wami thixo wami ungishiyelani na?
Thixo wami thixo wami ungishiyelani na?

My lord my lord why has thou forsaken me?
My lord my lord why has thou forsaken me?

TU She was devastated. You could see the picture she painted in her face. You know what? I used to think that God is a huge man behind the sky, but that day I felt God right there at the pass office. The women started mumbling something, and I knew they wanted to offer help. One woman did something even I did not anticipate. She started a song.

ANNELEN *(Starts a song and all the women rush forward to* QEDUSIZI *and lay hands on her.)*

Bambelela Kusona
Ngizo kubambelela kuso
Ngize ngizuz'umqhele wami

That was the song that did it.

(After the women circle QEDUSIZI *a few times they stop and* ANNELEN *is the only one with her hands on* QEDUSIZI *and she starts praying for her.)*

Nkosi yamazulu Jehova Sebawoti, wen'owadala izulu nomhlaba. Sisebusweni bakho namhlanje Thixo wamazulu Nkulunkulu wawo Hintsa. Sithi nayi imvu yakho Nkosi iguqe ngamadolo phambi kwakho icela usizo. Yehla wena emazulwini wenze imimangaliso yakho, njengoba wayenza ekudaleni kubantwana base sirayeli nkosi. Yehla emazulwini ukhulume nkosi. Ulungise izindlela zalomtwana umkhanyisele. Sicela egameni lendodana yakho Ujesu khrestu owafa wasifela Amen.

TU Then a miracle happened. The white man who had told Qedusizi to leave Johannesburg in seventy-two hours came back and took her passbook, put a different stamp on it and told her that she could now work anywhere she wanted. The Lord works in mysterious ways.

Nine

RUBY LEE In the spring of 1961 I started thinking seriously about moving back to Marion. I got word that my mother was low sick and I needed to return home as soon as I could. Lots of people were travelling through the south at that time because it was getting close to Mother's Day...May 14th, 1961. So I figured that I better get on a bus to Montgomery, where I would transfer and I might make it to Marion on time, that would make my mother so happy. I didn't even tell my white family that I wouldn't be back, I just left. *(Laughter)* I noticed that something was different as soon as I got on that bus. You see, there were coloured folks sitting in the front of the bus. I mean, right behind the driver. And there were white and coloured folks seated together throughout the bus. They all seem to know each other. As soon as the bus left Greensboro they started clapping their hands and stamping their feet in rhythm. Then they started chanting some kind of slogans...you know like at a college rally or something...

Let's go, let's go to victory
We shall win, we shall overcome
Let's go, let's go to victory
We shall win, we shall overcome
Let's go, let's go

Then some of them turned to me and tried to make me understand what they was about.

CARLA We are on a freedom ride.

IRENE We want to sit anywhere we want on these buses.

STEPHANIE We want to use the white facilities.

VALERIE Like the water fountain.

GINA BREEDLOVE Don't forget the bathroom.

GINA TORRES We want to be able to go into them white restaurants.

CARLA And eat in them too.

Bust Jim Crow
Bust Jim Crow
Bust Jim Crow

RUBY LEE I listened to everything they said and was afraid for them. See, we had been up South all that time and were headed for

Alabama and Mississippi and them crackers down there did not play, and would try to hurt them. When I told them this they said they were counting on them rednecks to do something foolish so they could compel the federal government to enforce the 1946 Bus Desegregation Laws. Now, that is when I considered changing buses in Atlanta and waiting for another bus, but I did not want to get home too late. Well, the first city as soon as we crossed the Alabama state line was Anniston. Now, Anniston is the thick of Ku Klux Klan country.

So when the bus pulled up into the station we were met by an angry white mob. They surrounded the bus and started yelling all kinds of obscenities. They had sticks, knives and bricks. Anything they could get their hands on. When the riders wouldn't get off the bus, they tried to force their way on the bus. So we formed a human barricade by the doors. That only made them madder...If that was possible. They started slashing the tires and beating on the outside of the bus with their axe-handle sticks. Inside we started yelling for the driver to get out of there!

FREEDOM RIDERS Move on! Move on! Move on!

RUBY LEE The driver got out of the station as soon as he could...So the mob jumped in their cars and pickups and followed us. We almost made it to Highway 78 but the bus started leaning to the side and the driver realized that the slashed tires were going flat. So he was forced to pull over to the side of the highway. He cut off the engine and high-tailed it into the woods like a jackrabbit.

VALERIE I was on that bus!

RUBY LEE Right!

VALERIE Yes I was there, when they started throwing bricks and stones and bottles.

CAST Right!

VALERIE And through a broken window, they threw a firebomb and we all went belly down in the aisles of the bus.

CAST Oh my goodness.

VALERIE Then the seats caught fire and we all scrambled towards one another in a huddle for safety. The flames were growing, engulfing the bus in one crazy inferno. Then the smoke became thicker and thicker. We could not see. People were coughing and choking and gasping for air. We all rushed to the door. Then a miracle happened. The doors of the bus opened and I flew out of the bus, and as soon as the last of the riders got out it exploded, sending debris flying everywhere.

Ten

TU

Qezu Ngane yakwethu
Kuth'angizinqume khona namhlanje
Qezu ngane yakwethu
Kuth'angizinqume khona namhlanje

VALERIE (*as* SCHOOL TEACHER) *(Is in front talking to the rest of the cast, as* STUDENTS, *sitting and standing around the boxes.)* Wonderful students. Now do you understand the concept I am trying to teach you?

STUDENTS Yes teacher!

QEDUSIZI You see, it is the same method found in Western choral music. Are you listening?

STUDENTS Yes teacher!

QEDUSIZI You see when the missionaries came, they heard our intricate harmonies and took that concept from us. The only difference is that they wrote it down and we didn't.

NOMATHEMBA Amandla!

CLASS Awethu.

NOMATHEMBA Yes mistress. These white people came to our land took our brothers and sisters to foreign lands in America and changed their names. Then they came here and gave us the Bible. How we have the Bible and they have the gun and our land. Ah mistress, now our music too. Awu ngeke, Kanti koze kube nini. Amandla! [How long can this nonsense go on?]

CLASS Awethu!

NOMATHEMBA Mistress, did you read the newspapers today about Mthuli?

ANNELEN That man they killed fighting for our culture.

THULI Ja! Yesterday, last night, twelve midnight. The police and the soldiers came with those big machines and shattered his tombstone to pieces.

TU They pushed him in front of a moving train, mistress.

NOMATHEMBA He was defending our mothers, mistress.

QEDUSIZI Mthuli Shezi.

CLASS Yes.

QEDUSIZI Germiston Station.

CLASS Yes.
QEDUSIZI December, 1972.
CLASS Yes.
QEDUSIZI He was defending me. Yes! I remember that day very well. December 12, 1972. I was at Germiston Station with another woman, Mrs Mazibuko waiting for the train. There were a lot of people at the station that day, and suddenly I saw these two white railway officials coming towards us. I did not pay them any mind. Then one of them got very close to me, that is when I knew something was up.
ANNELEN (*as* THE WHITE OFFICIAL) Hey, Kaffir maid, what are you doing here.
TU NOKWE (*as* MRS MAZIBUKO) We are waiting for the train, my baas.
EBONY JOANN Ek praat nie met jou nie, I am not talking to you, I am talking to this Kaffir woman. Wat maak julle hierso?
QEDUSIZI We are waiting for a train makhulu baas...

Before I could finish the sentence, he (CAST *claps hands at the same time.*) slapped me across the face. Then a young black came out from the crowd. I just knew that he was going to intervene on our behalf.
THULI DUMAKUDE Aga man, Lezinto ziyadelela, they need to learn to respect our mothers.
QEDUSIZI Then a scuffle broke out between the two whites and the black man. A train was coming. And they pushed him in front of the train!

Eleven

RUBY LEE You see, while I was away from home I had lost contact with the church community. But after returning, I devoted all of my time to my mother. It was then that I saw how the congregation rallied around my mother in her last days, making it easier for her to accept her fate peacefully.
IRENE

I love the Lord he heard my cry.
I will dwell in the house of the Lord for the rest of my days.

RUBY LEE Seeing that, and just the series of things that had happened to me, made me wonder if the Lord was trying to tell me something, telling me that maybe I was looking for my good in all the wrong places. I then decided to stay in Marion, and recommitted myself to staying in the house of the Lord.

(Back to the song, which was being sung quietly under the monologue.)

RUBY LEE THEN, on February 18, 1965 all hell broke loose in Marion. You see, Albert, and other civil rights activists, had started holding voter registration mass meetings at the Zion Methodist Church. That night, Jimmy Lee Jackson had stopped by my house, after dropping his mother and his grandfather, Cager Lee, at the church. They were both very active in the voter registration movement. See Jimmy Lee had come down with a cold and had wanted me to fix him some of my mother's favourite cold remedy. After giving him some of that remedy, I insisted that I go to pick up his family for him because he looked mighty sick. He insisted on going, so I went with him to Zion Methodist Church.
STEPHANIE I was in that church that night. The night of the beatings. We had been gathering in the church regularly for almost two months because the voter registration movement was growing. We had been expecting Dr King that night, but he couldn't make it so he sent a representative, a Willie Bolden. Bolden's mission was to get the folks stirred up and he did too, because by the end of his speech we was all fired up, singing those freedom songs and ready to march to the jailhouse.

Woke up this morning with my mind
Stayed on freedom
Woke up this morning with my mind
Stayed on freedom
Woke up this morning with my mind
Stayed on freedom
Hallelu, hallelu, hallelujah

We lined up two by two. I was in front of the line, not too far from Turner and Bolden, the two march leaders. As soon as we stepped out of the doors of the church we were greeted by what looked like a scene from hell. Hundreds of white mens were standing there waiting for us, with the meanest expressions on their faces. They was carrying axe handles, billy clubs, hoes and picks; some even had guns. Then there was about three hundred state troopers there too. Then the local sheriff came up and said that we were assembled illegally. "You all better disperse, else there'll be some trouble here tonight." Then he started counting. Then as he was counting some of those white mens pulled out their guns and shot the streetlights. Pow! Pow! Pow!

RUBY LEE The streetlights started going out, as soon as we pulled up in the parking lot in front of Mack's Cafe, right next to the church. Then we heard gunshots, sounded like firecrackers. Then we saw people, lots of folks running towards from the direction of the church in the dark. We could see shadows as they passed the truck. They were holding their heads and running. They were screaming...

STEPHANIE (*as* WOMAN IN THE MARCH) We were running. I had Mr Cager Lee by my hand, Jimmy Lee's 82-year-old grandfather. I was trying to get him to run a little faster but Mr Cager Lee was an old man. Soon the troopers caught up with us and started beating us up. I had to let his hand go as they beat him down to the ground. I overheard one of them say "B.J., that's old Mr Cager Lee. Don't beat him no more." When they left him I came back and tried to help him up.

RUBY LEE The only light that was left in the area was right in front of the cafe. Then Jimmy Lee's mother ran past us towards Mack's Cafe with the troopers hot on her heels. That is when Jimmy jumped out of the truck and followed. She did not even get inside the cafe when the troopers got her and dragged her out of the cafe. And started beating her up. She put up a hell of a struggle but a group overpowered her. By then Jimmy Lee had gotten to where she was and tried to intervene. When they saw him they left his mother and turned onto Jimmy.

They started beating on him with those clubs. When they could not knock him down I saw one of the troopers pull out his gun, put it up against Jimmy's side and shot him. Pow! Pow! Pow!

RUBY LEE He shot him three times!

QEDUSIZI Jimmy Lee.

RUBY LEE Somehow Jimmy Lee broke free, only to run smack dab into another group of white men, who proceeded to beat him again, all upside his head. When he managed to break away this time he was facing the pickup. Seemed like he could see me. I tried to signal to him to come to the truck, while I tried to remain hidden from the others. But Jimmy couldn't see me. He ran past the pickup and continued up the hill. Stumbling but never falling. When he got to the top of the hill he just disappeared. I had never seen nothing like that before. It looked to me like Jimmy Lee went straight on up to heaven.

(Lights fade)

(THULI *starts a song,* "Nxa Ebizwa Amagama", *and the women join in.)*

(As the lights come up the women start hugging one another, and get up and get into one big clump of a hug. Lights fade briefly and come up as the women sing):

WOMEN Amen Amen.

(As the women sing Amen, Amen, RUBY LEE *and* QEDUSIZI *reach for each other's hands. Then the rest of the cast gets up and they start hugging in one big tight clump. When they break free they get into a wide circle, holding hands, and bow inwardly once, and then run towards the boxes and start clapping hands, recognizing* KHALIQ, *the musician. Then they leave.)*

(Curtain!)

Magi Noninzi Williams

> Not much has been said about who we are and of our dreams and aspirations. I believe that it is time we break away from our patriarchal shackles and liberate ourselves because nobody is going to do it for us.

Playwright, producer, actress, and director, Magi Williams is one of the most produced black female playwrights in South Africa. She is the author of *Kwa-Landlady* (winner of the 1993 First National Bank (FNB) Vita Award for Most Promising Play, equivalent to the American Tony Award), *Sisters of the Calabash*, (FNB 1994 Vita Award for the Best Ensemble Work), *Rise and Shine*, *Ma-Dladla's Beat*, *Ebony & Ivory*, and *Voices of the 90s*.

Magi was born in Alexander township, but her family later moved to Soweto, where she was educated and spent most of her life. Her interest in the arts began at an early age with encouragement from her father, an actor, playwright, and musician. As a child, Magi traveled with her father and his musical groups during the holidays. On many occasions, she would perform Christmas carols with group members. She also watched a great deal of theatre written/produced by prominent playwright Gibson Kente, whose work inspired her to act. In high school she performed in Shakespearean plays such as *The Merchant of Venice*. At the age of 18, Magi appeared at the Market Theatre in *Die Van Aardes Ban Grootoor*, by Pieter Dirk Uys. Since that time she has appeared in numerous productions, including Benjy Frances' *Burning Embers*, and *Othello*, *Julius Caesar*, *The Good Woman of Sharkville*, *Black Age*, *Joseph and the Amazing Technicolour Dreamcoat*, to name a few. For television, Magi appeared in *Egoli*, *Soul City 2*, *Sister Mercy*, and *Umuntu Ngumuntu Ngabantu*. She has travelled to Europe as a performer in *Burning Embers* and *The Good Woman of Sharkville*.

Magi's writing career developed through poetry during her twenties, just jotting things down about life while living alone. She was inspired to write her first play from an actual incident, which centered on a young rape victim. Magi's radio and television set had been stolen, and when she went to the Orlando township police station to report the incident there was an eleven-year-old girl who arrived bleeding – a victim of rape.

> A policeman interrogated the young girl in front of everyone in a very rough way. This was a turning point for me to write plays. It affected me deeply. The play looks at the stigma of rape that stays with you, and how it affects you throughout life. The play deals with a married woman, who is a nurse, who is raped and who has to go through a backyard abortion. It is a very angry play that has never been produced.

Most of Magi's plays deal with strong social issues, with an emphasis on the plight of African women. *Kwa-Landlady* (1992) is her second play and also explores abuse of women. In this, as in her other plays, she does not write totally in English. She incorporates Zulu, Afrikaans, and Sotho. "I have to write that way. I feel that as black people there are some things we express better in our own language. Humour is completely different and lost if translated." *Sisters of the Calabash* (1994), her next piece, is a celebration of womanhood through song, dance, and poetry.

> We are trying to revive the culture of storytelling through the use of poetry. We perform these poems which we have

written ourselves and we fuse them with vibrant dances and our traditional songs. We also fused them with songs from the African-American women's group, Sweet Honey in the Rock. Mainly a celebration to also say that women have been a part of the struggle, and we haven't just been in the house looking after babies. We were there in 1976 as well. We won't be shuffled to the background.

Her next play, *Ebony & Ivory* (1995), focuses on a relationship between a black woman and a white woman from different backgrounds, living together in a Yeoville flat. Her play *Ma-Dladla's Beat* (1996), is a one-woman piece about a single mother from KwaZulu-Natal who travels to Johannesburg to find her lost husband, but also to seek greener pastures. "She comes with big dreams, particularly in the new South Africa, only to find that things haven't changed." The play premiered at Lincoln Center in New York City for the second Woza Afrika! Festival during July of 1997.

Rise & Shine (1996) examines four women in an insane asylum. The work deals with abuse and why the women are there. "The play also informs us how some people in the asylum are some of sanest, because society is so insane."

Most of Magi's plays have premiered at the Windybrow Centre in Johannesburg: "Any other way is difficult [referring to the Windybrow]. People don't value women writers. It's also very difficult for a black woman in South Africa." Her most recent piece, *Voices of the 90s: Woman to Woman*, provides a critical view of contemporary society and women's views on relationships, careers, men, and children: "This drama, with poetry and music, is also a mouthpiece for a liberated woman, who still has many bridges to cross in the so-called free culture we live in."

Magi considers herself a self-taught writer, but would love the opportunity to work with a mentor. In 1993, she formed Inkaba Players, consisting of four women. *Inkaba* means "origin of a people" and at the same time it means "umbilical cord" – representing motherhood, warmth, and sustenance. Magi resides in Johannesburg, where she does voice-overs and radio plays, in addition to her writings.

ARTISTIC STATEMENT

Kwa-Landlady is a play about female abuse, but in a different way. (*Kwa-Landlady* means "at the landlady's place".) Abuse in the sense that people who are in power will abuse you, and even black people abuse each other when they have power. This is from my experience living in a back room (I left home quite early); experiences that I went through such as being abused by men who were landlords. Because I'm an actress, I was looked upon as odd. I was very strange to them. I dressed differently, and I'm a free spirit.

I work strange hours as an actress, and I go to work when most people are returning. So for them "She's not working, we don't see her on TV, she says she's working but where? She must be lying, she's not working, she has lots of strange friends that visit, she's not married, so she must be a prostitute in the Hilbrow District." People never understood even if you explained, because at that time, the 1980s, people were not used to going to the Market Theatre, the Civic, or the Windybrow. It was mainly whites who attended those theatres. Black people would attend Gibson Kente and other township plays, and for them those were the only plays. So if you were not involved with Gibson or not on television, you were not an actress. You had to be lying and must be a prostitute. So those are some of the things I had to deal with as an actress living away from home in that environment. Also, general abuse – you have to do certain things, certain laws that are so stupid. So I created *Kwa-Landlady*, where people were expected to be home at certain hours, sweep their yards at certain times, or other foolish things. Using power to abuse people that live there. It's about abuse multiplied – it's a vicious cycle.

THE ROLE OF THEATRE IN SOUTH AFRICA

The role of theatre in South Africa is to communicate or depict events of the past and present in an informative, stylized and entertaining manner. Our theatre is not only political, but it also touches on all different aspects of our diverse societies. Lastly, it creates a forum for debate. It makes people think.

HAVE SITUATIONS IMPROVED FOR BLACK WOMEN IN THEATRE IN THE NEW SOUTH AFRICA?

As a black South African woman, you work on certain levels. You have to deal with so many negativities and rejections as a woman in this business. I'm still looked upon as a newcomer. It's so much to deal with. There's so much fighting that has to be done. So many male plays have been written and performed, but not enough about women's issues and their contribution. I don't see things getting better without continuous fighting. I would like to see women network more, and share ideas. Confidence is a big problem with many of the women. Other problems exist such as women having to deal with families, jobs, and transportation – these are all issues. Getting sponsorship has been a problem. I'm considering going toward television in order to supplement my theatre work, since theatre pays so little. I also find it crazy how South Africans have to establish themselves in another country to be recognized by their own.

HAVE THINGS IMPROVED IN GENERAL IN THE NEW SOUTH AFRICA?

The new South Africa. What does it mean to an average person in the street? Streets cluttered with vendors, homeless children, squatter camps mushrooming everywhere. Have we really moved on? Affirmative action, yes – but what does it mean without proper education? As far as I'm concerned the rich are still rich, the poor are poorer. We need empowerment if we are to go anywhere as people.

PRODUCTION HISTORY

Kwa-Landlady premiered in 1993 at the Windybrow Centre for the Arts in Johannesburg. Magi Williams and Pat Maphiki Maboe directed the play. Performers included Thembsie Times, Pat Maboe, Magi Williams, Pretty Nomhle Tokwe, Lindiwe Cebekhulu, and Ernest Ndlovu.

Interview conducted July 1996 and July 1997, in Johannesburg.

Photo by Mothalefi Mahlabe.

10 Kwa-Landlady

Magi Noninzi Williams

Characters
DADDY
NOZIZWE
LINDA
MA-CUMMINGS
RAHABA

Act I

Scene 1

(Scene takes place in NOZIZWE*'s room.* DADDY *knocks – carrying a bottle of gin and tonic.)*

DADDY Nozizwe, can I come in?
NOZIZWE *(Surprised)* Yes. Come in, Daddy.
DAD Thank you *(Sits down)*. Can I have some glasses Nozi, I'm so thirsty. *(Gives him some glasses, sits down and looks down, sadly.)*
NOZI Hayi Daddy, I'm having problems with job.
DAD Awu shame, that's why I haven't been seeing you at the bus stop. A lot of people are losing their jobs these days.
NOZI Yes Daddy.
DAD Ag Nozi, don't worry, Daddy is here, have a drink.
NOZI Hayi Daddy, I don't drink beer.
DAD This is not beer, this is gin and tonic – it will cheer you up, it'll make your blood run.
NOZI Hayi Daddy.
DAD C'mon Nozi – drink baby. *(Nozi drinks and chokes. Daddy laughs.)* Don't worry, you'll be fine, it's always like that when you start drinking.
NOZI Thank you.
DAD Nozi tell me something, now that it's the end of the month – how are going to pay your rent?
NOZI I don't know, Daddy.
DAD You mean to say your boyfriend doesn't pay your rent, buy you food, or clothes?
NOZI Hayi Daddy, mina angijoli.
DAD I don't believe that such a nice-looking girl like you hasn't got a lover. Wow! Look at those dimples, umhle Nozi, you know. *(She blushes.)* You know what, bayangazi – they know me, la elokishini. Some call me the Boss, some call me Mr. Executive. Ek is Ou Bra Z van kofifi. I've got money like...like dust. Let me see what I've got here... *(Searches his back pocket)* Yea, let me see. *(Counts money)* Here, have this. Will this be enough?
NOZI Hayi Daddy imal'engaka, shoo, so much money. No I can't!
DAD C'mon take it. *(*NOZI *stands up nervously.)* Take it, this is nothing. *(*DADDY *pushes money into* NOZI*'s breast.)* Nozi, Nozi, I want you and me to be like...this *(Indicates)*...like this! *(*NOZI *is alarmed by his tone.)* Do you hear me? Do you hear me my girl?
NOZI Y–Yes Daddy.
DAD And not a word to anyone about this, okay?
NOZI I...
DAD Do you hear me? *(She nods, then* DADDY *smiles.)* See you tomorrow night! *(He exits.)*

Scene 2

(Same evening – room is dark. LINDA *enters, tries to put the light switch on, stumbles on furniture, ends up finding a candle; she is mumbling to herself all along.)*

LINDA No, no, no. This is too much. I can't take this anymore. Lomfazi usile, you know. Mh! The lights are switched off, the plugs haven't been working, how am I supposed to read my script? Where's those matches?

(Searches her bag, lights candles, and as she tries to pump the Primus stove NOZI *enters)* Hayi suka, this is too much.

NOZIZWE Hawu sis Linda kwenze...

LI Nozi what are you doing here, you gave me such a fright!

NOZI I was afraid in my room, but why are you talking to yourself?

LI Asi-hilesidwedwe ebathi Uma-Cummings.

NOZI Who?

LI This Ma-Cummings woman, man.

NOZI Oh, Uma-Cummings. What's her story this time?

LI Phela, she has put the rent up again. Imagine.

NOZI Kanjani?

LI Haven't you heard? I got a circular last night when I came back from rehearsals.

NOZI No, no, sis Linda, this is unfair. We can't afford this rent going up, up all the time.

LI Apparently, we are being called to the "round table" again. You know mos it's a meeting again at eight o'clock tonight. "Don't be late," she said. When am I supposed to do my cooking?

NOZI But sis Li, what are we going to do?

LI First thing tomorrow morning, I'll be going to the Post Office to phone Zupra, and I want to speak to Mr. Zungezile, nqo ezimpondweni.

NOZI What is Zupra?

LI Zupra, Nozi, is a union. If they can help the twilight kids, they can fight for us too.

NOZI But how can they help us?

LI I'll just report Uma-Cummings to them and they will deal with her accordingly, because they know exactly how much people must pay and where.

NOZI Hayi but Ma-Cummings is so hard in die bek, and besides she's got that lawyer friend of hers – we don't stand a chance. Who are we to fight against the Cummings family? They are so powerful.

LI Bullshit! Nozizwe, wake up! You must not be intimidated by anybody. You've got rights too, didn't you know that Nozi?

NOZI Ai! Ai! Yazi mina ngiyabesaba. Phela mina, I've got nowhere to go. So I've got to be nice to Ma-Cummings and do what she tells me.

LI Nozi, there's no way that I'm going to go back home. I can't stand my stepfather you know. I can't stand the way he looks at me, undressing me with his eyes. I hate it! I cannot stand that man, strue's God. He is...so...Yechi! *(Shudders)*. So I am as homeless as you are.

NOZI But you've got brothers, and sisters, and a mother there.

LI You see, those kids of his are so precious to him that they are treated like glass. Ekbeteken vokol [I don't mean anything]. As for my mother, she is just this meek lamb. I don't know what she sees in that ugly man.

NOZI But, I thought you once said you come from a well-to-do family.

LI W–well yes. They are rich. A big house, taxis, shops, but it has nothing to do with me. I want my own career.

NOZI It's always the case, when people are lucky. I don't understand. If I had parents like that, I would be proud of them! I would!!

LI Listen Nozizwe, don't upset me now, I don't want to talk about those people. Let's concentrate on Ma-Cummings and tonight, and what we are going to say to her.

NOZI But, sis, what is there to say?

LI We are not paying the increased rent. Uyangizwa, I don't care whether my lights are brought back or not. I'll somer use my candles and Primus stove, until Zupra fixes her, or I'll have to leave.

NOZI Oh, sis Linda, if you go what will happen to me. I'm already treated like a dog in this yard. Those two are always talking about me.

LI No, I think I won't go. Where to? A place like Phomolong Extension would be triple the amount we are paying here. No, I won't go. Why should I give her that pleasure. I'm going to fight Ma-Cummings to the bitter end. *(Indicates)*

NOZI Uma-Cummings not Rahaba. Amathe nolwimi, so close.

LI You know this makes me so mad. Hayi, Jesus, uyazi uyahlanya lomfazi. This is a complete rip-off, I mean manginangena – the rent was R80 per month, after six month it was R120, then R160 and now R250. Ga, she thinks we've got money-machines in our rooms. Imagine ama-R250 a zowa-collecta end of this month. I mean this is ridiculous.

NOZI Hayi! Mina angazi sis Linda.

LI Don't say you don't know Nozi. Let's make a stand now, together! And nothing will defeat us. Uyazi ukuthini. Unity is strength. So please I need your support, my sister.

NOZI Sizobona *(Shrugs)* Hayi? Kodwa i-R250 is too much manje man.

LI For interest sake, how much are you getting

a month wena Nozi. I'm sorry I'm trying to pry into your life.

NOZI Yo! sis Linda thina kwa Masipala si thola R640 a month.

LI Oh shit!

NOZI Uyazi kahle, kahle mina sis Linda I have a problem.

LI What is it?

NOZI There's a big (wages) strike at work. It's tools down. For two weeks, we don't go to work.

LI Uthin' apha kum.

NOZI From next week Monday nobody is allowed to go to work. So I don't know what to do.

LI What do you mean, you don't know what to do?

NOZI Hayi phela sis Linda, how will I pay my rent?

LI How will other people pay their rent, Nozi?

NOZI Phela other people have their homes right here in Johannesburg, some don't even have to pay rent.

LI Manje u concluder ngokuthini sis.

NOZI Hayi mina, I am going to work – whether they kill me or not.

LI Heyi wena, don't talk like a child.

NOZI I mean sis Linda, what will I eat?

LI Sikhona, we'll see what to do, we'll share.

NOZI If you were me, what would you do?

LI I'd be strong and join the strike.

NOZI Ngibe usayinyova, a terrorist. It's easy to talk neh!

LI I mean, do you call i-R640 per month a living wage – ke wena?

NOZI Hayi akufani nokuhlala. It's not like sitting.

LI Listen Nozi you are working very, very hard, more than…

NOZI Thina sesa jwayela, I'm not a lazy person.

LI You are virtually keeping the whole township clean.

NOZI Hayi, into ezincane lezo – small matters?

LI So, you cannot betray your fellow-workers. You've got to support them and then you'll enjoy the fruits nawe, afterwards.

NOZI Ama-fruits? What fruits sis Linda, umasipalate won't give us fruits, he can't even give us mieliemeal. I know them ngeke ba-change-labelungu. [Those whites don't change.]

LI Nozi I don't mean those fruits. I mean, the sweat from your labor. If you unite and do this together those whites will be forced to give in.

NOZI Anyway angizelanga lezozinto all the way from Swaziland. Crossing borders, sleeping on the road, hiking, going through forest at night until Johannesburg.

LI Oh well, it's up to you really, if you feel you are worth i-R640 fine. But if it was me, I would fight for my rights. Anyway I've got to go and get some junk food somewhere. *(Picks up a tray of eggs.)* What a waste of money.

NOZI Hayi mina, ngi-awright, I've already eaten.

LI Okay see you later.

Scene 3

*(*UMA-CUMMINGS *is in her house. She has curlers on her head – hums softly as she paints her nails –* RAHABA *enters.)*

MA-C Hu! You look so dolled up, where are you off to?

RAHABA To church my Dali.

MA-C On a Thursday, ag man Rebs, don't lie.

RAH I'm taking this cake to Ntate Moruti, so that he mustn't just drink tea with ordinary bread.

MA-C Mhn! I'm impressed, you really like him, hey.

RAH Like him is another story. I adore him. He is God's chosen child, Ngoana Modimo. He is so powerful.

MA-C Awu Rebs, do you know him that well? Mh! Rahaba please help me with these rollers.

RAH *(Takes off* MA-C*'s curlers)* I hear there's a newcomer in the yard.

MA-C Hayi shame, poor girl.

RAH Why do you say that?

MA-C Sy's net a plaasjapie. You know mos-so. *(Indicates)*

RAH Ummoni, he-he? *(Laughs)* Ke se katane. She puts on tshalis, utsoba se neifi. And what's that stuff she puts on her face?

MA-C She calls it ummemezi.

RAH Ja memeza.

MA-C No Rebs it's called – ummemezi. It's from a bark of a tree, they grind it *and* mix it with water. It's supposed to give you this lovely complexion.

RAH Maar why bother, she's already ugly, kesekobo.

MA-C That girl works in the sun the whole day, she applies it to save her skin.

RAH Ubusy ka-compi, unyile kedi-chubaba – sunburns.
MA-C Hayi Rebs you are so rude!
RAH Heysh, sorry God will forgive me, but can she be really so backwards this is not Swatsini.
MA-C Hayi shame Rebs, leave her alone motlogele tle.
RAH Did you see her room? – empty, empty, empty-hayi!
MA-C She'll cover up, as long as she's got a roof over her head.
RAH Hu! Nna ngoana Mokgamapane, I will never sweep the streets of Soweto. It's the lowest of the jobs.
MA-C You are so fancy, how do you afford my rent wena anyway?
RAH Nna kebo tlali, I'm clever, I've been saving all my life – ntse ke sa bechetse banna, I've never been a sugar-mommy.
MA-C But you've never worked since I've known you. How?
RAH Phela my government. It pays for my injured leg so why should I worry?
MA-C Actually what happened? I've been wanting to ask you all along ke tsaba gore utla mpoqa I'm afraid.
RAH I was working in a butchery one year, and we had to remove these big chunks of meat from the freezers, then one day it was my turn to take the meat out, it was cold and slippery so I could not hold it properly, it fell on my leg and I've never been right since. Yaka u bona jana. *(Opens the bandages)*
MA-C Ag shame Rebecca. Now, tell me something – have you ever been married before?
RAH No, I've never been married in my life.
MA-C But why?
RAH I hate men!
MA-C How come?
RAH My father was a priest ke Lutheran Church. He ran away with one of the women in his congregation. Mosadi oa thapelo. We never heard anything from him since. My mother struggled bringing us up, so I don't see the necessary of getting married. Men are dogs – Ke dintja!
MA-C Ja – my dear, that's life. Anyway, I must get ready for my tenants, they will be here soon. *(Looks in the mirror)* Oh Rahaba my face! *(Stands up)*
RAH He Comza! What about that bitch who lives in the garage. I hear she's been long in the field.
MA-C No comment, Rebs I must run – the doorbell will ring any minute now. Bye!

Scene 4

*(*MA-CUMMINGS *in lounge,* RAHABA *sits down holding a tin cake.* LINDA *enters, jogging.)*

LINDA Hallo Sis Rahaba.
RAH Hu! Modimo! Ruri mo ha Ma-Cummings ho a dulwa tog ne! She really keeps all types. Keng yona nthwe? What's this?
LI I said hallo Sis Rahaba.
RAH Nyis Nyahaba, ke ousie wa gago nna. Do I look like your long sister?
LI Hau keng jwanong?
RAH Usa re keng jwanong. I don't actually talk to low-class rubbishes.
LI Sis Rahaba, what wrong have I done to you.
RAH Nguanyana nkatuge, cut me out, ngxege skete, before ke go bontsha. Something.
LI I don't believe this.
RAH You'll believe this like it or not. I've been watching you my girl.
LI Really I would like to find out how have I offended you, because all I said was – hallo Sis Rahaba.
RAH Ng'ka go junjuluza obe di piece soos nou.
LI Sis Rahaba you don't have to bother doing that, I am not a fighting type.
RAH You think because you are education, and u-appear-a mo telebyshini e ya gago ya masipa, u-great, ke tla go bontsha, ek sal jou wys. Ten Holy Bibles mme wa tswa, kind. Uit!
LI What do you mean? What are you on about? I mean I don't get your drift.
RAH Drift! *(Laughs)* E teng mo stationereng. You go speak your rotten English friends – ko disco tsa lona ko-Hillbrow, ko lelatla molenze teng. Ja! Nie hierso nie. Mo ke gwa Mrs. Ma-Cummings.
LI Ous Rahaba ake sebetse ko Hillbrow, I work in Rosebank.
RAH Ha! Don't make me laugh wena, you bitch, letrapula tuwe. You think I'm stupid ne! Tell it to the birds in the sky. Ja!
LI I wonder where these people are? Hayi, I must go and rehearse my script.
RAH Nye-hearsa – nyehearsa. Ha! Whatever that mean. Utla ekrea patala – Dali Utlallela metsotso. You'll curse the day you were born again.
LI I don't have to listen to this shit you are telling me you know, I really don't have to.

RAH I'm not through with you yet, ngoanyana. U ska nagana gore this is your father double-storey mansion Mme wa tsoa, out! I am Rahaba, Rebecca, Rachel Mokgampane nna, from Kimberley out. Ke tla gobontsa, wanya man! Jy kaak ne!

LI Jesus man, you are so pathetic you know that, you really are.

RAH Pathetic or not pathetic. Utla bona marago a noga, I'll show you a thing or two Ke kgale – long ago, ke go bona gore wa tella ka sekgowanyana sa gago satiki-Cheap English.

LI It's not my problem that you didn't get some education.

RAH Ke zaba nawe esitikini Mnci stru! Ke a e kana ka Barolong ba ntswetse. Who do you think you are, Princess Diana Sies?! Jou nonsense!

LI I don't have to waste my time with scum like you. You are such a hypocrite.

RAH And I'll see to it – gore – Snowy my friend in Jesus wa gontsa. Out! Of that room! Out of this yard! Jou vuilgoed.

LI I am going to be sick! I'm going to be sick!

RAH Ba nagana gore they can take advantage – ho Snowy Cummings kele teng. Ha never! Over my dead body! Sies! *(LINDA moves around fixing chairs, ignoring her.)*

Scene 5

(Evening at MA-CUMMINGS' lounge. Tenants assembled, UMA-CUMMINGS enters chewing as usual, greets them. PALESA – the daughter – enters. She is introduced to everybody, then kisses her mom goodbye.)

MA-C A warm welcome to kwa Ma-Cummings at Phomolong – to all the new members of the family. I call you people family, because you will be spending a large percentage of your time living in this yard. Remember dearies, I am very, very strict. In fact if my father was alive, Upa-Cummings, he wouldn't have allowed this to go on, especially with unmarried women, but seeing that there is a shortage of houses la elokishini, I thought – *(DADDY interrupts her.)* Yes put some onions in the pot, Daddy – I thought I would actually help out, not that I need more money. You know, I did my two years at the University of Makerekere and I would be going back soon because ngishoke my husband wanted me back, you know he cannot, just cannot live without me. By the way our two wonderful babies are back from boarding school, please I want you to make them feel at home, at home I repeat. After all...After all it is their home, isn't it? Now, when it comes to uBaba wa lapha ekhaya we will all call him uDaddy, siyezwana. *(DADDY comes in with two onions.)* No, no, put some baked beans man, you don't listen! *(She pushes DADDY out.)* Where was I? Yes, I demand that respect from each and every tenant. *(Pointing to them.)* Well I do hope, we live in peace not pieces in this precious home of ours. Akere Rebs. *(RAHABA nods.)* And if there are any problems, don't hesitate I repeat don't hesitate to call me even if it's 2 a.m., really dearies I don't mind. By the way, I will personally be checking up your rooms, weekly. Another thing people, we will fafaza the rooms, you know mos ne, so that my muti should be effective. Ke fedile ke baloi, I hope everybody is clear on that point. And now I would like you to introduce yourselves. Yes, Nomazizi tell us who you are and where you come from.

NOZIZWE My name is Nozizwe. My name is Nozizwe Vilakazi. I come from e-Swaziland, kwa-Manzini. I come from a very poor family. My father had three wives and many, many children, I think we were fifteen at home – so I ran away and landed here in Johannesburg. I had lot of problems with a place to stay. I ended up staying here kwa-Cummings. Mina ngisebenza kwa-Masipalate – at the Municipality, and there's a problem with...

MA-C Next.

LINDA I am Linda Gwaqu from Ebhayi, Port Elizabeth – Kwa-Zakhele. My parents moved to Jo'burg in the sixties. They lived in Alexander Township for sixteen years, then moved to Pimville. My mother was a domestic servant in Highlands North and my father was running his own koffie-kar. They divorced in 1975, my mother remarried – oh well, she's well off. I matriculated in Mashinini High School, went into acting and that's it.

MA-C Next.

RAH Nna ge, ke Rahaba Rachel Rebecca Mokgampane, from Kimberly out. I didn't see the necessity of school. My mother could not cope with all of us, so I found a job-o as a domestic servant girlie in Bloemhof for a while. Then I moved to Christiana, then to

Emmarentia. Be ke kreya mmereko ko-butcher-eng, ke mo ke ele ka bola leoto teng. Lacy, one ke bereka le ene, ampolella ka room kwaga Mrs. Cummings. Ruri mosadi wa modimo a-nkeketlela ang?

MA-C Thank you, thank you Rebs. As you all know, my name is Snowy Cummings from Cape Town, Bontheuwel. My father, was a Coloured and my mother was a Khoza [Xhosa], a nursing sister at Groote Schuur. My father was a welder at Sasol II. Us children were left alone with my mother. I'm very educated. You know, I just got bored with life in Cape Town and I landed in Sophiatown, where I met uDaddy. It was love at first sight, and then we got married immediately. We were moved to Phomolong in 1959 and we are still here. You know they call me Snowy, because when I was in Cape Town I had this lily-white complexion. Look at me now. You know this Jo'burg. Nx! And now for the house rules:

No single ladies – unless steady boyfriends.
The outside toilet must be cleaned – every day.
No brats allowed, no ups and downs, ins and outs, no cars, no parties, no dogs and no cats.
The rent must be paid before the 7th of each month.
The gate is going to be locked from now on.
My children are not to be sent to spaza shops or shebeens.
Every Thursday there will be a prayer meeting – in this lounge, and that is compulsory.
I must keep all the spare keys.
Last but not least, all the intercoms in your rooms must be switched on at all times.

Those are your Ten Commandments. Thank you ladies, any queries?

LI Yes. *(She stands up.)*

MA-C Yes, I heard that there are people planning a strike action against me. Well, let me warn you la ku kwa-Cummings you'll do as you are told or else. Gate!

LI But that is not, what I…

MA-C Just shut up! I'm talking here. If you think you can keep control here, you've got a nerve my girl. This is not P.E.

LI I'm sorry for the mis-u…

MA-C Ku kwa Snowy Cummings la, niyandiva. Ek slaan die kater, and wena, Linda, I'm keeping my eyes on you. Nozizwe, can you bake? *(She nods.)* Before the prayer meeting please come and bake some scones for me. Ma-Cummings must eat cakes after the prayer, because I get so thirsty and weak afterwards. Okay, dearie. Everybody else is dismissed. Rahaba, my dear can I have a word with you. Goodnight ladies, goodnight. (LINDA *and* NOZIZWE *exit.)*

Scene 6

(MA-CUMMINGS *and* RAHABA *lounging over a cup of tea and biscuit, gossiping.)*

RAH Wa itse keng Ma-Cummings o hlokomele ngoanyana – o bare. Ke. Mang?

MA-C Which one?

RAH O'bare o tlaga mo TV eng wa ectara.

MA-C O! You mean Linda – the TV star.

RAH Eke! Ke ogo. You know that girl is dangerous. O mo hlokomele watch her.

MA-C What do you mean she's dangerous.

RAH Mh! Ona le mokgwaenyana, I've been watching her.

MA-C What has she been up to this time?

RAH Hai, my blood boils when I look at her. Mnci-stru! There's something, somewhere, with that girl. I'm warning you.

MA-C Come to the point Rahaba. What's wrong?

RAH Ke mashayela-top! She thinks she's better than everybody else, here mo-Phomolong.

MA-C Tell me my friend, weditseng?

RAH Just because she appears mo – TV – ye yagage. She puts on these miniskirts and sagage. She thinks she's got it all worked out. Oho!

MA-C Come to the point Rahaba hle.

RAH You know what, nna ake na sebaka sa mosetsana o makgakga. Sy's verspot! Ng ka mo tshwara – tshwara. And just do one pattern.

MA-C No, no, Rahaba you are wrong now. You can't fight a person for no reason. Besides, o mosadi wa-Joini.

RAH Hela Ma-Cummings, Joini or no Joini I don't have time for silly nonsense. She always gives me this vuil kyk – una le go ntsheba ka-is.

MA-C Oh! Oh! But that doesn't make sense dear. I think Linda is the friendliest girl in this yard, it's just that you don't understand her.

RAH Hela Ma-Cummings Pasop! O tlare aka go jwetsa.

MA-C Anyway Rebs, mamela, what I called you for, is unfortunately about Linda again.

RAH Wa bona. Aha!

MA-C Listen first. Wa itse keng? Linda wrote me a very hot letter, ke e! *(Shows her the letter)* Saying that she won't pay my R250 rent increase. And...

RAH Ke go boleletse, my ancestors told me, phela ke ngoana wa badimo – I knew this was coming.

MA-C And she threatens to take me to Zupra.

RAH What are you waiting for? Chuck her out of that room, Ma-Cummings o emetse eng?

MA-C No, my friend we've got to dissect this slowly, plus I still have to show it to Daddy. You are the first one to see it, Mokgotsi.

RAH Wa itse wena o-soft! If it was me, she would have been, in the streets by now soos nou.

MA-C Easy, easy Rebs. And another thing, that little worm called Nozizwe has also put her signature in agreement with her.

RAH Igama le Nkosi malibongwe. I've been long telling you about this devil Linda girl of yours. Ke Satane ka nnete, a devil!

MA-C Rahaba, come to your senses, you are not helping me a bit to solve this problem.

RAH Bakobe! O metse eng! Chuck them out man, bakobe! Out!

MA-C Here! You can't talk like that. You know I'll be losing R600 – not at least R500 if I throw them out, and I can't afford that. My babies are here and food is very expensive these days – cost of living phela, Sisi.

RAH Okay, okay, I won't say a word about your precious little friends.

MA-C Wa itse wena o-funny. You pray every night, you go to church every Sunday but you are so hardened.

RAH Can you blame me, Lala gasenna, it's life.

MA-C Bua nnete, Rebs. I think you are jealous of Linda.

RAH Me! Jealous, ka-bicth-ele Ses! You'll tell me, one day.

MA-C Mind your language Rahaba. The girl keeps to herself, she doesn't talk too much, she begs for nobody's food. You can't really complain, really, you can't.

RAH Hela Ma -Cummings, Hela, open your eyes! This is Jo'burg.

MA-C I know that, so what's new?

RAH You must watch out girl! Daddy wa tsamaya! Skoonweg!

MA-C That's a blue lie.

RAH Hela, you think I don't know what kind of a girl she is? Why did she leave home?

MA-C Why?

RAH Batho ba bua, man. You are busy sleeping. Urobetse!

MA-C What do you mean?

RAH Haven't you seen the way she looks at Daddy. Don't you see the way she dresses?

MA-C There, I think you are mistaken Rahaba. Linda is not interested ko-Daddy, she's got a lot of men friends; besides she's an actress, that's how they dress. Haven't you seen ba Bra-Congo? Admit it Rebs, she's got a gorgeous body. I envy her. I used to be like that, when I was a teenager.

RAH Body or no body! People talk. And your yard will lose the dignity it had before she came.

MA-C Rebs, leave the poor girl alone.

RAH Snowy, you are harbouring a prostitute!

MA-C You can't talk like that Rahaba, that's a serious accusation.

RAH Ha! Why is she always working at night.

MA-C Because she's doing shows.

RAH EVERYBODY u – chaisa ka – five, yena ka-five she's going to work.

MA-C Phela, that's the work she chose to do.

RAH Agona mosadi, who can be gallivanting in the streets at night. Unless...

MA-C Unless what?

RAH She's a prostitute Sy's 'n hoermyt man! Kelehure! She's a whore!

MA-C Rahaba, thanks for being with me, good-night for now.

RAH *(Changes subject.)* Lentswe la Modimo lere: Mmele wa motho, ke tempele ya Jehova. Jehova says if you've turned your body into a Sodom and Gomorrah it shall be turned into a statue of salt.

MA-C Rebs, you've got your facts wrong. Sodom and Gomorrah was a place in the Bible. It's got nothing to do with anybody's body, especially Linda's.

RAH Kere – she will be doomed forever and she shall not see Kingdom of Heaven ever!

MA-C My friend, I think you should go to bed. I'll see you tomorrow.

RAH Never! Ever! Mend your ways, mend your face. Mother, Father, Child, for Jesus is coming! *(Trance-like.)* Mend your ways whilst He is still listening. The doors of heaven are wide open. Bare ka sekgowa, English, make hay whilst the sun shines.

MA-C *(Leads her out.)* Thanks for your advice my friend, I'll think about it.

RAH I'd like to say a little prayer before I leave.

MA-C Sorry Rebs, uDaddy is waiting to serve me supper Bye, Hu! *(Bangs door.)*

Scene 7

(Before the prayer meeting there's an exchange of words between MA-CUMMINGS *and* LINDA, *then with* NOZIZWE. RAHABA *enters spraying water all over, then people sing. Everybody in church, Zion regalia except for* LINDA.*)*

RAH Ba...bazwale, Ba...batsoale – my dear friends, relatives and foe, kekebohloko ka letsatsi la mahlomola, letsatsi la matswalo. I don't know what to say tonight my dear sisters. I look at you, I pity you all Bofang. Bofang mabanta bo sesi? Your belts. Letiye, and be strong in the name of Jesus. Amen, say Amen bazalwane. Kere ha ke tadima? Ke tadima kanqane ho thaba – mountains, ke bona legoloi – an angel, lengoloi la Modimo Mr. Gabriel. When I look at him he is smiling usmilela nnake le ese – one. Why? I ask myself bazalwane, because I am. Child of God. Pave your ways before the dawning of the day. The day shall come my sisters – to you, and you, and you, over there. Lomini! Mh! Hai! Jaha! Lomini iyeza nakuwe, Nakuwe, Nakuwe.*(They sing.)*

Oh yes Lord, yes Jesus, I'm all yours, I'm your lamb Nkulunkulu, Nku ya gago. Lentswe la Modimo – God, lere: Ntho tsa le fatshe di ya fita. Material things won't bring you Glory...Glory in the name of Jehovah, Ba bang they think gore ke di beauty queen, bakenya di make-up, di-cutex, ba-perma, they put on? Ba kenya marokho – pants, you don't know if a person is a man or a woman. Ba bang ba etsa they do, di-abortion, they throw their babies mo di-draineng. They sell their bodies ko di Hillbrow. Ba feba, sies! Julle's vuill. Le ditsila man, lankga. You stink! Kodwa sisters, verily I say unto you, those who feel they want to drink from this cup. Those who feel they want to make their bodies the temple of Jehova. Rise up and shine. Report sisters, before it's too late in the name of Jesus. I shall say a Hallelujah O Lord, I thank you Lord, that you love me even if I am a sinner. (DADDY *pinches* NOZIZWE*'s bum)* You died on the cross for me and paid the price of all my sins, today I am a new creature. I am saved in Jesus' name. Amen. (NOZIZWE *moves forward.)* – Rahaba Ngoanyana, come to my room at nine o'clock sharp tonight. Wa nkutlwa? Thank you brother. Thank you bazalwane. *(Song.)*

Act II

Scene 1

(RAHABA *still praying,* NOZIZWE *enters.)*

NOZI Kokoko Sis Rahaba.

RAH Come in, ngoanyana. Igama lenkosis malibongwe, praise God Hai bo!

NOZI Awu sesi are you alright.

RAH Hai! Hai! Hallelujah, Mh! Ja!

NOZI Sis Rah...

RAH My girl, things are bad.

NOZI Where?

RAH Bad, bad, bad.

NOZI Yini manje futhi.

RAH My girl, my dream will never let me down, kengoana wa badimo. My ancestors told me gore wakula, girl – you are sick, sick, sick!

NOZI Hawu Sis Rahaba, me?

RAH Ja kanti, what you take me for? I am gifted child of Jehova, his chosen prophet I am here to deliver you, and you over there.

NOZI Hai mina...

RAH To deliver you from the chains of Satan.

NOZI What do you mean by...?

RAH Hela ngoanyana bare kego bolelle gore you've got demons. Amadimoni.

NOZI Me!

RAH And if you don't do anything about it, watsamaya. Jy loop.

NOZI Ngempela.

RAH Yes, yes that's why I'm here. Come to me my child, come to Jesus. Bring all your problems to me and I'll fix you up.

NOZI But, I don't understand this if you say I've got demons, what do you mean?

RAH Nosiso my girl, why do you scream so much at night?

NOZI Well I, I, I...

RAH Eke! Rerig, I knew it mos. Igama leNkosi malibongwe.

NOZI But I haven't explained anything yet, I...

RAH Save your breath my child, because I am here my child, sent by Jesus. Gore ketlogopholosa. To save you.

NOZI Hai emhlabeni kunzima, *(Sighs.)* I miss

my home makunje. Anyway, thank you very much Sis Rahaba, I need people like you.

RAH Hey, Lala ema pele kagontankisa. Don't thank me yet. Money speak it.

NOZI Sesi mos mina I'm out of work.

RAH Ain't my problems ngoanyana. If you don't wake up you'll sleep and you'll sleep forever.

NOZI What do you mean?

RAH Ho lewena obua sekgowa – English ne! Monkane wagago – Linda is after your blood. Gona jwanong why are out of work? Bagoloya. They are bewitching you.

NOZI Hayi ubani onga loya mina.

RAH You ask too much. All you need is sewasho and a prayer.

NOZI What is sewasho?

RAH Sewasho is water filled with shiboshi, spirits, and ash.

NOZI Shiboshi?

RAH Shiboshi is Jeyes fluid – which is to chase away your filthy demons. And methylated spirit is to burn them out – forever. And Molora, which is ash, is to cool your spirits down, so that you must never, ever scream like a demon at night.

NOZI Well thank you Sis Rahaba, but now...

RAH You must wash with this mixture, you scrub your floors with it and drink three spoons, and mark you, I said three spoons or utlabona Mmago wamo Swatsi – your mother, girl.

NOZI Hai kodwa u...

RAH Heyi, kneel down. *(She kneels.)* Eee ekae tuku. *(REBS fetches doek and blows into a bottle with liquid.)*. Phuma madimoni, Tswaya Satane. Spirit Rejoice leave the body of this girl now! Joy and Shadii put together – Hei–148 Zambezi River. Amen-Direct from God Tsamaya! Loop! And don't look back.

(NOZI exits.)

Scene 2

(At LINDA's place. She is in a cheerful mood drinking sherry and smoking. Cool music playing. NOZI enters.)

NOZIZWE Hau Sis Li, ushaya ziphi namhlanje?

LINDA Hm! *(Laughs)* Nozi I'm just having a sherry. Want a sip?

NOZI I-Sherry intwenjani? I'm not used to it. Thina sijwayele abo G and T, Sis Li?

LI Try it Nozi – it's a lovely drink. It relaxes you and it's good, especially tonight; it's a bit chilly.

NOZI *(Tasting)* Hai, but this is warm. Are you not supposed to put it in the fridge?

LI No, Nozi, it's not meant to be. Drink. *(Laughing)*

NOZI Mh, Ah…a. *(Drinking)* Hai, it's not bad, really, pour me a glass Sis. Anyway and then? *(Pointing towards main house.)*

LI *(Laughs)* Ho, Loyo, I think that letter shook her a bit. Hey, thanks again Nozi for your support Nangomuso.

NOZI I actually felt better, after speaking to you. Hai phela thina asiholi kwa-Masipalate.

LI It's okay Sis. Phela in life, you learn from other people.

NOZI Kodwa Sis Linda. I think I've gained a lot from you. You are such a lady. You know, u-friendly, you are so free and you are so conrident about everything.

LI Ha, I wouldn't say so. Nobody's perfect. I mean you can't walk around with a frown on your face if you've got problems.

NOZI Hai, kodwa Lili, wena udla soft. The world is at your feets.

LI Now, you are embarrassing me. Look Nozi, life is what you make it.

NOZI No-no, look at me, I'm so miserable. No man looks at me. Ngibathe ngiya- Jewisha, hai, kuyala. *(Claps hands)*

LI Yazi yini Sis. In life – you come first, you've got to live according to your means, and live your life to the fullest.

NOZI Kanjani? It's impossible.

LI Do all the things that make you happy. Wena Nozizwe, forget about other people and men.

NOZI Come to the point Sis Linda. *(Bit tipsy.)*

LI And stop calling me Sis Linda, 'cause we belong to the same age group mina nawe Lalela, all I'm saying is that if you like buying expensive clothes, buy them. If you like going to movies, go. If you feel like gin and tonic, have it. If you feel like dining in the Carlton, dine. If you feel like going to shebeen alone, go. Nobody must stop you like people talking about you, they won't do anything for you. They'll just talk. As for men, that's another story, they are just a waste of time.

NOZI Phela nina niyizifundiswa. You know all these things.

LI This has got nothing to do with education. It's got something to do with what I want in life.

NOZI I don't even know what I want in life.

LI I do know what I want but I'm not sure about my future, especially with my career.

NOZI Ha Sis Linda, Nina niyizinginga you are rich, I always see you on TV.

LI That's nothing Nozi. Anybody can do that. All I'm saying is that you've got to have confidence in life, and know that everybody has got a right to live, or has a purpose on this earth.

NOZI Ho-ho thina laba-sesaba yinhlekisa o Rahaba saying that I've got demons. Au bheke nasi nesigqokovane this bottle, uthi wena uyangiloya. You're bewitching me.

LI Mina! Do you believe that? *(Pause)* You know, talking about these two, makes me sick. Anyway, I've always believed that you are treated the way you want to be treated by people. Uma unyatseka, bazokunyatsa nawe.

NOZI Sis Li, abantu abanje ngo Rebs no Ma-Cumms, what can you do against them. Hai mina ngiyabesaba.

LI You don't have to fear anybody. You have a right to be in this yard. You pay rent and you don't beg for their food, so usabani?

NOZI They are just overpowerful.

LI Overpowering yani? For instance, in that prayer meeting you didn't have to go forward, ukuthi uMpostoli Rahaba faking and behaving like this Great Prophetess. Hm! *(Laughs)* Nx! She's so funny.

NOZI Hawu kanti asiwumprofeti?

LI Hay suka anybody can do that. It's just an act. Mhm! She's so funny *(Mimics)*. Bofang mabanta, your belts – le tiye bosesi. Kere ha ke tadima, Kanqane hothaba mountains, ke bona lengoloi la Modimo an angel. Mr. Gabriel. Ha ke mo sheba, look, wasmila U smilela nna keleesi-one. Because I am a child of God. Hallelujah.

NOZI Hai, you are so good. Lomini! That day! Lomini iyeza nakuwe, nakuwe. *(They go on mimicking* MA-CUMMINGS *and* RAHABA *and improvising.)*

LI What about uLandlady?

NOZI We will all call him uDaddy siyezwana, ngisho-ke my husband ubaba walapha ekhaya.

LI Uh! She's such a Kugel.

NOZI What is koogle ke manje?

LI Oh well, we call all these rich, spoiled white housewives, the Sandton types, koogles. Shame, she can't even say the University of Makerekere.

NOZI Kanti it's Makerere not Makerekere like she says.

LI Then you wonder if she really went.

NOZI You mean she could be lying to us?

LI Let's face it, can you really go all the way to Uganda for a nursing diploma? I mean, please.

NOZI Don't hesitate, I repeat. Don't hesitate to call me even if it's 2 a.m. Really dearies I don't mind, I've long been asking myself maar what kind of English is that?

LI Be kekreya mosebetsi-jobo ko Christiana leko Emmarentia – be ke sebetsa ko butchereng ke mo kele ka bola loto teng. Ruri Lazy ngoana Modimo angkeketlela ang-ka ankesa ko Mrs. Cummings.

(Laughter)

LI Hai Nozi let's stop this gossip, it's not right. But these people – they like to undermine other people.

NOZI *(Deep in thought)* Sesi, Linda awung't-shele how do you feel about acting, I mean don't you get shy? I mean I'm sure a lot of people watch you.

LI Hai, that's very difficult to answer. But I can simply say when you are on stage you are sort of...possessed like – Rahaba. You just do your thing.

NOZI Just like that?

LI Well, it's not an easy job sis. It takes a lot of work to be a good actress. It takes a lot of reading, memorizing like uma wenza u-two times one are two, two times two are four, etc. Plus discipline, plus rehearsal meaning that you repeat the same thing over and over again ... the whole day.

NOZI Kusho ukuthi niyasebenza man. I didn't know that.

LI Ja, asi wuku-smila nje kwi TV, it takes a lot of hard work and perseverance. And there are a lot of sharks out there jong. *(*NOZI *is drunk.)*

NOZI Hei maar wena u-nice Sis Linda?

LI Nozizwe, I want to ask you something: tell me how have you been paying your rent for the past three months, ungasebenzi?

NOZI Hayi Lili man, ungangibuza wena.

LI No seriously, Nozi, I want to know.

NOZI Oh well uDaddy. *(Passes out)*

LI UDaddy wenzeni? Nozi, Nozizwe, Nozizwe Hai, I will have to take you to bed now. *(She picks her up and they exit.)*

Scene 3

*(*MA-CUMMINGS *and* RAHABA *gossip over a cup of tea)*

RAHABA Ke go bolleletse. I told you and you didn't want to listen.

MA-C Ene, they say they saw her last week in a disco in Hillbrow, with a white man. Hai tshwara mo my friend. *(Shakes hand.)*

RAH Ke ngoana wa badimo nna. I get shown these things at night. I told you she is a saleslady. *(Both drink the tea.)*

MA-C Ke eng saleslady?

RAH Awu, don't you know a pro, a pro man a Jezebel.

MA-C Ho! *(Laughs)* You mean a prostitute.

RAH Kanti! Take this child of Satan out of these surroundings. Wang shemosa man! Ke jesebela!

MA-C But it's her life, as long as she doesn't bring her whites here, as long a lahla mlenze daar ver ko Hillbrow. I couldn't be bothered.

*(*LINDA *comes in and clears her throat.)*

MA-C Sit, sit down dearie.

LINDA I'm afraid I don't have much time Ma-Cumms. I must run.

MA-C Rahaba please make dear Linda a cup of tea.

RAH Me, you are mad Snowy, Nna, nna moradi wa Mokgampane I must make this rubbish girl tea. Watlola waetse!

MA-C O! Please Rebs, just behave like a saved person. Linda is not a bad child.

RAH Ha!

LI Yes, what is it, Ma-Cummings?

MA-C First and foremost, about this letter Linda. Tell me why you don't want to pay my R250? It's not a lot for you, besides you are a TV star, and... and... *(*RAHABA *nudges her elbow on her ribs.)* Ee Chuwi! *(Giving* RAHABA *a dirty look)*

LI *(Impatiently)* And what?

MA-C Oh well, never mind.

LI Listen Ma-Cummings, I am not prepared to pay that kind of money in a one bloody room. That's it, case closed.

MA-C But Linda this…?

LI Right now, my mattress is rotting because of your leaking roofs. I had to paint the wall myself, and I've been asking you since I lived in this yard to please fix my window. I freeze to death in winter. This is crazy!

MA-C No-man, I'm not fighting with you. I mean I can understand Nomazizi when she can't pay. Ag shame poor thing, but you can.

LI May I enquire as to who is Nomazizi?

MA-C That one who always puts on Tshalis. Poor girl she's still so backwards.

LI She is Nozizwe and you'd better leave her out of this, and tell me exactly what you called me for.

RAH Utlwa hore ogo cheeka jwang in your bloody house and in your bloody yard nogal Sis! UPrmantig man.

MA-C Ema, ema man Rebs, tell me my dear actually what are you and who are you?

RAH Mhm! *(Nodding)*

LI What do you mean? *(Standing up.)*

MA-C No-no sit down and relax. This is woman-to-woman talk, a kere Rebs?

RAH Ja, the truth is the truth, shame the devil. Ha! I've never ever seen you on TV. Are ke ectara. Actress Yakokae? Where?

LI Hei, please people I don't have time to…

MA-C People talk, you know.

RAH Ja ha!

LI What do you want from me, he?

MA-C Sisi tell us truth. What kind of work do you do?

LI I am an actress.

MA-C But we know that already. Tell us what do you do?

LI Stop asking me stupid questions, Ma-Cummings.

RAH Wa mmona!

MA-C But you can't hide it anymore, not with all these men you hang around with.

LI Hide what?

RAH Mhn! You think we don't know, he!

MA-C So, how much does he give you per night?

LI Who?

RAH O sa botsa. You know, wa etse wayidaftisa

MA-C Your white boyfriend.

LI Oh gosh! Oh no! Oh please man, give me a break.

RAH It was bound to come out. Remember I told you about my dream last week Ma-Cummings.

LI I'm going to bed. This is bullshit!

MA-C Heyi ntombozane come back.

RAH Wa utlwa! The ladies of Babylon – mhm!

MA-C Mh-m. Think back – disco. Last Saturday.

LI Oh! That was François, my colleague. Gosh this is ridiculous! *(Laughs)*

RAH François, nyatswa. *(Mimics her.)* Look at

this Jezebel! You and your lot will never escape the wrath of God. That Sodom and Gomorrah called Hillbrow – is the first place to be destroyed by the fires of Hell on the Judgment Day. He'eh! Utla utloa moya! Rona re tla be rere. O Jerusalema. Vulani amasango singene. *(Sings)* To the Lord Angels. Singing hosanna.

LI I'll just say goodnight Ma-Cummings. I don't have to listen to all this nonsense and insults. This is shocking!

MA-C No-no, dearie. Don't run away.

LI Firstly, wena Ma-Cummings, you are a mother. I'm not talking about barren women, who are hypocrites hiding behind the word of God. I don't expect you to talk to me like that.

RAH Hei wena – letrapula towe! Ek sal vir jou takel! Ketla go junjuluza!

MA-C Sh–sh Rebs. Well me, I know who I am. At least I've got a loving husband uDaddy and a roof over my head, my diploma, my profession, wena.

LI Jesus man. I'm still young Ma-Cummings. I'm only twenty-four years. I'm living my life. I love my independence and I love my career, and I'm still going to grow in it.

MA-C But where's your future. You've got no home Sis.

LI If I can tell you about my family, you'll be surprised. It's another chapter. You know I should actually invite you to come and see some of the work I'm doing; then you'll appreciate theatre.

MA-C Linda, don't tell us lies girl by saying you are working. You are working kuphi wena? You always talk about, a job or ngisaya kuma-auditions and you come late at night, jumping over my gate every night. You always put on pants, I've never seen you in a decent dress and I'm sick and tired of your telephone calls and I hate honkies anyway.

LI Well Ma, I do apologize for my late night and my telephone calls. But you must understand it's my job. It is how I earn my living, otherwise I wouldn't be able to pay your rent.

MA-C How much are they paying you?

LI It depends on what you are doing Ma-Cummings.

MA-C Maybe we can come to some agreement. *(Softening)* But, tell me Linda. Do these things of yours pay? I would like ukuthi u Karabo no Palesa my angels, to appear on your TV station.

LI Well Ma. I'll try and organise that. I'll speak to the producer.

MA-C But you know Linda, you are such a nice lady, never mind you do these jobs of yours enginga zi-understandi. Bakudlel'u mona. *(Taking tongue for Rebs.)* They are all jealous of you.

LI You know Mama I don't know what to say to you. But I'm doing serious work. I'm not only doing TV shows. I also do theatre. We work with retarded children. We do children's theatre and do plays on abused women. For instance, do you know how many women are raped daily in South Africa?

MA-C How many?

LI Two hundred women have been raped daily in South Africa for the past three years.

RAH Ag Ummaka man.

LI *(Ignoring her)* And only one in twenty rapes has been reported.

MA-C But why?

LI Do you know how traumatic it is. Do you know how ashamed these women are made to feel. Some are married women. Nurses, lady teachers, university students, schoolgirls, let alone children, it's sick.

MA-C But you can't keep quiet about things like that.

LI Exactly, the society shuns you as if it's your own fault. There's a stigma attached to being raped. You are married, you've got kids, imagine how you would feel. University students are usually gang-raped on their own campuses. There was an interview on TV recently with a university student who spoke about her ordeal for the first time after nine years. Imagine if all these rape victims were to get AIDS. What about jackrollers?

MA-C Yes they drag schoolgirls out of their classrooms. Apparently one young girl is retarded at the moment after being raped by them.

LI I read in the *Sowetan* that a two-year-old girl was raped and killed. Pigs like that should be castrated in public, 'strue's God!

(NOZIZWE *runs in, clothes torn, hysterical.)*

RAH Jo, jo, jo, nnawe Barolong bampontsa eng!

MA-C Oh my God what happened?

LI Nozi, Nozizwe, what have they done to you? *(No response.)* BASTARDS!

MA-C Should I call a doctor?

RAH There are no doctors this time are bolelle let her tell us.
LI Shut up Rahaba. Nozi will talk to me.
RAH Jaa, iza nazo.
MA-C Let me get an aspirin.
LI Nozi, if you tell us we can do something about this.
NOZI I want to go home.
RAH Ja, this is Jozibele kind utla tsoga. I've been long telling you about this memeza business of you trying to attract men in the streets all day. Batlago jackroller.
MA-C Rebs give her a break tog.
RAH Two times – two deposit James bond and the seven dwarfs – corner of Jacksonvale in Peking.
MA-C Rahaba go and drink your salt water please.
LI Please people, let's all calm down, Nozi will talk to me. Yini Sis?
NOZI I was...*(Sobs)*
RAH Bathong I'd like to say a little prayer.
MA-C Not again please, later.
RAH Oho! Kene kere keyalethosa.
LI You were what Nozi?
NOZI Well, as I was...*(Sobs)*
RAH Heyi man, boa talk!
MA-C Be patient. The poor child has been through a bad time.
RAH Deliver her to me now, I'll take the devils out, quick, quick.
MA-C Hm Rebs, you seem to know everything.
RAH Yes, yes, I knew it mos, praise God.
NOZI U...Udaddy ungi-rapile.
MA-C He what?
NOZI He...he raped me.
LI Oh my goodness.
RAH Lies, lies, filthy rotting lies.
NOZI Ngempela sesi Rahaba.
RAH Hey man, maar hoekom le le-so, so cheap he?
LI Shut up Rahaba and give her a chance.
MA-C I really don't believe this.
LI How did this happen?
NOZI After you dropped me in my room. UDaddy came to my room and...and it was dark. And he... He... He... He...
RAH Se, seketory se.
MA-C Please start from the beginning Nozizwe. *(MA-C shakes NOZI.)*
NOZI UDaddy has been coming to my room, and he has been buying me ama-gin and tonic, when I said he must go away because I don't want trouble, he said I'm the boss here la kwaMa-Cummings ku khonya mina, and you'll do as you are told.
MA-C And then?
NOZI And then he said...he said if I want to last in this yard, I've got to listen to him and play the game.
MA-C Which game?
NOZI What happened was that – after I lost my job kwa Masipala, uDaddy ebeza kimi-used to come to my room – athi he'll pay my rent and look after me.
RAH And you said yes.
LINDA Hai Rebecca khaume tog.
NOZI No...yes at first I kept on refusing. One Friday he came with R300 and a bottle of gin and tonic. We started drinking and later he...he... *(Then cries)*
MA-C He what, Nozizwe?
NOZI Well he took off my clothes.
RAH And you said yes.
NOZI He was forcing me 'strue, he *was* – he strangled me and said if I dare talk, he would choke me to death.
LI That's enough, Nozizwe, it's alright, at least we know now. Come and sit down Sisi.
RAH He... 'e Ja!
MA-C Keng Rebs?
RAH I've been wondering all along.
MA-C What?
RAH That's why this girl screams so much at night. Wena Snowy all along I thought this girl had demons. Hayi two times two deposit, something is wrong. Hai bo!
LI Look people, let's stop all this drama and let's help Nozizwe.
RAH Hai bo! Yinkinga le, talk to me Holy Spirits.
MA-C So how long has this been going on uthulile nje?
LI But she was threatened all along – can't you see how frightened she looks? Hm! To think all this time uNozizwe has been trying to tell me something about uDaddy.
MA-C He...E uDaddy!
RAH uDaddy what?
MA-C That man has not touched me once, for the past, for the past three months.
RAH He? E? Mokhotsi wareng jwale.
MA-C So, ubona gore this little girl Nozizwe is better than me Snowy Cummings – ha!
RAH Mokobe my friend, chuck him out, man.
MA-C He's been calling me names – saying that I am a cold fish. He...e...amadoda.
RAH Men are dogs, kedintjoa!
MA-C To think I've done so much for this

bastard. I gave him my life. I gave him my youth. I scrubbed his stinking feet, bought him suits; he coughs, he farts in my bed; nale sugar diabetes yakhe. Folk! He'll get it from me. Where is he?

RAH Sisters, let us pray for his sins. *(She sings.)*

MA-C Shut up with your prayers. Shut up Rahaba, shut up!

RAH Anyway lenna lemo gona, he tried his luck.

LI Heh! With me too, you know.

MA-C UDaddy.

LI AND RAH Yes uDaddy.

MA-C Kusho ukuthi uPalesa my daughter is not safe with this man around. Uphi umgodoyi the bastard, aphume aphele endlini yami. *(*DADDY *comes in drunk. They all hit him and throw him out.)*

LI Well done girls.

RAH Ja mosadi wetsa jalo. Hy moet fokof hy's net 'n hoerjas.

LI No Ma-Cummings you are wrong. You cannot talk like that because abuse leads to more abuse. There's a lesson in this for you too.

MA-C What do you mean?

LI You, for instance, you abuse people and you are power-crazy.

MA-C Me?

LI You can't raise the rent after every two months – look how shit those rooms are, anyway.

RAH Ja maar...

MA-C I was only trying to help.

LI Help what? That's downright abuse of your fellow human beings and you've been doing it since I lived in this yard.

RAH Ja maar Snowy, I think this girl is talking the truth for the first time, and nna ke...

LI Even these prayer meetings zenu nabo Rahaba, you can't force us to be Christians even if we don't belong to this church yenu. It's all bullshit anyway.

MA-C I was not aware.

LI I think you should meet with your tenants, discuss their problems and find out how they feel about certain things.

RAHABA Snowy – we. Dis waar, I would really, like to make a very short prayer.

LI AND MA-C Hai, hai.

RAH Bathong you are always against me ka-Prayer.

NOZI Hai I also didn't know what to do?

LI It's okay Nozizwe, we know now. I know it hasn't been very easy on you. Tomorrow morning I am going to take you to POWA, they will help you. POWA is an organization fighting for abused women. Nozi you were very brave. Keep it up! The play we were working on was about all these rape incidents. There's a woman from Zaire called Doris Nyembo, who did research in South Africa and wrote a play about her findings. She writes plays about women and their problems because here at home we are too shy to write anything about our lives. Siphethwe hi abantu bazothini.

MA-C What do you think we can do?

LI We need women like you Ma-Cummings, like Rahaba, like aboNozizwe. Bafazi, Women, Masibambane ngezandla. Let's stop pointing fingers and laughing at each other.

RAH Othinta thina unthi'nt 'imbokodo.

MA-C What are we going to teach our children? We need a better tomorrow.

LI And I believe that we the women of today can change the face of South Africa. Give it a new perspective. Starting from today.

NOZI Usathi today. Now.

LI Now. Khonamanje uma ubhekisisa we African women, we are actually oppressed double.

NOZI How do you mean?

LI By the law and by our men. Black women are not protected by the law. Our men and the male police have been getting away with a lot.

MA-C Women are being battered by their husbands.

LI Women are abused bodily and verbally and assaulted by men in the streets, in taxis and in trains.

RAH Nothing is done about it.

LI The law does nothing about it. Khonamanje why can't we be paid the same salaries as men. There are a lot of qualified women around these days. I mean, it should be equal pay. There are women digging trenches, women like abo Nozizwe, right in the streets of Soweto. Same job, same power.

NOZI So what do you suggest we do? What can be done?

LI Let's fight against oppression. Let's fight for equal Rights! Let's demand fair treatment at work and with the law, and let's fight for equal pay.

RAH Are yeng Basadi! Phambili!

MA-C Power to the women!

(All women respond by saying Phambili!!!)

LI *(Moves to audience)* We are going to take a walk my sisters. A walk through the night. We are going to march through the streets of Soweto. March for our Rights. March for our Freedom. We are the Now, we are the Future. Come with me, let's join hands and let's be one. Tonight we are going to march to Regina Mundi church with our lit candles. Sisi, Bhuti, we need you. This is our course. Let's march together in peace. Tonight. See you there.

ALL Phambili!

(They sing a freedom song.)

(In the meantime the three actresses distribute candles to the other women in the audience and they all exit – singing.)

Bibliography

Selected published plays by and about black South African women

DIKE, FATIMA. *The Sacrifice of Kreli*. Cape Town: Space Theatre, 1977.

——*The First South African*. Johannesburg: Ravan Press, 1979.

——*So What's New? Four Plays*. Ed. Zakes Mda. Florida Hills, South Africa: Vivlia, 1996.

——*So What's New?* Women, politics and performance in South African theatre today (III), *Contemporary Theatre Review*, Vol. 9, No. 3 193–229.

ESSA, SAIRA and CHARLES PILLAI. *Steve Biko: The Inquest*. Durban: The Upstairs Theatre, n.d.

FUGARD, ATHOL. *My Life and Valley Song: Two Plays*. Johannesburg: Witwatersrand University Press, 1996.

KLOTZ, PHYLLIS, THOBEKA MAQHUTYANA, NOMVULA QOSHA, XOLANI SEPTEMBER, POPPY TSIRA, AND ITUMELENG WE-LEHULERE. *You Strike the Woman, You Strike the Rock: More Market Plays*. Ed. John Kani. Parkland, South Africa: AD Donker (PTY) Ltd, 1994.

MANAKA, MATSEMELA. *Ekhaya*. Orlando, South Africa: Blues Afrika Productions. n.d.

MAPONYA, MAISHE. *Umongikazi/The Nurse. Four Plays*. Ed. Zakes Mda. Florida Hills, South Africa: Vivlia, 1996.

MDA, ZAKES. *And the Girls in Their Sunday Dresses: Four Works*. Johannesburg: Witwatersrand University Press, 1993.

MHOLPHE, GCINA. *Have You Seen Zandile?* Bramfontein, South Africa: Skotaville Publishers, 1988.

MHLOPHE, GCINA, THOMAS NEVIN and NERISS PHILLIPS (adapt.) *African Story Theatre: A Collection of Dramatized Folk-Tales*. Johannesburg: Heinemann, 1996.

MUTWA, CREDO V. *uNosilimela. South African People's Plays: Plays by Gibson Kente, Credo V. Mutwa, Mthuli Shezi and Workshop '71*. Ed. Robert Kavanagh. Johannesburg: Heinemann, 1992.

NAIDOO, MUTHAL. *We Three Kings: A Farce in Two Acts*. Durban: Asoka Theatre Publications, 1992.

Selected books on black South African theatre and black South African women

BANHAM, MARTIN, ERROL HILL and GEORGE WOODYARD (eds) *The Cambridge Guide to African and Caribbean Theatre*. Cambridge: Cambridge University Press, 1994.

COPLAN, DAVID B. *In Township Tonight!: South Africa's Black City Music and Theatre*. London: Longman, 1985.

DAVIS, GEOFFREY V. and ANNE FUCHS (eds) *Theatre and Change in South Africa*. Amsterdam: Harwood Academic Publishers, 1996.

ETHERTON, MICHAEL. *The Development of African Drama*. New York: Holmes & Meier Publishers, Inc., 1982.

JAMES, ADEOLA. *In Their Own Voices: African Women Writers Talk*. London: James Currey Ltd., 1990.

KAVANAGH, ROBERT. *Theatre and Cultural Struggle in South Africa*. London: Zed Books, 1985.

——(ed.) *South African People's Plays: Plays by Gibson Kente, Credo V. Mutwa, Mthuli Shezi and Workshop '71*. Johannesburg: Heinemann, 1992.

KERR, DAVID. *African Popular Theatre*. London: James Currey Ltd, 1995.

LARLHAM, PETER. *Black Theater, Dance and Ritual in South Africa*. Ann Arbor: University of Michigan Research Press, 1985.

LAZAR, CAROL and PETER MAGUBANE. *Women of South Africa: Their Fight for Freedom*. Boston: Bulfinch Press, 1993.

MDA, ZAKES. *When People Play People: Development Communication Through Theatre*. Johannesburg: Witwatersrand University Press/London: Zed Books, 1993.

MDLOVU, DUMA. *Woza Afrika: An Anthology of South African Plays*. New York: George Braziller, Inc., 1986.

ORKIN, MARTIN. *Drama and the South African State*. Manchester: Manchester University Press, 1991.

Journals

South African Theatre Journal
Theatre Research International
Speak (South Africa)
Agenda (South Africa)